T0296806

Securing VoIP
Keeping Your VoIP Network Safe

Securing VoIP
Keeping Your VoIP Network Safe

Regis J. (Bud) Bates

ELSEVIER

AMSTERDAM • BOSTON • HEIDELBERG • LONDON
NEW YORK • OXFORD • PARIS • SAN DIEGO
SAN FRANCISCO • SINGAPORE • SYDNEY • TOKYO
Syngress is an Imprint of Elsevier

Acquiring Editor: Steve Elliot
Editorial Project Manager: Benjamin Rearick
Project Manager: Paul Prasad Chandramohan
Designer: Greg Harris

Syngress is an imprint of Elsevier
225 Wyman Street, Waltham, MA 02451, USA

Copyright © 2015 Elsevier Inc. All rights reserved

No part of this publication may be reproduced or transmitted in any form or by any means, electronic or mechanical, including photocopying, recording, or any information storage and retrieval system, without permission in writing from the publisher. Details on how to seek permission, further information about the Publisher's permissions policies and our arrangements with organizations such as the Copyright Clearance Center and the Copyright Licensing Agency, can be found at our website: www.elsevier.com/permissions.

This book and the individual contributions contained in it are protected under copyright by the Publisher (other than as may be noted herein).

Notices
Knowledge and best practice in this field are constantly changing. As new research and experience broaden our understanding, changes in research methods, professional practices, or medical treatment may become necessary.

Practitioners and researchers must always rely on their own experience and knowledge in evaluating and using any information, methods, compounds, or experiments described herein. In using such information or methods they should be mindful of their own safety and the safety of others, including parties for whom they have a professional responsibility.

To the fullest extent of the law, neither the Publisher nor the authors, contributors, or editors, assume any liability for any injury and/or damage to persons or property as a matter of products liability, negligence or otherwise, or from any use or operation of any methods, products, instructions, or ideas contained in the material herein.

British Library Cataloguing-in-Publication Data
A catalogue record for this book is available from the British Library

Library of Congress Cataloging-in-Publication Data
A catalog record for this book is available from the Library of Congress

ISBN: 978-0-12-417039-1

For information on all Syngress publications
visit our website at http://store.elsevier.com/

Working together
to grow libraries in
developing countries

www.elsevier.com • www.bookaid.org

Contents

Technical editor biography

Tom Ring is currently employed by IQ Services, a Minneapolis-based company that provides performance load testing and availability monitoring services for Fortune 500 contact centers. He holds a dual position at the firm, serving both as the Lead Sales Engineer and as its Security Manager.

Mr. Ring has been employed in the telecommunications industry for over 30 years. His positions have included: Senior Systems Administrator at Pixius Communications, Support Engineer at Harmonic Systems, Level 3 Engineer/Programmer at Norstan Communications, Field Support Engineer at Ericsson Development, and National MD110 Field Engineer for Honeywell Communications Services Division.

While he rarely takes his Engineer's cap off, Ring enjoys amateur radio and autocross in his spare time. His favorite passion is maintaining his 1985 VW Westfalia Camper.

Favorite flavor – capsaicin.

About the author

Regis J. "Bud" Bates has more than 48 years of experience in telecommunications and information services and has long been considered a technology "Guru." He currently contributes to these fields as an author, consultant, expert witness, speaker, course developer, and teacher. He has written numerous books on the technologies.

With clients spanning the range of Fortune 100–500 companies, Mr. Bates has been involved in the design of major voice and data networks. His innovative ideas in implementation have been written up in trade journals and magazines. Many of his projects deal with multiple sites and countries using various architectures. A significant amount of Mr. Bates' work has also been in the wireless communications area. In his work with venture capitalists, he has consistently been on the mark with his projections for various analyses and studies.

Mr. Bates is known for his dynamic keynote speaking. With a style that is power-packed and a delivery that is exciting, he knows how to captivate, engage, and motivate his audience. He motivates the sales force, customers, management team, and capital investors trying to figure out where the technology is heading for the future and where to invest. Regis Bates also develops and conducts various public and in-house seminars ranging from a managerial overview to very technical hands-on classes on Voice over IP, VoIP security, Wi-Fi networking, WIMAX networking, MPLS, DWDM, and IPv6. In the recent past he has focused much of his development and training activities on the convergence of three key areas: VoIP, security, and Wi-Fi.

He developed much on the wireless curriculum including Wi-Fi mesh, RF design, and Wi-Fi hands-on classes. He is very familiar with the Cisco routing and switching products, security products, and wireless products. He has served as an SME for many other training and development projects in the past.

As an independent consultant, Mr. Bates regularly lends his expertise to third-party assessment companies in the analysis, review, and recommendation of technology patents. In particular, Mr. Bates has assessed several portfolios from several large telecommunications and information system vendors, rank ordered the patents and technologies on a technical superiority basis, and monetized many of the portfolios so that his clients could acquire a reasonable portfolio for a reasonable price.

EXPERTISE

- Convergence technologies
- LAN, WAN, Ethernet, MPLS, ATM, frame relay, switching and routing
- Optical networks

- CATV networks
- TCP/IP
- Telephone equipment or operations
- Voice over the Internet Protocol (VoIP)
- Voice over Wi-Fi
- Wireless networks and technologies (cellular, GSM, CDMA/WCDMA, 3/4G GPRS, and SMS/IMS/MMS)
- Wired networks (PBX, voice, data, VoIP, 800 services)
- Disaster recovery/business continuity planning

PUBLICATIONS

Bates' books and seminars have been used by more than 166 colleges and universities around the globe, and Mr. Bates teaches many communications/computer courses and seminars in over a dozen countries globally.

BOOKS

1. Principles of Voice and Data. McGraw-Hill Educational Group, 2006
2. Voice and Data Communications Handbook, fifth ed. McGraw-Hill, 2006
3. Co-author on Wireless Networks Dictionary. Althos Publishing, 2006
4. cdmaOne and cdma2000. McGraw-Hill, 2003
5. General Packet Radio Services (GPRS). McGraw-Hill, 2002
6. Broadband Telecommunications Handbook, second ed. McGraw-Hill, 2002
7. Voice and Data Communications Handbook, fourth ed. McGraw-Hill, 2001
8. Optical Networking and Switching. McGraw-Hill, 2001
9. Voice and Data Communications Handbook, third ed. McGraw-Hill, 2000
10. Wireless Broadband Communications. McGraw-Hill, 2000
11. Nortel Networks Layer 3 Switching Handbook. McGraw-Hill, 2000
12. Broadband Telecommunications Handbook. McGraw-Hill, 1999
13. Client Server Internetworking. McGraw-Hill, 1998
14. Voice and Data Communications Handbook, signature ed. McGraw-Hill, 1998
15. Voice and Data Communications Handbook, first ed. McGraw-Hill, 1996
16. Wireless Networked Communications. McGraw-Hill, 1994
17. Disaster Recovery for LANs. McGraw-Hill, 1994
18. Introduction to T1/T3 Networking. Artech Publishing, 1992
19. Disaster Recovery for Telecommunications, Data and Networks. McGraw-Hill, 1991
20. Securing VoIP. Syngress, in press

ARTICLES

Mr. Bates has written several articles for different magazines over the years extolling the benefits of convergence, movement of information across broadband networking strategies, and user-oriented how-to documents:

1. IPTV Magazine Home PowerLine Networks, May 2006
2. IPTV Magazine Wireless Premises Distribution Networks, March 2006
3. IPTV Magazine Cable Premises Distribution Networks for IPTV, January 2006
4. CIO Magazine Pundit "Wireless Carriers Have the Goods," 2002
5. CIO Magazine Pundit "The Fiber Glut Myth," 2002
6. CIO Magazine Pundit "Cable vs DSL," 2002
7. Crisis Magazine "Disaster Recovery Planning," 1998
8. International Journal of Management "Managing Telecommunications," 1997
9. Disaster Recovery Magazine "Planning for Telecommunications Disasters," 1997

Acknowledgments

This book is designed to make you aware of the threats to Voice over IP (VoIP) on your wired network, introduce you to some of the issues that have already arisen, and guide you through an audit of where your network is exposed. Then, we will give you some ideas on integrating your IT security plan with your VoIP plan, preventing wherever possible the risks of eavesdropping and replay. Next, we will look at the wireless side of the VoIP networks that pose even greater risks. I hope you enjoy it for what it is, an overview to get you started.

This is not my first published book but it is my first with Elsevier. I once worked with the publisher, Steve Elliot, at another publisher and had lost track of Steve. It was he who found me again and convinced me to write this book. So I thank him for his perseverance in prodding me along the way. I also appreciate Steve's patience in my delays due to work schedules.

I would like to acknowledge Ben Rearick, Editorial Project Manager also at Elsevier Publishing, for his patient mannerism and encouraging attitude. Ben was responsible to keep me on track, a job that no one should be tagged with due to my fluctuating schedule. But through Ben's active role of keeping after me and prodding me to continue, we finally got the book completed.

I further want to acknowledge and thank my technical editor, Tom Ring. Tom had to keep me straight and offer his guidance in steering some of the content. He is an active VoIP'er so his input was invaluable. I look forward to working with him again someday.

I would be remiss if I did not acknowledge Gabriele, my wife, for her help in getting the graphics together. She was instrumental in taking an idea and rough drawing and creating a graphic that works for this book. Gabriele also made sure that I stayed on track as much as she could. It was her endless encouragement that led me to making the time to complete this work.

Finally there are a lot of people in the background, too many to mention. These are the production staff at Elsevier and the proofreaders. Moreover, the numerous vendors who welcomed me into their Partner programs and shared information with me freely are some of the unsung heroes here. They know who they are and I thank them for all their time and efforts.

Lastly, let me thank you, the reader, for two things. First, thanks for buying and reading this book. Second, thanks for being a part of this industry and helping it grow and mature. No book can solve every problem; no author can satisfy every reader's needs. Jointly, we all work together to improve the industry and help to make it what it is. You deserve the applause for all you do.

Thanks to you all!

Introduction

CHAPTER OUTLINE

SECURING VOICE OVER INTERNET PROTOCOL (VoIP): KEEPING YOUR NETWORK SAFE

This book is intended as a primer for various organizations and individuals who may be planning to roll out a VoIP system. Generally speaking, if you have not experimented with VoIP in the past, a lot of new issues may surface that had not been considered in the older days of telephony. This book is structured in such a way as to handle those issues. In this chapter the following issues will be addressed:

1. History of telephony and why it was always considered to be safe
2. History of the Transmission Control Protocol/Internet Protocol (TCP/IP) suite and why it was always considered unsafe
3. The convergence of voice with data networks, and introduction to VoIP

4. Ingrained weaknesses in the deployment of a VoIP system including:
    a. Technological weaknesses
    b. Policy weaknesses
5. Statements of what is at risk when you deploy VoIP
6. Some of the threats that are known problems
7. Toll fraud
8. Theft of services
9. Loss of confidentiality
10. Eavesdropping
11. Hijacking
12. Voice mail hacking
13. Infrastructure attacks
14. Man-in-the-middle (MITM) attacks
15. Disruption or denial-of-service (DoS) attacks

As the reader might see, the issues can be many, yet they are not insurmountable. For example, when looking at the list overall, there are some pieces that can be considered and can be shorn up together. Actually, it is best if the security policies and procedures that organizations adopt and implement fully complement each other. Moreover, when dealing with VoIP, it is imperative that the security policies and procedures match those of the organization's information technology (IT) security, audit, and business resumption plans and they all coalesce as a single document. In fact, the closer the ties built in to blend the security, the better the installed system should work as a homogenous plan.

HISTORY OF TELEPHONY

In the very beginning of the voice telephony networks, the systems and services were always considered safe. The reason for this stems from the "Bell Telephone Company" philosophy. The Bell companies always ran a telephone wire from the Central Office (CO) to the customer's location. Different ways were used but for this discussion, the telephone wires were dedicated wires that ran from the CO along a wiring telephone pole line route to the end user's location (i.e., residence, business, etc.). In Figure 1.1 is shown a markup of how the wires were run from the CO to the end user over a pole line route. Because these bundles of wires were large, it was difficult for anyone to break into a pole line route or a buried route of 600–1200 pairs of wires and tap into them. It was possible but less than practical to break into such a link. Note that at the end user's location a single pair of wires was run into the customer location and a telephone set (typically an analog phone) was terminated on the wires.

Alternatively the dedicated wires were bundled together in a conduit or buried directly in the ground. For efficiency sake, the telephone wires were bundled in 600 or 1200 pairs of unshielded twisted pairs. As the larger bundles of wires were run closer to the customer site, they were split off at manholes or handholes where the pairs ultimately got separated to bring one to four pairs to the door. Shown in Figure 1.2 is the pole line and conduit combination.

FIGURE 1.1

The telephone company wires were run on a pole line route.

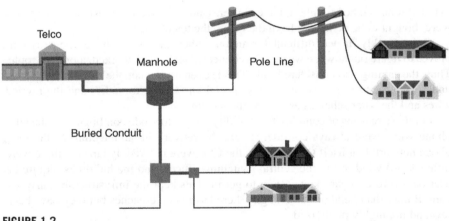

FIGURE 1.2

A mix of buried conduit and pole line route can also be used.

Throughout history, the telephone company CO has always been kept under lock and key. No outside personnel were allowed into the CO. The reason is obvious; the Bell Telephone Company was a natural monopoly and had total control over their wires. Entering the customer's site was a two- or four-pair cable as might be seen in Figure 1.3. This graphic shows a four-pair connection that is typically color coded so

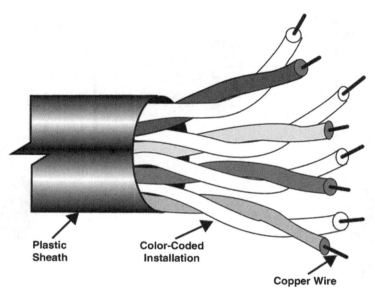

Plastic Sheath

Color-Coded Installation

Copper Wire

FIGURE 1.3

A four-pair wire was terminated at the customer location.

that dial tone can be brought to the end user. Under normal circumstances, the wires were thought to be dedicated from the CO to the telephone set.

Quite frankly, it was difficult for anyone other than a telephone company employee to figure out how the wiring was connected and how it worked, along the route. Thus, the cabling was considered safe. This is even truer when the cables were buried under the ground in a conduit. It took special knowledge to understand the myriad wires and the color schemes as well as the labeling.

For these reasons of complexity, visibility, and color code combinations, the telephone wires were always considered safe. Moreover, the architecture of the telephone network lent itself to security as the COs were not visibly labeled, there were little (or no) windows in the central switching offices, and the buildings required a user password or a card key system to get in. This kept the infrastructure fairly secure. Rather than belabor this thought, there have been breaches but they have been few and not highly publicized.

HISTORY OF THE INTERNET PROTOCOL

Without a doubt, much has happened since the inception of the Internet in the late 1960s. To be sure, the Internet was always considered an open access network. The intent was that colleges, universities, government agencies, and certain large corporations would use the Internet to share information. Thus, it had little security placed on it in the beginning. The entire purpose was for users to openly access data, files, and text messages (mail) that could be transferred between and among computers.

To facilitate this sharing a set of protocols was developed called TCP/IP. This protocol set was referred to as the DoD model in the beginning as the Internet was actually designed for the DoD under the auspices of the Defense Advanced Research Project Agency (DARPA) budgets for just this sharing of data.

Because DARPA needed the openness to share the files among many different computer systems, the protocols developed were open (no real security). As long as you knew how to connect, the access was wide open. Later, after several iterations, the need for securing the TCP/IP suite became rather obvious. Therefore, the TCP/IP in use today (still mostly IPv4), which was developed for use in 1983–1984, has been fixed like a patchwork quilt. New features were added, new security tools were added, and other tools were developed. Whereas the network was used primarily for the DoD use, it took a long time in coming. Yet in 1991 depending on how you view the evolution, the Internet became a public network to serve as the "information highway" of the future. It was then that the use and the exposure of the Internet exploded to a worldwide network accessible to all. The beginning network used a model of switches and routers that were different than the telephone companies. In fact, where the circuit-switched telephone network was used for voice and dial-up data, the Internet was based on a packet-switching network using TCP/IP. Figure 1.4 shows a mapping of the TCP/IP stack; although there are many different ways to show this stack, it is fairly easy to display many of the protocols in this one figure. As can be seen there are basically four different layers in this model. The bottom two layers include the hardware interfaces (looking at many different LAN and WAN connections) and the networking layer Internet Protocol (IP). At the transport layer Transmission Control Protocol (TCP) and User Datagram Protocol (UDP) are shown. These two different protocols are different to each other in terms of their function. Where TCP guarantees delivery, UDP does not guarantee delivery. It can be that VoIP runs on a TCP connection or a UDP connection. More will follow on that later. At the application layer in the TCP/IP stack as it was developed there are many applications that are supported. It was later that at the application layer new protocols were added to TCP/IP to support the VoIP services.

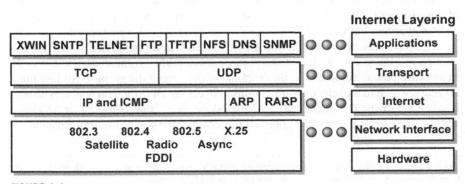

FIGURE 1.4

The TCP/IP stack as it existed early on.

After several years, breaches occurred across the Internet. As a result, a series of add-on features were created to patch the problems. These fixes included firewalls, new routers, more protocols to create a secure(r) environment, etc. It was these patches and fixes that helped create the Internet the way we know it today. Yet, some of the fixes got in the way of developments (i.e., in VoIP) that created the need for a workaround. Regardless of the issue, the protocols needed to be created to simplify and shore up the network, but the "evildoers" across the globe sought out many of the loopholes in the protocols and began exploiting them. Many of these exploits will be discussed later in this chapter and throughout others.

It was only a matter of time that voice and data convergence would rise to the forefront of the industry. Early on there were two separate directions that led the way for voice and data communications: the first was the voice telecommunications departments that often worked for finance or administration in corporate America. As such circuit-switched voice was the primary goal to satisfy the needs of the organization. The voice networks were deployed for daytime use (primarily) and the circuits sat idle off-hours. Consequently, the MIS[1] departments saw an opportunity to get a free ride for the data transmissions after hours by using both dedicated (leased) lines and circuit-switched lines. Second, after enough haggling and arguing, data transmission volumes began to overtake the voice traffic and newer methods of shipping data across the organization were needed. Packet switching was one of the methods. X.25 protocols were developed to handle reliable data transfer (guaranteed delivery and low error rates). However, this reliability came with a price. The costs were high and the delays encountered from retransmissions were high. Thus, a new method had to be found.

WHAT GOES AROUND COMES AROUND

As mentioned above, the Internet was developed for open communications between and among computer systems of different organizations. However, the original Internet protocols (such as IP) did not guarantee delivery, did not sequence the data properly, and did not provide error-free traffic. Consequently, the X.25 protocol was developed and rolled out as the salvation (1976) and went through several iterations of improvement. The X.25 network as shown in Figure 1.5 was primarily set up for dedicated access but was later used as a dial-up connection for smaller sites.

X.25 operates at layer 3 of the Open Systems Interconnection (OSI) model as seen in Figure 1.6. With that there was considerable overhead associated with transmitting data. Remarkably, the X.25 networks served the purpose for less than 20 years, which in the telecommunications networking environment was very short-lived.[2] One of the drawbacks of X.25 was slow speed, that being 56 or 64 kbps. The IT departments were fast approaching critical mass with the transmission of

---

[1]As it was called in the earlier days, management information system has gone through several iterations of naming until it became what is known today as the IT departments.
[2]X.25 was continued in use for certain organizations for years after this discussion but the masses began moving away from it earlier.

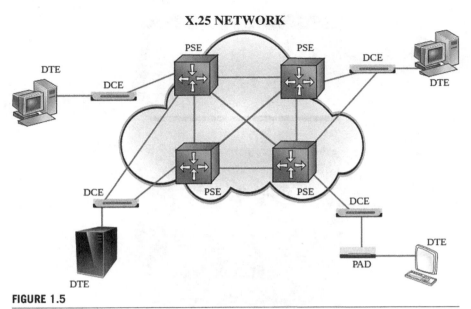

FIGURE 1.5

The X.25 network as it evolved.

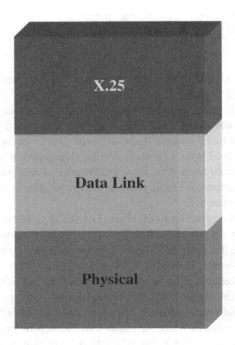

FIGURE 1.6

X.25 operated at layer 3 of the OSI model.

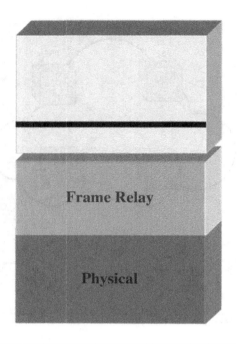

FIGURE 1.7

Frame relay used a reduced overhead at layer 2 of the OSI model.

data and had to find a lower-cost method to satisfy the data needs as well as faster networking speeds.

In 1992 both frame relay and ATM were introduced as means of moving away from the slower and more costly X.25 networks. With the implementation of frame relay the networks reduced overhead and allowed data to move at speeds of up to 2 Mbps and a streamlined layer 2 protocol. With reduced overhead and faster linkage frame relay spanned data rates of 56 kbps to 2 Mbps and reduced the error checking on the frames of information. Frame relay at the lower portion of layer 2 of the OSI model is shown in Figure 1.7.

Frame relay worked fine and still does, but the data needs were outstripping everything that frame relay could handle. As a result, a faster packet technique called Asynchronous Transfer Mode was developed to handle the speeds available on optical fiber networks. Speeds in ATM ranged from 50 to 622 Mbps, using a reduced overhead. Reducing the amount of error checking needs was an obvious fit for the telecommunications industry because fiber optics produced data at much higher throughput and lower errors. ATM then works at the bottom half of layer 2 of the OSI model similar to frame relay, as can be seen in Figure 1.8. The upper portion of layer 2 is called the ATM adaptation layer that is used to prepare the traffic based on the traffic type (circuit-switched voice, packet-switched voice or

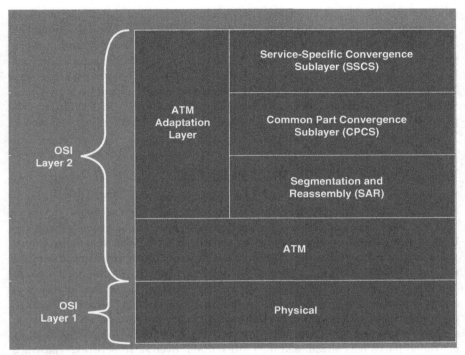

FIGURE 1.8

ATM operates at layer 2 of the OSI model.

video, packet-switched data, etc.). The figure shows that there are different steps to get the ATM cells ready for the network.

After all the work that was placed on the networks to ready the data for movement, what began as the IP (from the original ARPANET) became a better way to move data. In 1984 the TCP/IP stack version 4 (IPv4) was introduced as mentioned above as a means of DoD units to move data between disparate machines and protocols. This worked for many years and in 1995 the information highway of the future (as it was called) was brought about with the commercialization of the Internet. TCP is a smart protocol that was designed for reliable data transfer on an end-to-end basis, much like X.25 protocols were designed to carry the data reliably. TCP works at layer 4 of the OSI model.[3] IP is designed as a dumb protocol that guarantees nothing. IP does not guarantee delivery, is not concerned with proper sequencing (arrival) of the data, does not worry about error checking, and does not necessarily arrive on time. As a result, TCP is the protocol that handles these issues. One must remember that by this time the optical networks were delivering data (and voice) at higher,

---

[3]The DoD model had only four layers but comparisons are always drawn between TCP/IP and the OSI model. So for the purposes of explanation, the industry refers to TCP as a layer 4 OSI equivalent.

more reliable speeds and throughput, so the industry realized that all the overhead could be minimized. Looking at the TCP/IP stack as seen in Figure 1.4 it should be evident that the protocol stack includes a lot more than just TCP and IP. In fact, when guaranteed error checking and delivery techniques are not really needed, UDP can be used at the equivalent of layer 4 instead of TCP. Underlying protocols that carry TCP/IP or UDP/IP packets include ATM, frame relay, and X.25 and LAN protocols. So the layer 3 (X.25) protocol and subsequent protocols that were developed to re-place IP from its old days have been displaced by IP at the layer 3 of the OSI model. What goes around comes around!

VoIP NETWORK AND POTENTIAL PROBLEMS

Before diving into the problems, one question that should be answered is "why both-er?" VoIP and IP telephony should be understood as two different things.

First, VoIP is a means of sampling and packetizing real-time voice so that it can be sent over a data (or voice) network in packetized form. What this means is that voice is sampled, a packet is created, and the packet is routed or switched across a network. Sometimes the voice information is merely sent across a corporate network or a leased line network. Other times, the packets are routed across the Internet. Still a third option is that the packets are carried on a corporate data network (Ethernet, e.g.), and then passed out to the public switched telephone network (PSTN) through a gateway function such as a media gateway. This of course means that voice is converted into a data stream and then just sent out over an IP network. The voice is sampled at normally a variety of millisecond increments.[4] That being the case, a sample is 160 bytes of voice traffic. Logically then, there will be 50 samples/s. Added to each sample, for example, is the overhead associated with the various protocols.

Looking at the overhead allocated to a voice packet the Ethernet overhead in-cludes 14 bytes of header and 4 bytes of trailer. Then inside the data frame is the IP header, which is 20 bytes long. Following that is the UDP header consisting of 8 bytes. Finally, the Real-Time Protocol (RTP) header, which is 12 bytes, is added. Summing these numbers up produces 58 bytes of overhead (14 + 4 + 20 + 8 + 12) combined with the typical 160-byte voice sample. One can see that the overhead is extensive. This frame of VoIP is shown in Figure 1.9 as a snapshot of the RTP frame.

Using the above numbers, the overhead amounts to over 36%; this is a lot. There are ways of compressing the overhead with IP header compression and RTP com-pression, but for now this is the easiest way of describing the overhead.

Second, IP telephony includes all of the above, but adds more features and func-tions such as call forwarding, call hold, conference calling, etc. In the IP telephony world, systems such as IP PBXs are used, whereas in the earlier service called VoIP all that is needed is a means for converting voice into packets. VoIP is just packetized

---

[4]The sampling actually takes on different increments from 5 to 30 ms. The G.711 standard (64 kbps) used a 10-ms sample and was then formatted into a 20-ms packet. There are differences but for this discussion, a packet of 160 bytes in G.711 is used.

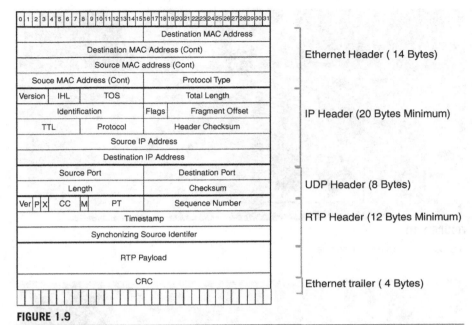

| 0 | 1 | 2 | 3 | 4 | 5 | 6 | 7 | 8 | 9 |10 |11 |12 |13 |14 |15 |16 |17 |18 |19 |20 |21 |22 |23 |24 |25 |26 |27 |28 |29 |30 |31 |

FIGURE 1.9

The VoIP frame with all the overhead.

voice, whereas IP telephony includes packetized voice and all the add-ons. It is fairly difficult to separate the two services because of the devices used to provide the packetization and the features.

An example of the devices in the simplest form is an analog telephone adapter (ATA) such as that provided by companies such as 8x8, Vonage, or others. An ATA allows analog telephone sets to be plugged into them [and treated as what is called foreign exchange station (FXS)]. A typical adapter may have one or two interfaces (RJ-11 telephone jacks) to plug in the sets. On the other side of the ATA is the LAN side with a standard Ethernet connector (RJ-45 jack). Now the two analog sets are plugged into the ATA and a data cable is connected to the LAN. This provides the voice to data transition. Typically connecting a PC with a standard browser to the ATA allows the user to configure the various options available in the IP telephony realm. An ATA provided by Sipura,[5] for example, is shown in Figures 1.10 and 1.11. The figures show the various components in the adapter.

The benefits of VoIP

VoIP allows users to make phone calls over the Internet, or any other IP network, using the packet-switched network as a transmission medium rather than the traditional

---

[5]The Sipura is a Linksys company.

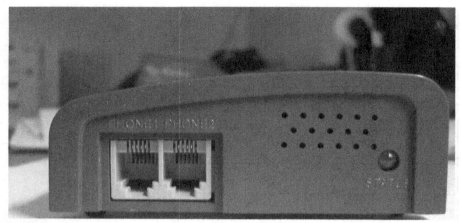

FIGURE 1.10

A Sipura ATA adapter, front view.

FIGURE 1.11

A Sipura ATA adapter, rear view.

circuit transmissions of the PSTN. If a quality Internet connection is available, phone service can be delivered through this Internet connection instead of from the local phone company. This assumes that the Internet connection is from someone else other than the local telephone company such as a CATV company or a wireless provider.[6] As the technology has become more reliable in recent years, enterprise

---

[6] It is also possible to get the Internet connection from the local Telco on an xDSL service that produces an asymmetrical (normal) speed for up and down links.

organizations and residential customers have been moving to VoIP for a number of reasons:

- Consolidation of voice and data on one network reduces costs and results in a lower network total cost of ownership (TCO).
- Operating expense savings include lower long-distance charges, reduced support costs, and savings via workforce virtualization.
- Newer and increased functionality, specifically automatic routing of calls to the VoIP phone set no matter where it may be.
- Using an ATA users can talk and surf the web at the same time on a single connection.[7]
- Companies also use the migration to VoIP as an opportunity to replace aging telephony equipment with feature-rich technology such as teleconferencing and collaboration/multimedia applications.
- VoIP supports increased mobility, since remote workers have the same access to voice features as corporate office employees.

SOME INITIAL THOUGHTS ON VoIP

Another area of concern before going too far is that whenever a VoIP system is considered, many organizations read the news and the state-of-the-art conditions. However, some things that must be considered are given in the following.

One of the reasons that hacking is so predominant and that network penetrations occur is that the industry has a propensity to elevate the "hackers" to a level of awe. Everyone thinks that there is some mystique associated with a hacker who can penetrate a network and steal information (no matter how large or small). Colorful terms such as "ethical hacker" or "white hat hacker" are even used to give these people some form of status. No matter what the name tag that the industry chooses to use the resultant hack into a network (for whatever reason) is still an illegal activity and should be punished. Regardless of the motivation, anyone who penetrates a network without authority to do so is a crook! There is little difference between a person who holds up a bank with a gun and a hacker who accesses your private information via a network with some form of terminal device.[8] A hacker who breaks into a website deserves no more honor than a thug. Regardless of the motivation, illegal activities are just that, illegal! However, this celebrity status that the industry assigns to hackers is phenomenal. Quite frankly, this is unfathomable that dual standards exist and that praise for the evil hacker is so prominent.

Whenever a VoIP system is installed, whether an employee, an owner, or another position, the reader has to consider the risks that come with the territory. Any organization that has had to defend or recover from a penetration; has also spent hundreds or thousands of hours, wasting several equivalent salaries, to defend or recover from a hacker's attempts; and has had the taste of what the government calls a "victimless"

---

[7]The assumption here is that the service provider is providing a QoS that is higher than what the browser will use and the telephony is given a higher QoS. For many homes and SMBs this may be a challenge.
[8]Actually, it has often been said that the hacker gets more than the bank robber with a gun.

attack knows the frustration and the embarrassment of that hacker's achievements. Because of this mystique assigned to the evildoers, the risk of crime and penetration goes up exponentially.

Given this rationale for elevating the hacker/evildoer to a level of awe, several reasons exist for the attempted hacking of a VoIP system (or any other system for that matter). The hacking involves eavesdropping by listening in on conversations. These reasons, however weak they may appear, are as summarized in Table 1.1.

WHAT ARE THE REASONS FOR THE VoIP HACKING ATTEMPTS

The reason that so many attempts have occurred in the VoIP network space include such things as what has been going on with VoIP and IP telephony. For example, a VoIP system originally included strictly taking a voice sample and packetizing it into an IP packet, and then forwarding it along the route to the final destination. However,

Table 1.1   Reasons for Eavesdropping on a VoIP Call

Reason	Description
Joy riding and bragging rights	The attacker views hacking as an exciting game of discovery and exploration, and does not intentionally wish to damage the property of others; the attacker wishes to demonstrate technical prowess to his or her peers. This group includes casual hackers and many novices
Revenge	The attacker feels as though he or she has been treated unfairly, and is seeking retribution or financial compensation. The most common members of this group are disgruntled employees
Theft	The attacker is in search of personal gain through unauthorized financial transactions or theft of intellectual property, proprietary information, user data, or network services. This group includes career criminals, hired professionals, and organized crime rings
Politics	The attacker defaces a website, destroys data or computer systems, disrupts service, or reveals confidential information (e.g., sensitive financial data, personnel records, or medical histories) to further a political agenda. This group includes political activists and members of terrorist organizations
Corporate espionage	The attacker is hired to gather information on a rival company (e.g., information regarding upcoming mergers, earnings reports, or unfavorable transactions) that, when leaked to financial markets, may affect stock prices or sabotage the company's public image. The attacker may also be hired to steal intellectual property or trade secrets. This group includes hired professionals
Information warfare	The attacker is a member of a military organization focusing on intelligence gathering, dissemination of misinformation, military or corporate sabotage, and/or destruction of commercial and communication infrastructures. This group consists primarily of highly trained and experienced government spies, intelligence officers, and members of terrorist organizations

A Stair-Stepping Approach to Added Features of VoIP

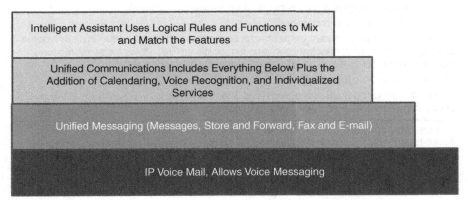

FIGURE 1.12

VoIP features in stair-stepping approach.

as time progressed, many new features and functions were added to the VoIP system of choice. Consequently, what started out as strictly a voice solution has emerged to being a fully converged business solution. For example, the VoIP infrastructure included several solutions offered by the providers. These included such things as voice mail (IP-based voice mail). From there the vendors created a unified messaging system that included message store and forward, facsimile, and e-mail messages all in a single mailbox for storing and later retrieval. Step three in this evolution included such services as a unified communications solution (which most equipment vendors offer today). Unified communications includes the addition of linkage to calendars, voice recognition software, and whatever individualized rules and policies the user chooses. Ultimately, given all the features and functions of VoIP features allowed in an IP telephony solution, the final end game is an intelligent assistant that can use logical rules and functions to offer any mix and match of these features as the individual rules establish. One can see that the myriad different possible combinations stress any security solution for a VoIP environment. This can be seen in Figure 1.12, which shows a stair-stepping approach to adding features of VoIP functionality.

With every addition of features and linkage, the complexity of the network grows immensely. It is up to the individual owner to secure these systems based on the individual needs. Looking at this list of features and add-ons for a VoIP system the add-ons shown in Table 1.2 can be considered.

THE NEED FOR VoIP SECURITY

Multivendor implementations require more than just knowing that the technologies will work together. There can also be a significant support commitment and cost in maintaining resident experts on multiple vendor products. In addition to having to

Table 1.2 Features Added With VoIP/IP Telephony Solutions

Single integrated voice and data network, over the same IP network
Simplified add, moves, and changes
Resilient deployment; different elements can be located in different communication rooms as long as there is IP connectivity between the locations. This allows for better recovery but adds to the complexity and risks using a decentralized approach
Excellent application support, for example, unified messaging
Reduced fixed wiring cost; only a single Cat 5 (or better) cable is required; the PC and phone can share the same cable back to the wiring closet*

In many cases this converged network does not produce the expected gains and results. This may be due to higher expectations or that the wiring facilities won't deliver the performance due to other limitations.

know how to install and provide production support, someone must be a security expert on each vendor line to keep on top of security announcements, vulnerabilities, patches, upgrades, and so forth. The future can change the balance completely. While products from two vendors might "play well together" initially, what happens in the future when a new technology develops and one vendor chooses a standards-based approach while the other chooses a proprietary solution, or maybe not to play at all?[9]

As with any technology, people tend to try to overcome a technology's capabilities to secure the system. Hackers have always prided themselves on their ability to break into or through a system's security procedures. Much of the time, the hacker is looking for the same type of satisfaction as outlined in Table 1.1. What better way to show off than to break into some large corporation's system and then use the bragging rights to "earn" recognition. Thus, any system (computer, voice mail, VoIP, PBX) needs to be protected from the people who have nothing better to do than chip away at the system security.

Think about it, some youngster may have no social life and spends his/her spare time just trying to break into systems. They have all night to hammer on the system. Moreover, the manager of the system is trying to satisfy the masses within the organization, troubleshooting problems, planning the next step of deployment or upgrades, and keeping the system fine-tuned. So the manager has little (if any) spare time to devote to checking for the hacker banging on the door from the outside. This creates an opportunity for the hacker to continue to pry at the security in hopes of getting through. By design, inherent vulnerabilities are associated with VoIP by sheer nature of the discussion above regarding the IP. What this implies is that there may be little that can be done to shore up the risks associated with the use of VoIP. However, this does not mean that we should not try to secure VoIP and all its benefits.

---

[9]One such issue is that some companies' experiences have been that 95% of new installations where there are multiple vendors (and there are usually a half dozen or more in play with complex large installations) will have serious issues that can take weeks to months to fix (very good point). And they may never truly work as designed.

Above and beyond the inherency of risks associated with IP, there also exist additional risks and needs for securing VoIP by nature of its use. If someone is using a VoIP solution and does not take any precautions, then the risks are exponentially acquired against the use of the system. Let's assume that a VoIP system is installed and the using organization doesn't take any steps to secure the VoIP system and the customer traffic. If no firewalls are used, or if no encryption tools are used and if the VoIP is wide open, then there can be no perceived security. In fact, the door is wide open for the hackers to attack and gain access or control of the system.

Let's assume that the installation of a VoIP solution is not controlled. How can that be? One should be able to assume that security is inherent! Wrong! Nothing can be further from the truth. In fact, some of the areas that can be exposure points for an organization are described in general below and then summarized in Table 1.2:

- The system servers: Many of the VoIP systems are Linux/Unix based and have a number of open doors that can be exploited. (More on this a little later.) Back doors, patches that are not applied, updates, and direct access to specific ports that are open all create some of the opportunities for lost security.
- The local area network: One can read any day of the week about networks that were penetrated in an Ethernet environment. These are targets for access to voice as well as data networks. Now more than ever, when the LAN carries gigabit speeds of data (or even tens of gigabits) there are so many applications open for use by internal and sometimes external personnel. If in fact the Ethernet is not protected, it will be hacked and open a back door into the VoIP network. Ethernet, after all, is an internal network; there is no physical access to the cables or the switches as they are locked up in special closets. That at least is the story that many organizations select to believe. Remember the earlier discussion of the telephony network, where the wires were accessible only to the telephone company employees.
- The wireless LAN: It never fails. As soon as the access to the LAN was attained, users wanted it to be ubiquitous. It must be accessible everywhere. It must be better, faster, and cheaper, whatever. Then the untethering of the Ethernet occurred with the WLAN using a wireless NIC card and an access point. Unfortunately, wireless LANs have been hacked in the past due to improper use, lack of authentication that is effective, and lack of good encryption. Now overlay the wireless LAN with VoIP and a new problem occurs. Not only could the WLAN be attacked, but the voice conversations will also be subject to the same attacks (i.e., MITM, replay, redirection, eavesdropping, and just plain fraud). The system will not know where the user is when connecting wirelessly and the opportunity to hack the Wi-Fi network is a new risk. Many cases of user networks that are wide open (no security) whatsoever have been recorded in the press. Add to that many new tools available to the hacker to eavesdrop or launch DoS attacks and the risks are greater than a basic wired network.

- The telephones: Telephones are devices that can be plugged into any open port in a switch, or a jack in the wall. The devices are initially programmed to openly register on the network (the LAN) and if there are no restrictions in place, they are ready to use. If a SIP phone is used, for example, then any SIP phone may be able to register. Let's add to that the fact that the phone might be moved. One of the inherent features of a VoIP telephony solution is the fact that moves, adds, and changes are so easily accommodated. If a phone can be arbitrarily moved from one room to another, all security may be lost.
  Let's add to the fact that, as mentioned above, many of the telephone systems are driven by a Unix-based platform. The kernels in the phones are subject to manipulation. There is more than one incident where a VoIP phone being remotely controlled by a wrongdoer turned on the microphone on the phone in a senior executive's office. That phone then becomes a microphone listening device whereby confidential or proprietary information may be disclosed unknowingly. Although the manufacturers are working to solve this problem, it remains a potential target.
  Another risk with the telephones is a DoS attack whereby a hacker or wrongdoer might launch a TCP or UDP flood on the LAN causing the telephone to compete for the resources and potentially force it to drop the connection. A secondary risk is a distributed-denial-of-service (DDoS) attack where a number of hacked devices may launch a number of different types of attacks such as DoS, DDoS, and others.
- Tools to authenticate and encrypt: Many of the phones may not have a reasonable method of being authenticated on the network. Thus, as mentioned above, any phone can be attached to the network and use services. Suppose a phone can be authenticated (either none required or some simplistic approach is used); then it is granted access. However, if the phone can somehow be required to use an 802.1X authentication using a preinstalled certificate, so much the better. Most manufacturers are considering using an 802.1X solution, but the upgrades to many systems may be too costly. Once the phone is authenticated, there needs to be a mechanism to secure the signaling and the traffic. This means that the phone should be using an encrypted format to secure the voice as well as the signaling. Tools as well as protocols are being developed to encrypt the traffic and signaling information. Tools to solve this will be discussed a little later in this book.
  Incidentally, SIP is a protocol of choice in most cases and it in itself was not designed to be universally open. SIP runs over UDP, a nonsecure protocol, and then over IP, which as stated in the beginning of this chapter is a wide open set of protocols.

Now in a table format the list may look as shown in Table 1.3.

There is also a potpourri of handset-type devices that spans the IP phones, PDAs, softphones, and a range of VoIP applications as shown in Figure 1.13. Unfortunately, many of these devices are manufactured by different vendors, have different operating systems, are available in different revisions of the code, and have different

Table 1.3   List of Risks and Vulnerabilities in a VoIP Network

IP phones
Core routers
Media gateways and session border controllers
SIP proxies
Gatekeepers*
Location servers
Layer 2/3 switches
Application layer gateways (ALG)
VoIP voice mail systems
VoIP fax and modems
Any infrastructure equipment in VoIP

Gatekeepers are particular to an H.323 network.

FIGURE 1.13

A potpourri of devices creates other risks.

procedures for using the system. This all adds to the complexity of the management and security of a VoIP solution. The term that has emerged in the industry is bring your own device (BYOD), which places the onus on VoIP management in an IT or other department. These devices add to the overhead and management of the overall system, while also exposing the VoIP networks because the end user owns the device but chooses to use this device in a corporate network, exposing back doors, entry points, and other risks because the end user is likely not securing the device and management has no "real" right to adjust or mandate how a user device will function. The only thing that can reasonably be done is to limit the access and secure areas that a BYOD device can be allowed. This creates new conflicts between the management and the end user who feels that total access should be available wherever, whenever, and however the user wishes.

Additionally different skill sets and risks are associated with different types of hackers. As mentioned above, there may be a youngster who is looking for bragging rights, or a different type of hacker who is looking for free use of a telephone network for personal use. That basically leads to several different types of hackers who are risks to corporations, small businesses, and just about anyone else. The hacker groupings shown in Table 1.4 are risks to not only a VoIP but also a data network. Also shown in Table 1.4 is a summary of the different types of hackers and the degree of risk that would typically be associated with them.

Table 1.4 Types of VoIP Hackers

Group	Details	Skill Level	Threat
Casual hackers and crackers	Varying levels of skill, ranging from beginners to seasoned veterans. Often they rely on widely available automated tools to locate (scan) and exploit weaknesses	Low–high	Low–moderate
Employees and insiders	Direct access to internal resources. May have detailed knowledge of an organization's computer and VoIP systems and security mechanisms	Low–high	Moderate–high
Thieves and career criminals	May be highly skilled at evading discovery and capture. Detailed understanding of financial and accounting systems	Moderate–high	High
Corporate spies and hired professionals, industrial espionage	Proven skill sets. Often are insiders with direct access to confidential information, or are hired (moles) to gain such access	Moderate–very high	High–very high
Foreign governments and terrorist organizations	Highly trained with very high skills. They are focused on intelligence gathering and effective information warfare tactics	Very high	Very high

A word about a few of these types of hackers may be in order here, given incidents and conditions in the world today. For example, when it comes to the casual hacker, it might also include a novice such as a "script kiddie." Now most folks have heard of script kiddies but just what is the risk? Well for one, they launch what is called an unstructured attack. They really don't have the skills to develop the tools themselves, so they basically scan the web or other blogs to find a tool developed by someone else. They use it without really knowing what they are doing; then whether successful or not, they usually pass it on to someone else (like a friend or co-student, etc.). Script kiddy is normally considered a derogatory term, which if used when discussing these novices can actually cause them to become infuriated and launch even more attacks. So a word of caution is to use the terms carefully. The difference between an unstructured attack and an all-out DoS attack may well be that the attacker in the latter case has been offended!

The second issue is that of the employee or insider. This may well be a contractor, subcontractor, or whatever. The newspapers as of 2012–2013 have been rife with stories of "insiders" who have blown a whistle over something that they feel is a violation of their moral code or of customers' confidence and trust. Examples of insiders that recently were in the press include Pvt. Bradley Manning who chose to release thousands of confidential e-mails and messages to the outside (WikiLeaks). Although these were e-mail and messages, the point could have easily been the fact that voice mails and voice messages could have been equally breached.

Still another of the (in)famous whistleblowers is Edward Snowden who released information about NSA including leaked information and details about several top-secret mass surveillance programs. Snowden was a contractor working at NSA who revealed programs of mail interception, telephone call details, and Internet usage. So as an insider he was able to breach security systems within NSA by bypassing logs and accessing information to which he supposedly did not have access. As an insider, he was privy to many of the systems and security measures within NSA.

The above incidents are a sampling of insiders defeating systems and posing security risks. Given the tenacity of the two insiders, one can imagine what others might be doing to probe and attempt to breach VoIP and data systems. It has always been a statistic used in the data processing world that 80% of security breaches and violations to organizational rules are performed by employees or insiders.

The third type of risk is the thief. Once again the newspapers are always full of breaches and theft of information within an organization. Data centers are always being probed; credit card information is being lost or stolen on a regular basis on the belief that the information can be sold or used for profit or for identity theft. These breaches were from data centers. But equally important is the theft of services (e.g., voice) that can amount to significant losses for an organization. One such example is the case of Edward Pena. Pena from Miami was charged with stealing more than 10 million minutes of VoIP telephone service and selling them to unsuspecting customers at a highly discounted rate. He paid a West Coast computer hacker approximately $20,000 to help him illegally route Internet telephone calls through the networks of more than 15 unnamed VoIP companies (carriers). He and his partner were able to present themselves as legitimate carriers and sell the stolen minutes to customers. Pena netted over $1,000,000. When captured he was charged with wire fraud for violating computer hacking laws. Pena was convicted in February 2010 of computer hacking and wire fraud. Pena and Moore, his partner, used brute force attacks against VoIP networks owned by the carriers. They penetrated the authorization codes and then sold the access to the unsuspecting customers.

Another such situation occurred in Los Angeles when hackers commandeered a hospital's VoIP telephone system. The hackers demanded that employees pay hundreds of dollars or they would take the phone system out of service. The hackers launched a denial of service (DoS)[10] attack on the hospital's phone system rendering it totally unusable for a couple of days. Scammers and hackers are now launching attacks that exploit the vulnerability of the VoIP systems by totally flooding the lines with call attempts causing the systems to seize up and creating buffer overflows. These attacks are becoming far more frequent. Although the process has been the techniques of scammers, it may well become the tool for malicious hackers and/ or terrorists to knock out services such as electric distribution centers, hospitals, emergency services, military installations, etc. Evidence now shows that these types of attacks are increasing in the hundreds. End users have been coerced into paying various amounts of money (hundreds to thousands) just to stop the attacks. The point, of course, is that the frequency and the vulnerabilities are increasing and that much has to be done to protect against and mitigate the risks.

The other two types are far more risky, but much less information has been exposed regarding the professional spies. This has one of the following two different possibilities:

- They are not discovered and they move on after garnering the information or doing enough damage.
- They are discovered but the organization does not wish to publicize the facts because it might make them look foolish.

Think about the ramifications if a professional hacker or a corporate spy causes any form of breach in security. In many cases the security and the public relations departments don't want to admit that they were defeated for different reasons. The security department doesn't want to look ineffective to peers in the industry, whereas the public relations department doesn't want to have the industry (bankers, stockholders, senior management) lose confidence in the organization's ability to protect its assets and proprietary information. This is a form of a "Catch-22" in that the organizational departments don't want the world to know what is going on, but the need to let others know what has happened is paramount to prevent future exposures.

Only recently has the threats of cyber security and attacks by terrorist organizations begun to surface. The industry personnel have probably known of this threat and been exposed to it, but kept it quiet. A recent comment from the departing Secretary of Homeland Security, Janet Napolitano, emphasized that the new Secretary

---

[10]More on this topic later.

would have to prepare for the Cyber Attack quickly to prevent exposure. Moreover, several news clippings over the period of 2013 have indicated that everyone is spying on everyone else. These are government agencies and terrorist groups that are trying to protect against or perpetrate the inevitable penetration. It is no longer a secret that different governments have the tools and the clout to eavesdrop on conversations whether on the landline (copper wires that we always thought were so secure) or on wireless technologies. This easily includes the capture and the decoding of VoIP conversations.

The above conversations are in no way criticisms of the need and the preventative steps that are taking place around the world. Instead, these are comments that no matter what the means of communications or what the protocols used, the ability to capture and decode a VoIP conversation exists and is used on a regular basis. The logical conclusion that follows is that industry must take whatever precautions to prevent the arbitrary capture and decoding of confidential, business information by anyone who does not have a need to know the information. This includes the casual hackers, the crackers, and the "script kiddies" along with industrial espionage agents and terrorists. This may sound a bit like paranoia but the historical facts are there and need to be considered while planning for a VoIP network solution. Another issue that should be considered is that VoIP networks also carry a lot of other type of information, such as fax, video, and data. Thus, whatever steps that can be taken must be taken.

NEED FOR SECURITY AND CAUSES

When considering the need for security on a VoIP system, there are several issues that prevail in any technology. Inherent weaknesses exist in just about any old or new technology. After all, VoIP is still in its infancy because it has only been developed since 1996 and beyond. In the telecommunications arena this still relegates it to a "new" technology. Therefore, it must be treated because of this newness using the following considerations:

- Technology weakness
- Policy weakness
- Configuration weakness

This list can be taken one at a time to understand just what is going on.

Technology

Every technology developed is typically a product in motion and therefore has its own weaknesses. This may include some of the source code, the physical chipsets, the operating systems, etc. Regardless, many of these technological weaknesses never get published by the vendors; instead the vendors might create a fix (patch) and just introduce the next revision of their software. Sure, some of the glitches make the news and get a lot of publicity, but there are many fixes that the vendors just do not speak about. Many of the glitches are discovered by research houses and universities, either on their own or under contract from a vendor. However, many are also discovered by hackers who are looking for back doors into the code or ways of usurping the security measures that the vendor put in place.

One such example is the kernel in a VoIP phone that can be manipulated. This is one of those issues that is not specific to a single vendor product or a single vendor! Indeed a hack[11] on the system exposed a point of exploitation that allows anyone with the correct set of tools to remotely turn on the microphone in a VoIP telephone. This is serious because if done, that microphone is like a hidden eavesdropping device to listen in on any conversation that takes place in the room. Now the particular phone tested (and any other manufacturer's phone could have easily been chosen and shown to be exploitable) was a Cisco 7xxx phone using Cisco Native Unix (CNU) code. Without exposing the actual problem and techniques, Columbia notified Cisco of the problem. Cisco agreed to fix the situation. The aim here is not to select and pick on Cisco; as mentioned any other manufacturer's phone could have easily been exposed to this same exploitation because they all use the same basic principles and coding techniques. Moreover, the issue was that the microphone could be remotely activated (e.g., with a wireless PDA) and any conversation could be listened in on. Note the VoIP phone is not carrying a VoIP conversation across the network but it is a listening device by nature of its function. Now think about the Cisco 7xxx series phones that are very popular in the industry and understand just who uses them: people such as senior executives in corporations, bankers, mortgage lenders, Homeland Security, DoD, the President of the United States, Director of CIA, FBI, and many others. What information, proprietary research, national defense, law enforcement, or personal information based on financial situations can be discussed in these offices where the VoIP phones that are exploitable are located? This makes a great opportunity for a terrorist group to learn about DoD issues and plans, opens the door for legal ramifications, and also creates the opportunity for identity theft. So the technology issue, of which one was listed, exposes a myriad of problems and risks. Remember also, TCP/IP was never originally designed to be a secure set of protocols. It was designed as an open set of protocols to allow different systems made by different vendors and using different operating systems to intercommunicate. Add the fact of TCP/IP's openness that operating systems made by different companies have known technological problems with patches, fixes, upgrades, and every other kind of known weakness. Included in this risk of technological problems is the entire list of network equipment (such as layer 2/3 switches, routers, firewalls, gateways, etc.). In reality, any time a VoIP system is being put together, it behooves the organization to look at every system component for holes. Make sure that all patches, fixes, and updates are applied to each component as recommended by the vendor.

Other issues that have been addressed in the past have been the fact that some systems can be forced into an unscheduled reboot, and during the reboot a hacker

---

[11]A study sponsored at Columbia University was published that exposed the problem with the code in the kernel of different VoIP phones. Columbia gets its research money from several different organizations including DARPA, Department of Homeland Security, IARPA, Cisco, and others.

can log in as "administrator" and take command of the phone system. This has been well documented in the past.

Policy

When addressing the issues, it is never clear just what group in an organization is responsible for the installation and operation of the VoIP telephony system. Logically one could assume that the IT department will be responsible for the management and operation of such a system because it touches every piece of network equipment as listed above. From Ethernet networking, layer 2 and 3 switching components, routers, gateways, and firewalls, the VoIP system uses all of the components in processing the actual calls. Add to that the fact that the data applications as listed above, such as integrated voice and data, calendaring, messaging, e-mail, etc., all realistically fall under the domain of the IT department. However, there are other organizations that split the management and the operation of such systems between departments (i.e., in some organizations the administrative services department may be responsible for the day-to-day administration, whereas the technical associations are handled by IT). What this creates is a void in the policy decisions that may exist. For example, most IT departments have their policies of access and proper use of the IT network well documented. Included in the policies of an IT department will be security procedures (e.g., passwords, hours of operation, frequency of use) that are approved and tested on a regular basis. Unfortunately in the VoIP arena, and particularly when shared among departments, there are usually no security policies written. Moreover, the VoIP telephony system is often not included in the organization's disaster recovery plan, so whenever a fault, downtime, or attack occurs, there are little policies and procedures on how to react and recover.

Another area that creates a potential security risk is the fact that few policies exist for VoIP telephony that include a process for change management. Whenever a data processing system needs upgrades or patches, there is usually a very logical process of how the changes are applied, and what the fallback procedure will be. Yet, with a VoIP telephone system, it seems that a vendor might log onto the system (either locally or from remote) and apply a patch in a "laissez faire" approach, meaning that they do what they want without any inclusion of the management or owners of the system. Thus, the nonexistent change management policies lead the way to disastrous situations. Monitoring of the systems is also forgotten in many cases. As long as the system is up and running, no complaints are received and no major glitches occur; then the policy is one of "if it isn't broken, don't fix it!" Recall that a system may be functioning properly, but when a single vendor makes a change to a system, it may well cause pandemonium when that change causes a different component to fail, or worse when a door is opened that causes a major security risk to the system.[12] A detailed list of what is being accomplished, what the changes are, and what the

---

[12]It should be noted that most large companies test, first in a nonproduction environment, and then, off hours, on the full production system if they can. If they can't, they are still very careful to monitor (different than test) the environment from the outside-in to catch problems due to changes. This is not always directly related to security, but the companies are very aware of risk of all types now, and change control is very strict.

fallback procedures are must be included before any changes to operating systems, processes, and the like.

Still another policy decision that must be taken into consideration is the employment policy within the organization. These policies are lacking. The fact is that most pundits will state that 80% of all problems with security – breaches, theft of services, theft of identities, etc. – occur from internal sources. How often has the news media picked up on a story whereby an internal employee creates a breach for one of many reasons such as:

- Revenge against the organization
- Profit
- Recognition
- Ignorance

Therefore, when dealing with securing a VoIP system as with any organizational tool (e.g., finance systems, data processing, human resources) just hiring a knowledgeable individual is not enough; a reliable and security-conscious individual trait is a must.

Although other policy issues may also exist, the last one addressed herein is the fact that internal conflicts may also exist that could jeopardize the security of the VoIP system. This is especially true when two different departments have shared responsibility for the management and operation of the system. Management doesn't deliberately create the situation, but inadvertently it could happen. Depending on the severity of the internal conflict, the resultant damage to the VoIP systems and security can be monumental. There have been documented cases of deliberate sabotage between and among different departments. Although that happens, it is the organization that suffers the most when users cannot complete their responsibilities due to lack of service, lack of access, quality of service, and more. Besides, and often more problematic, the group that implements the system is almost always not the same group that provides the long-term support.

What the above areas point out is that whenever a VoIP system is being considered, financial gains will not be achieved, seamless integration of voice and data is not achieved, and overall business goals are not achieved unless the weaknesses described are addressed.

Terms and attacks

Oftentimes the terms used in a data processing environment migrate over to the VoIP systems. The reason is simple; the VoIP system is computer driven, software based, and connects to the LAN, just like the data processing equipment. A router handling the packets of voice performs the same as a router for strictly data. However, many routers (gateways, switches, etc.) handle both the voice and the data packets. Therefore, the same terms and risks exist for VoIP.

Thus, when looking at some of the terms used in the industry as seen in Table 1.5, the same terms have been around for many years in the data environment.

Table 1.5   Common Terms Used in Data and VoIP Systems

Terms	Description
Virus	A program that can replicate itself with little or no user intervention; the replicated programs can also replicate themselves
Worm	A form of virus that spreads by replicating itself on hard drives, systems, or networks. A worm working, for example, with an e-mail system can make copies of itself to every address in the e-mail system address book. Examples of these worms are Code Red and Nimda. These high-profile worms caused significant damage in the recent past*
Trojan horse	A disguised program that appears to have some use or may be amusing, such as a game or a screen saver. However, in the background the Trojan is performing other tasks such as deleting or changing data and capturing keystrokes (key loggers) that constitute log-on and passwords. A true Trojan horse is not technically a virus because it does not replicate itself. It is, however, a very dangerous program

A quick note is that in a VoIP system, presence is now used to create friends lists, etc.; these are in the form of an e-mail address that is a target for the worm. These can also be unknowingly launched by a "script kiddy."

Moreover, beyond the terms used, the names of attacks fall under one of the following:

- Structured
- Unstructured
- Internal
- External

Some of the kinds of attacks on a VoIP system include such things as:

- Reconnaissance attacks
- Access attacks
- DoS attacks
- Data manipulation attacks

Each of the above-mentioned four categories is an issue that covers other forms of service problems. The VoIP system should be designed and tested to protect against such kinds of attacks as shown in Table 1.6.

Reconnaissance attacks shown in Figure 1.14 [note the five example points selected (arrows point to the example point) to perform the reconnaissance], as the name implies, are a form of intelligence gathering. Typically the networks are probed at various points to determine any openings and vulnerabilities. Some of the methods used to perform a reconnaissance attack include call walking and port scanning. Call walking is a term used in reconnaissance attacks whereby the attacker initiates a lot of calls to a block of telephone numbers (say 100 numbers) in hopes of obtaining some identification of the resources used to service these calls. Some people will

Table 1.6   Typical Types of Attacks on a VoIP System

Type of Attack	Description
Toll fraud (theft of service)	The IP version of the classic attack by a person impersonating an employee (social engineering) or Console Cracking (asking the operator for an outside trunk) to make long-distance calls. However, the attacker impersonates a valid user and IP address by plugging in their phone or spoofing the MAC Ethernet address
Service use and abuse (internal threat)	The abuser uses services for his/her own personal gain, could be long-distance service abuse
Eavesdropping (monitoring)	The attacker sniffs (taps into the LAN wireline or Wi-Fi connection) to intercept voice messages. Easily available programs such as Voice over Misconfigured Internet Telephony (VOMIT) perform this function. Other tools used are Wireshark,* Audacity, etc.
Call hijacking (session hijacking)	Attacker spoofs a SIP response redirecting the caller to a rogue SIP address and intercepts the call
Resource exhaustion (service disruption)	Also known as denial-of-service (DoS) attack. This attack reduces the number of available IP addresses, bandwidth, processor memory, and other router/server functions
Message integrity	Man-in-the-middle (MIM) attacks to intercept, alter, or redirect call. Also sitting between the caller and the system allows the MIM to capture log-on and/or passwords
Message-type attacks	Attacker bombards (repetitive) SIP server with BYE or CANCEL messages or Internet Message Control Protocol (ICMP) "port unreachable" messages

Earlier versions were called Ethereal.

remember the term "war dialing" used in the movie called *WarGames* where a modem was used to dial sequentially to a block of numbers (10,000) to discover any modems that would answer and then create a target list. The call walking is a newer version of the war dialing program. The first action undertaken by an attacker when attempting to penetrate a network is to perform a reconnaissance attack like call walking probe. A successful probe would determine how the network equipment, users, and services perform as a means to be exploited or disrupted. This information could then be used to launch a structured attack against the network. This could then lead to one or more of the following:

- Dictionary attack
- Stealing presence of a SIP user
- Single user flood (UDP flood or number of calls flood)
- Multiuser flood (UDP flood or number of calls flood)
- Call walking
- Playing a SPAM message in audio format

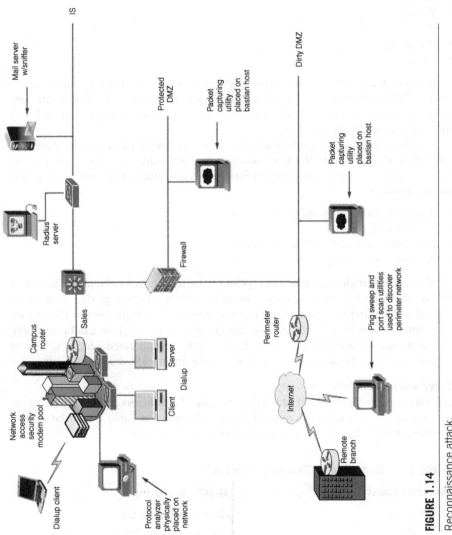

FIGURE 1.14

Reconnaissance attack.

Some of the commonly used reconnaissance tools are given as follows:

- NMAP
- Nessus
- Port scanner (advanced port scanner)
- Strobe
- WHOIS
- Ping
- Nslookup
- Trace

Access attacks include password crackers as means of gaining access either through MIM or through a form of reconnaissance attack. Table 1.7 lists a sampling of the password crackers used by evildoers. One cannot underestimate the tools that are readily available on the web.

One thing that should also be taken into account is the fact that social engineering can nullify all the benefits of a VoIP security plan. Regardless of what techniques are used, a social engineering (a different form of access) attack will virtually wipe out all the benefits of:

- Authentication of the end user
- VPN connections
- Firewalls and VoIP-enabled firewalls
- Network monitoring

Newspaper articles regarding the social engineering attacks abound. It is natural for an employee to feel somewhat intimidated when a person posing as a senior executive calls and says that they lost their password or their log-on. Either they are granted access by the employee looking it up or they are given a default access. This is an access attack in which the hacker gains unauthorized access as seen in Figure 1.15. Note the arrow pointing to where the unauthorized access occurs.

Other vulnerabilities

Several of the protocols posed added risks because the evildoers are always searching and probing the network. As a result the protocols shown in Table 1.8 can be considered the added risks and vulnerable points in a VoIP network.

Table 1.7 Sampling of Password Cracker Tools

Windows Based	Unix/Linux Based
L0phtCrack4	Qcrack by Crypt Keeper
PWLVIEW	Cracker Jack by Jackal
Pwlhack 4.1	John the Ripper by Openwall
PWL-Key	Crack by Alec Muffet
ntPassword	FastJack
SIPVicious	SIPVicious
Cain and Abel	

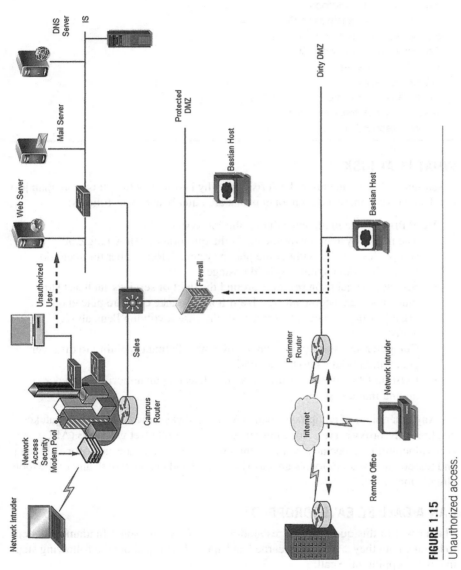

FIGURE 1.15

Unauthorized access.

Table 1.8 Vulnerable Protocols and Architectures in VoIP

Voice transport protocols
    Real-Time Protocol (RTP)
    Real-Time Control Protocol
    Stream Control Transmission Protocol (SCTP)
Signaling protocols and architectures
    Session Initiation Protocol (SIP)
    H.323 protocol suite
    H.248 MEGACO
    Media Gateway Control Protocol (MGCP)
    IAX2 from the Asterisk systems
    Skinny (Cisco SCCP)

WHAT IS AT RISK

A summary of just what might be at risk and why is shown below. It is more than just the data packets; there are components that are equally at risk as follows:

VoIP PBX, voice mail, and call distribution systems:
- The risk of system downtime poses the question of "How long can companies survive without the phone system?" Remember the scenario where the LA hospital was held hostage.
- Second, the question revolves around the theft of services such as "How much loss can a company survive if long-distance calls are placed on the organization's expense?" Remember the case involving Pena above.

Modems:
- Computer access may be obtained by a war dialing capability to discover penetration points into the network.
- Existing IP perimeter security may not detect an unauthorized intruder dialing into a system.

Any other piece of equipment such as VoIP gateways, media gateways, gatekeepers, firewalls, proxy servers, location servers, application layer gateways (ALG), etc., is a vulnerability especially in the signaling protocols that are used for call setup and teardown. These protocols are easily captured and decoded with any of the tools already mentioned.

CAN A CALL BE EAVESDROPPED?

The answer to this question is a resounding yes! There are some fundamental steps to be taken but they are quickly learned and applied. Think about the following steps in eavesdropping on a call:

1. Understand the fundamentals of IP telephony. Just what are the nuances and ways that the protocols present the voice over an IP network?
   a. The most important fact is, independent of vendor and signaling protocol, all IP telephony implementations use RTP.

    b. RTP does not use a fixed UDP port but instead relies on the call server to dynamically select a port from a predefined range. Each IP phone learns of this UDP port via the signaling protocol.

2. Obtain the necessary tools. This chapter has already expressed a number of tools that are readily available (free of charge in most cases) on the web. An evildoer will have no problem acquiring the necessary tools.

    a. Commercially available software application (e.g., Fireberd DNA-323) is an easy-to-use H.323 analysis tool.

    b. The tools enable the user to capture and play back IP telephony conversations.

    c. Most are Windows-based applications; however, there is a UNIX-based application available called voice over misconfigured Internet telephones (VOMIT).

    d. Many tools such as Wireshark[13] and Audacity are also readily available and free.

    e. One of the more interesting possibilities is the potential for network eavesdropping. An attacker with local access to a VoIP LAN can sniff network traffic and decipher voice conversations using Wireshark, Audacity, or VOMIT.

    f. Calls may also be hijacked by spoofing a SIP response.

    g. Potential for toll fraud exists if an attacker can impersonate a valid user/IP phone to ride along a VoIP network for free long-distance calls.

3. Connect the tools to the IP network. The reconnaissance attacks, access attacks, and social engineering attacks are all examples of how simple this can be.

    a. If configuration access to the switch was unavailable, ARP spoofing could be used to ensure that the tool captures the RTP packets.

    b. ARP spoofing is used by hackers to alter the normal flow of IP packets. It involves generating a spoofed ARP response packet in response to a valid ARP request packet.

    c. This process enables the hacker to direct the flow of IP packets through a compromised workstation from where the packets can be captured.

4. Attack by performing a packet capture and then decoding.

THERE IS NO HOLY GRAIL OUT THERE

Despite all the hype that has been placed on securing VoIP networks and calls, there are peculiarities in the industry that work against an organization. Because no one vendor necessarily installs all of the components, it is likely that differing approaches will be at work.

- Every company that has a product is unique; what works for one may not work for another.
- No one vendor has the perfect solution; if the vendor suggests that they can be the one solution that can provide sufficient security to prevent the risks already

---

[13]Formerly Ethereal.

discussed above, have them prove it. Guarantees with substantial penalties work to flesh out the wheat from the chaff.[14]

- No solution is complete because there are several different layers to the problem – much the same as an onion, when peeling off one layer at a time to find what is in the center. The same applies to a VoIP system that works in the OSI reference model; layered approach works best. Many vendors that offer a LAN, for example, address layers 1 and 2 of the model, but VoIP sits at the application layer, so different vendors may have to integrate their products to complete the network. The same holds true when securing the VoIP system; layers must be addressed.
- The layered defense starts with the people touching the system, operational, managerial personnel, and users alike. With the people come policies and procedures on what to do and how. These are critical components in securing a VoIP solution.

SUMMARY

Thus far, the issues are dealing with the possible risks and the types of attacks that can be deployed against an organization's system. These are many in the real world because there is so much at stake. In the next chapter, additional risks will be addressed and how these attacks will work against an organization.

---

[14]The phrase "separate the wheat from the chaff" is a holdover from an adage of the past meaning that you select what is useful or valuable and disregard what is useless.

Policies

A computer security policy is a formal statement of the rules by which people who are given access to an organization's technology and information assets must abide.
IETF *Site Security Handbook*

CHAPTER OUTLINE

In Chapter 1, several issues were pointed out dealing with the reasons that a person or persons would want to attack and eavesdrop on a Voice over Internet Protocol (VoIP) call. The list was not exhaustive, but clearly pointed out many of the issues and the reasons why. Those in the industry are concerned that a new line of exposure has been created that few people understand what VoIP is all about and fewer people know how to protect it. End users look to their vendors to provide the necessary security tools to protect the VoIP. Yet, as seen in Chapter 1, many vendors have minimal security. Aside from that, the interconnection of different vendor products to create a VoIP network creates a whole new set of problems. What works for one company very likely may not work for a different company. Additionally, whenever a vendor upgrades a product that is interconnected, the changes necessary in operating system, security processes, etc., can break a different component's security process. What did work before the change no longer works after a change is implemented. This could be understandable in that a single vendor is concerned only with the products that they sold; all the other products are not their concern. Yet, as the owner of the network (and all the associated components that make up that network) the user department (IT, IT Security, Administration, etc.) must be concerned with what happens. A secure solution that was painstakingly built now no longer is secure. Worse, the user department may not even know what has changed or what is no longer working the way it was.

Beyond the vendor situation that can certainly cause disruptive problems, the actual end user of the service creates a new set of problems. In today's networks (wired or wireless) end users feel entitled! They want to bring in their devices (regardless of the device, such as a cellular phone, PDA, smartphone, tablet, etc.) and use it in the office environment for their personal satisfaction. Most organizations were not prepared for this onslaught of requests (or demands) from the end-user community. As a result, policies and procedures were not in place to deal with the "bring your own device (BYOD)" practice. When dealing with a company-owned piece of equipment, the organization can pretty much dictate what the security policies and procedures will be. In fact, equipment can be bought (or initially configured) that conforms to the company security policy. Not so with a BYOD device, in that these devices come from a myriad of outside agencies such as:

- Cellular companies
- Electronic boutiques
- Large department stores
- Web-based sales organizations

Moreover, these devices are leased, rented, or owned by different people (usually the employee) and it becomes very difficult to manage and control such a wide variety of devices, owners, operating systems, interfaces, applications, etc.

The variables associated with the variety of devices include (this list is not exhaustive but it does represent some of the more common):

- Type of device (PDA, smartphone, tablet, laptop, netbook, etc.)
- Versions of cellular environment (GSM, CDMA, WCDMA, CDMA2000, LTE, WiMAX, and so forth, also called 2G, 3G, 4G, etc.)
- PC laptop and notebook-based operating systems:
  - MAC OS (Cheetah, Puma, Jaguar, Panther, Tiger, Leopard, Snow Leopard, Lion, Mountain Lion)
  - Windows (XP, Vista, Win7, Win8)
  - Chrome OS
  - Android OS
  - Chrome–Android converged
- Versions of smartphone operating systems:
  - IOS version (versions 1–7 on an iPhone)
  - Android versions (i.e., Cupcake, Donut, Éclair, Froyo, Gingerbread, Honeycomb, Ice Cream Sandwich, Jelly Bean)
  - Even the Distro environment for the variety of Linux versions (i.e., Ubuntu, Fedora, Linux Mint, Puppy Linux, Tiny Core, Mepis, and more)
  - Symbian versions 6–10
- Wi-Fi devices (802.11 a/b/g/n/ac, etc.)

Just about all of the above devices create a new exposure into a VoIP and data network. Every one of them has some ability to handle VoIP as either a function of the operating system or an add-on feature or software application. This also includes the use of softphones that every vendor has some interface or added application to deal with VoIP softphones. Still another opening is an application that can run on a desktop PC, notebooks, cell phones, tablets (many), PDAs, etc. This includes Skype and others.

WHAT IS THE PROBLEM?

Just about any of the VoIP components such as IP-PBXs or IP phones (including the list covered above) are potential targets for compromise by any one of many packet-based attacks. These phones and signal routing devices have two potential weaknesses:

- First, they all rely on an underlying operating system as discussed above, which most likely has exploitable vulnerabilities. One needs only to read the trade press to understand many of these vulnerabilities. In Chapter 1, the "kernel" problem showed that part of the OS in many of the phones was an exploit target that has been uncovered.
- Second, beyond the operating systems, the devices (routers, phones, gateways, etc.) may have a variety of openings in them that present an opportunity for exploitation. The protocols used for VoIP traffic are relatively new (in terms of a telecommunications system, VoIP is still in its infancy). Protocols are in constant flux (look at the number of RFCs alone that deal with the signaling and media protocols); a distinct possibility exists of an as-yet undiscovered exploit that allows attackers system access, opportunities to crash devices, or allow improper phone usage (such as phone theft or the other issues to be discussed later in this book).

Think about this: when making a VoIP call two different communications channels are used at the same time:

1. The call control channel
2. The actual media channel (it can also be called the data channel because in VoIP; voice is data and data is too!)

THE CALL CONTROL CHANNEL – HIJACKING

Setting up a call begins with the use of a signaling capability across a control channel. Shown in the following sequence is a call establishment using the SIP protocol:

1. The calling party (Bob) decides to call the called party (Alice). A Domain Name System (DNS) resolve is needed to resolve the address for the called party.
2. The DNS server replies with the resolved address of the proxy server to use to send the call.
3. Bob's device sends an Invite message to the proxy server that handles Alice's device along with the parameters for the session description protocol (SDP).

4. The proxy server sends an inquiry (where is) to its location server asking to locate Alice's phone (or PC).
5. The location server sends a reply to the proxy server with Alice's PC address.
6. The proxy server now sends a DNS resolve for the called PC.
7. The DNS server sends back to the proxy server the address to use to reach Alice.
8. The proxy server now sends the Invite message and the SDP parameters to Alice's device.
9. Alice's device returns a "100 (trying)" message to the proxy server.
10. The proxy server forwards the "100 (trying)" message to Bob.
11. Alice's device sends a "180 (ringing)" message to the proxy server.
12. The proxy server forwards the "180 (ringing)" message to Bob's device.
13. Alice's device returns a "200 (success)" message and the SDP parameters for Alice's device to the proxy server.
14. The proxy server forwards the "200 (success)" message and the SDP parameters for Alice's device to Bob's device.
15. Bob's device sends an ACK to the proxy server.
16. The proxy server forwards the ACK to Alice's device.
17. The media channel is then opened.

Note that this is shown in Figure 2.1. The graphic is used to show the activities that occur on the control channel (the SIP protocol). SIP uses a well-known port (UDP 5060) to set up the connection and then after the agreement is completed between the calling and called parties, the media channel (RTP) is opened.

A perpetrator can terminate the call control channel, by communicating with the signal routing device that the call is over while at the same time taking control and maintaining the media channel. The system thinks the call is over but the talk path or media channel is still in use. The possible result is theft of phone services.

Now another issue is possible with the VoIP protocols allowing mobility:

1. Alice moves from her office to home. On logging on, Alice's device registers with the proxy server at the new location (Register).
2. The proxy server then forwards a location update message with the new location for Alice.
3. The proxy server then responds to Alice's device with a "200 (OK)" message.

This sequence is shown in Figure 2.2.

Once the mobility sequence occurs, the next issue is on redirection. This could pose a situation of hijacking a call based on a redirection. First, the following sequence describes how the redirection works:

1. The calling party (Bob) decides to call the called party (Alice). A DNS resolve is needed to resolve the address for the called party.
2. The DNS server replies with the resolved address of the proxy server to use to send the call.
3. Bob's device sends an "Invite" message to the proxy server that handles Alice's device along with the parameters for the SDP.

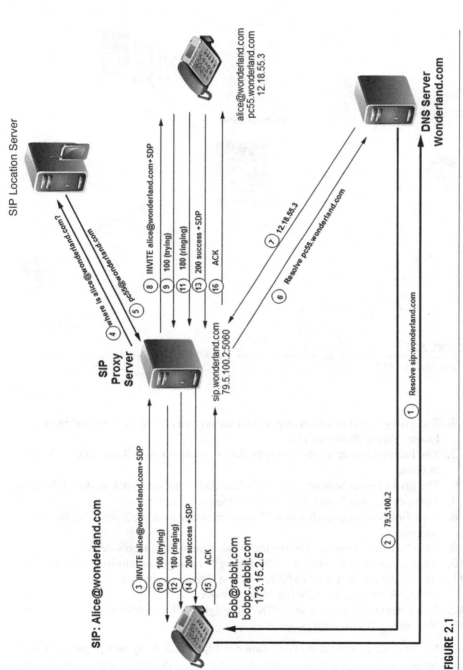

FIGURE 2.1

Setting up a SIP call.

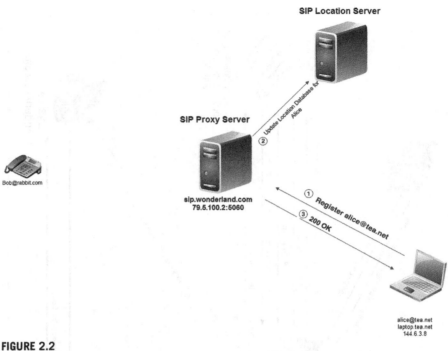

FIGURE 2.2

Using VoIP mobility.

4. The proxy server sends an inquiry (where is) to its location server asking to locate Alice's phone (or PC).
5. The location server sends a reply to the proxy server with Alice's PC address at home.
6. The proxy server now sends a "302 (Redirect)" message back to Bob's device.
7. Bob's device sends an "ACK" back to the proxy server.
8. Now Bob's device sends a new "Invite" message to Alice's device at the new address.
9. Alice's device sends a "100 (trying)" message back to Bob's device.
10. Alice's device now sends a "180 (ringing)" message back to Bob's device.
11. Alice's device then sends a "200 (success)" message back to Bob's device along with the SDP for Alice's device.
12. Bob's device then sends an "ACK" message to Alice's device.
13. Now the media channel is open.

The sequence described above is shown in Figure 2.3. Imagine a perpetrator who can corrupt the location database and redirect a call to a different location. Moreover, DNS poisoning could also be used to redirect the call to a different IP address.

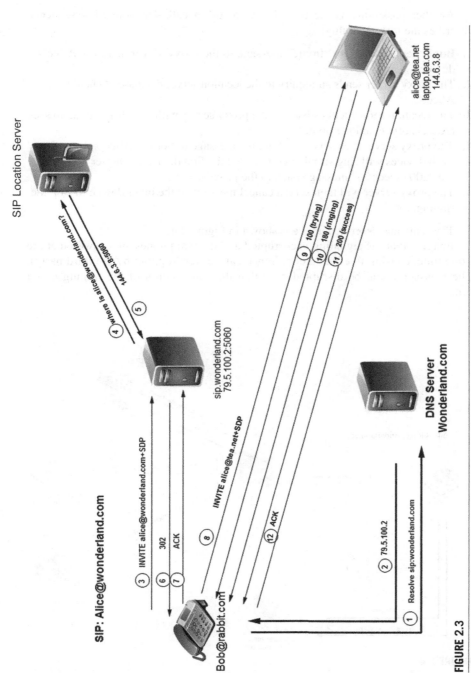

FIGURE 2.3

Redirection in SIP.

Another possibility is the SIP ability to fork a call. The following sequence describes the forking ability:

1. Bob's device sends an "Invite" message to the proxy server handling Alice's device.
2. The proxy server sends an inquiry to the location server database: "where is Alice?"
3. The location server replies back to the proxy server with two different addresses (Alice's office and her home).
4. The proxy server then sends the "Invite" message to both of Alice's devices.
5. Both devices will ring simultaneously, and the first device to answer will send the "200 (success)" message back to the proxy server.
6. The proxy server will then send a cancel message to the other device to stop the ringing.

The sequence described above is shown in Figure 2.4.

Imagine that the signaling is corrupted and the two phones are answered at the same time, causing in effect a conference call (eavesdropping by the third party). The message could be disrupted such that the cancellation of the ringing is not sent.

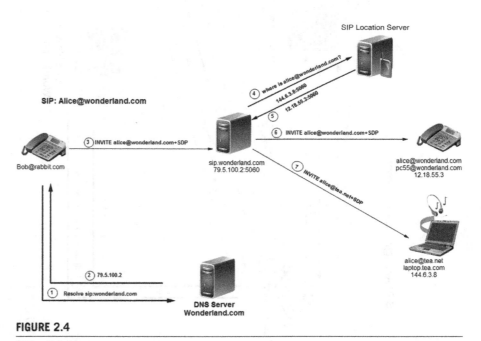

FIGURE 2.4

SIP call forking.

SOFTPHONE ISSUES

Now let's discuss one of the other devices mentioned above: softphones. Organizations can use VoIP softphones to connect remote employees without the need for expensive cellular phone bills or long distance. Headphones attach to a PC and use a software tool to provide VoIP services through the PC. Setup is easy, but adds a number of vulnerabilities. Viruses, worms, and Trojans are very common on PCs, which can expose the VoIP system to a number of threats, including eavesdropping, hijacking, theft, loss of confidentiality, and extortion. Moreover, the softphone is on the data portion of the network. What this means is a bridge is formed between the voice portion and the data portion of the network, allowing a user to access and sniff both sides of the network. The softphone – a virtual VoIP phone application that runs on laptop computers without the need for an actual telephone handset – is free in many cases. Some people will use a headset; others will just use the built-in speakers and microphone in the laptop. A typical softphone might look like that shown in Figure 2.5. This is a representation of the X-LITE offered by CounterPath and creating a connection with a free or very low-cost interface to an Internet telephony service provider (ITSP).

A softphone gives traveling employees a means to make calls as if they were inside the network. However, these remote computers can become an access point

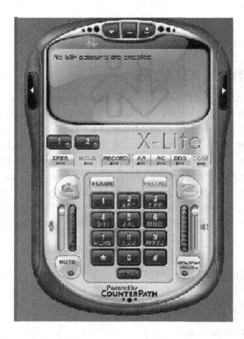

FIGURE 2.5

A softphone as offered by CounterPath.

for attackers if they are not properly secured. An unsecured computer can be easily compromised and used to collect data or access the corporate network. Additionally, most VoIP traffic is not encrypted by default as it travels over the Internet. VoIP deployment to remote users requires additional encryption techniques to protect the confidentiality of conversations.

The softphone can be used as a tool to attack the VoIP system. There are many cases in which a number of softphones have been used and configured to penetrate test a VoIP PBX system and/or usurp the security measures placed on the LAN. It is for this reason that organizations have a tendency to minimize the use of softphones within their environment. This is not a condemnation of the softphone because these devices clearly have a use in an organization and a practical means of accommodating the road warrior. It is, however, when the hacker looks for a tool that the softphone becomes an easy-to-use device in their quest to break into a system for other purposes.

The list of softphones (although not exhaustive) is quite large; just about all vendors have a softphone of some type, and each of these can be used in a penetration mode to overcome the security of the system. In Table 2.1 is a list of various softphones from the various manufacturers.

Softphones are also targets of a spoofing attack, whereby a client phone not registered on the network can be spoofed with an "Invite flood" that will cause the client software to crash. Tools are readily available for the attacker to find on the Internet. The use of a UDP flooder or a "SIP Invite" flood can also be used as a denial of service (DoS).

DENIAL-OF-SERVICE ATTACKS

Availability means that VoIP service is always available for use when needed. Voice networks have always been considered "lifeline" services. However, as much as data networks are exposed to many forms of attacks, VoIP services are equally at risk to a DoS attack. In such attacks, the attacker attempts to prevent your use of the VoIP system. DoS attacks can come in many forms. Policies have to be implemented before they become an issue. Many organizations forget to train the internal staff to report when things don't work properly. Lack of a dial tone, softphones continually crashing, servers crashing, and buffer overflows are all issues that users may experience but never report. Most DoS attacks result from an overload of resources:

1. Disk
2. Network bandwidth
3. Internal tables
4. Input buffers

Consequently, an organization may be under attack and never know it until too late.

Table 2.1 A List of Some of the Softphones Available on the Market

Manufacturer	Description
CounterPath	Various products that cover X-Lite, Bria, eyeBeam, etc. One of the more popular softphones
QuteCom	Previously known as WengoPhone
Firefly by FreshTel	Supports SIP and IAX, as well as a range of codecs
DIAX	Free, open source softphone supporting both SIP and IAX
Express Talk	STUN and SIP support
Zoiper	Supports both SIP and IAX
Damaka	"Peer to peer" SIP softphone
AdoreSoftphone	Supports SIP RFC 3261
MiniPax	Supports G.729, G.723.1, Speex, GSM, and G.711
MizuPhone	Extra features such as HD video, remote desktop over SIP, and ultra-wideband codec
FlashPhone	Adobe Air, web-based SIP softphone
FaramPhone	SIP softphone that utilizes the NGN, 3G network standards
Mirial Softphone	Supports SIP and HD quality
YakaPhone	IAX/IAX2 and SIP softphone
wxCommunicator	SIP Windows, C++, based on sipXtapi
Ekiga	Formerly known as GnomeMeeting, an open source VoIP and video conferencing application for GNOME
IAXComm	IAX softphone for Windows, Linux, and Mac OS-X
SJ Labs SJphone	Supports both SIP and H.323 industry open standards
Phoner	Free but not open source Windows SIP softphone. It also supports ISDN
3CX FREE VOIP Phone for Windows	Supports several SIP profiles, supports G.711 (A-Law and μ-law), GSM, iLBC, and Speex codecs. STUN support for NAT/firewall traversal

Source: VoIP Supply.com.

Looking further into such attacks, the following is a summary of some DoS attacks and distributed-denial-of-service (DDoS) attacks that can occur:

1. Vulnerabilities – DoS
2. Zombie recruitment
3. Attack tools
4. Bandwidth attacks
5. SYN floods
6. Established connection floods
7. Connections-per-second (CPS) floods

DoSs can be functionally categorized as an attack that comes from anywhere, including internal or external (across the Internet). Figure 2.6 is an example of a DoS perspective.

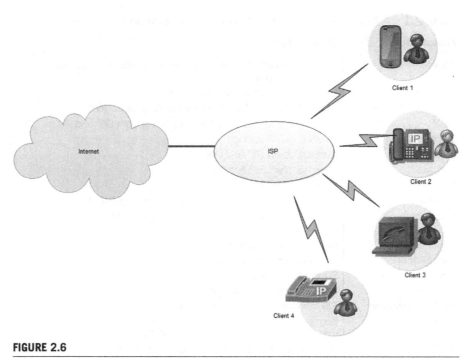

FIGURE 2.6

A typical scenario for a denial-of-service attack.

The hacker sends instructions to all of the computers in his or her zombie pool (also called a botnet) with the IP address and any specific parameters of the target machine. The zombies attempt to connect to the server over and over. The inundation of traffic requests slows the server down significantly for other legitimate users, or even causes it to shut down (crash) completely. Some well-known DDoS attacks include:

- *Ping of death:* This is when zombies send huge electronic packets to victims.
- *Mailbomb*: Zombies send out so much e-mail that it crashes the targeted e-mail server.
- *Smurf attack:* Zombies send Internet Control Message Protocol messages to innocent computers. These reflector computers are then made unknowing accomplices in the zombies' attack.
- *Teardrops:* When zombies send out pieces of an illegitimate data packet, the targeted system crashes from trying to reassemble the packet.
- *TCP SYN flood:* When the zombies send out a SYN–SYN–ACK sequence to the server (proxy, media server, etc.). The target machine receives a flood of TCP SYN messages that fills the backlog queue and ultimately causes the machine to slow down or crash from buffer overflows (see Figure 2.7 for the TCP SYN flood).

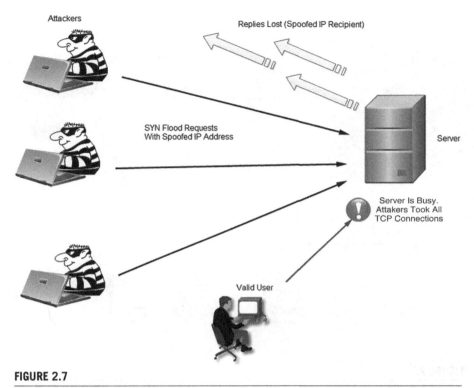

FIGURE 2.7

TCP SYN floods.

- *CPS:* CPS flood attacks flood servers with a high rate of connections from a seemingly valid source. In these attacks, an attacker or army of zombies attempts to exhaust server resources by quickly setting up and tearing down TCP connections, possibly initiating a request on each connection.
- *Established connection flood:* Attacks can be some of the most difficult to detect and block. These attacks originate from an IP address that is checked and accepted by a proxy server through a complete three-way handshake. Once an established connection flood attack enters a network, it strikes against the proxy server, intending to crash it. Once the proxy crashes, access to systems and servers behind the proxy server is blocked.

Zombie attacks fall into the category of a DDoS. In this case a series of attacks are launched at a target machine (proxy, gateway, signaling gateway, etc.). Figures 2.8 and 2.9 are a two-part example of a zombie attack on a media server.

In light of DoSs, there can be attacks based on flooding tools or there can be the DoS caused by abuse of protocols (i.e., SIP, H.323, TCP, etc.). These will include likely targeted devices such as:

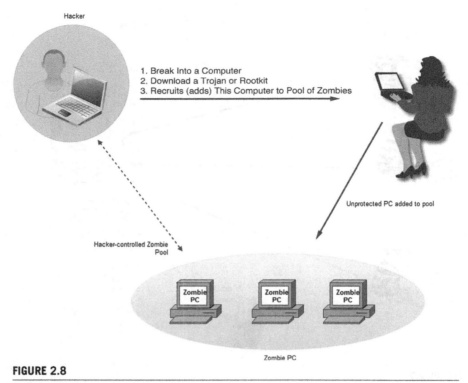

FIGURE 2.8

Zombie attack part 1.

1. IP phones (these are easy prey)
2. Routers and switches (would depend on the equipment)
3. Signaling gateways, media gateways, and SIP proxies (as described above)
4. Any other device in the path that a call takes from the originator to the termination

Some means of mitigating the zombie and DDoS attacks are when proxy servers detect a DoS attack; they enact a series of actions and notifications according to customized settings. Administrators can set the system to block, permit, or generate notifications for the system, users, and logs.

Every filter in the intrusion protection service (IPS) provides protection against a wide variety of attacks. Network administrators can customize the settings for filters, including the following:

- Actions for attack responses
- Notification contacts for alert messages
- Exceptions for specific IP addresses

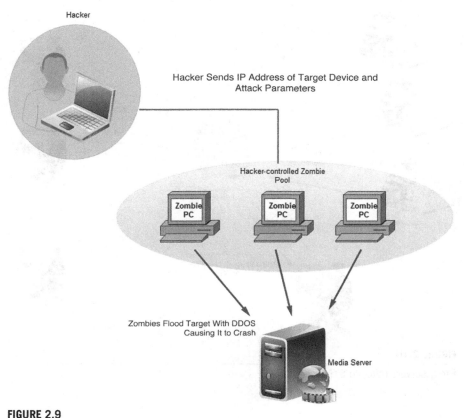

Hacker

Hacker Sends IP Address of Target Device and
Attack Parameters

Hacker-controlled Zombie
Pool

Zombie
PC

Zombie
PC

Zombie
PC

Zombies Flood Target With DDOS
Causing It to Crash

Media Server

FIGURE 2.9

Zombie attack part 2.

CPS flood filters working in conjunction with established connection flood filters and SYN proxy filters can provide dynamic and powerful protection for your network traffic.

Proxy servers can be used to mitigate SYN floods using advanced DDoS prevention as well as acting as a SYN proxy. This is shown in Figure 2.10.

SECURITY CONCERNS

Some added concerns that have to be considered is the fact that major issues exist with VoIP implementations because there is little effort that gets placed on securing the system. After all, it is only a telephone system! Oftentimes the person responsible for the VoIP system is not technically astute and not from the IT department. Many organizations have relegated the responsibility for the VoIP system to the Reception desk (Administration)–responsible person, in schools the Vice Principal, and in

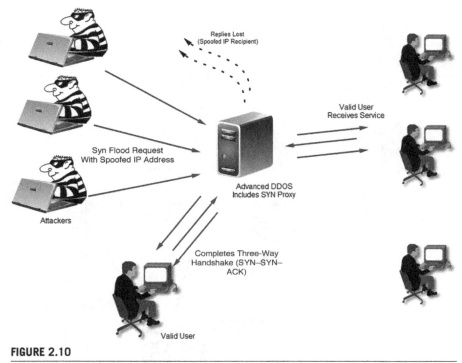

FIGURE 2.10

Proxy servers mitigate SYN floods.

medical offices it is the administrator for the front office. So, one can see that there will be other concerns that never enter the mind of the VoIP manager because this is all new to them. Some added concerns might include:

- Stealing bandwidth – In itself can cause many delays and system crashes. If users cannot make and receive their calls unimpeded, then they will not want to use the system.
- Eavesdropping – Discussed in chapter 1, the impact of this could be tremendous. For example, if the eavesdropping is accidental, then the impact is probably minimal, but if the eavesdropping was conducted by a competitor, it could mean a significant loss or impact. Moreover, if the eavesdropping is from a foreign terrorist group, then the consequences could be greater, possibly involving life and death situations.
- Stealing data – Stealing data can have all the same consequences as stated above in the eavesdropping issues. Usually, industrial espionage is involved and that could impact financial or market share postures. This can be done in a wireless environment with IP spoofing as seen in Figure 2.11. IP spoofing hides the attacker's identity.

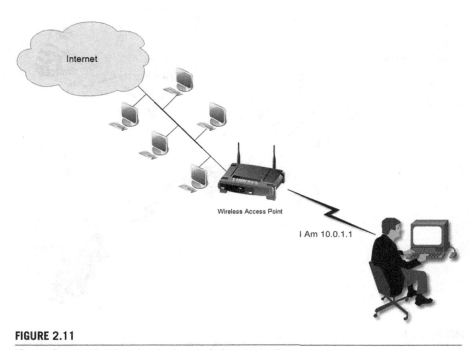

Wireless Access Point

I Am 10.0.1.1

FIGURE 2.11

IP spoofing can be done in wired and wireless networks.

- Impersonation – What if we divulge information to someone who says that they are someone else? Impersonation is a very big risk in wireless such as man-in-the-middle attacks. This is seen in Figure 2.12 showing the impersonator.
- Modification and insertion – Someone using portions of the voice and conducting a replay attack. This could be used for personal gain, disruption, or just inserting information to show off that it can be done. The replay attack can also be done in a wired or wireless network. Figure 2.13 is a graphic of a replay attack.
- DoS – Discussed above, the DoS and DDoS issues are very common. Besides those already mentioned there are some added ones that include[1]:
  - Trinoo (distributed bot)
  - Tribe Flood Network (variation of Trinoo)
  - Stacheldraht (Trinoo + DDOS) (German for barbed wire)
  - Trinity (Linux attack uses IP floods)
  - BlackEnergy
  - YoyoDDoS

---

[1]Many of these are older versions that were implemented around the 2000 time frame and were still being used in 2009–2010. Many of the capture tools and cleaners are now included in the virus scanners. However, like anything else care must be taken to stop these and others from getting on the network.

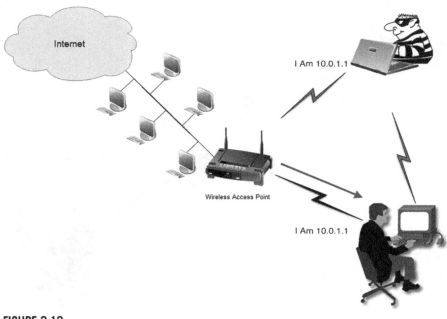

FIGURE 2.12

Impersonation is a risk, especially in wireless.

- Asymmetric attacks – These send normal rates of "high-workload" requests. For example, a single request from a client generates a large amount of work for a web server. The objective of these attacks is to consume large amounts of server resources such as CPU, memory, or disk space in order to severely degrade the service or bring it completely down.
- A flood of invalid VoIP registration requests that can cause the system disruption for days on end.

"Application-layer DDoS attacks" attempt to target specific well-known applications such as Hypertext Transfer Protocol (HTTP), DNS, or VoIP. It should be recognized that the VoIP phones and softphones have a web-based application in them for configuration purposes; this is an attack point. The DNS server is also a target for attackers because of the many vulnerabilities and the impact of a successful attack is potentially huge. The DNS servers perform the resolve for the addressing of a proxy and/or individual. If the DNS is poisoned, then the resolve will steer the caller to the wrong address. VoIP and specifically SIP and H.323 use well-known ports for their control signaling (SIP uses UDP port 5060 and H.323 uses TCP port 1720 for initiating a session). These ports as well as the servers must be protected. Moreover, the most serious threats to IP telephony are posed by RTP (i.e., media) flooding attacks that do not involve any handshaking, which makes detection far more difficult.

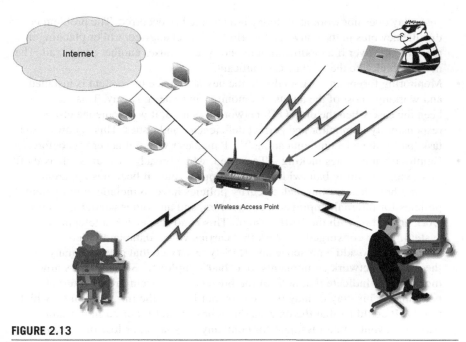

FIGURE 2.13

Replay attacks can be conducted as a modification or insertion.

SECURITY POLICY NEEDS

Given that many organizations have not taken a lot of steps to secure the VoIP system and the actual traffic, the need is paramount to create a policy to protect and defend the network. Many issues that can be attributed to the theft of services, penetrations into the VoIP networks, and the loss of confidentiality are listed as follows:

- No security policy written – This is a must do! Most organizations did not create a policy for the wired POTS networks because that was always considered the responsibility of the local telephone company. Now that the network has converged with the IP side of the business a policy must be written to secure and protect the VoIP services.
- No DR plan – For years IT departments have been building out disaster recovery/business continuity plans to recover in the event of a catastrophic loss. Once again, many organizations assumed that the local telephone company was responsible for recovering the voice network; therefore, this was not a requirement in the past but it is much more so now.
- Change management nonexistent – As covered in Chapter 1 many organizations have VoIP systems that include parts from a multitude of vendors. What might work together today may change overnight if one of the vendors creates a new operating system or updates some of the software. What worked well together

yesterday does not work at all today if a change has occurred. The problem is that the newbies in the converged world have no change control or planning in place to take over if a modification to one system causes another part to fail. The need to think like the IT staff is significant.

- Monitoring forgotten – Again due to the newness, once the system is installed and working, most of the audits and monitoring issues go away. This has been the case when the old POTS network was used; it was someone else's responsibility to monitor and correct deficiencies and issues. This is now on the task list for the telecommunications/VoIP manager where it never was before.

- Employment policies lacking – Too often, when breaches occur, such as theft of services, stealing bandwidth, eavesdropping, etc., it becomes apparent that the breaches are internal. Security policies have to include employment policies for internal employees, contractors, and any other vendor that may work around or with the VoIP system. This is no longer just a telephone system; it is a converged network that carries voice, data, and video. One could also add a presence and IMS-type service that exposes many of the internal network components to a "bad" employee. Several years now, most studies indicate that 80% of the breaches that occur are by internal personnel. This may or may not be true, but it is all the information on which to rely. It could be that the external breaches are not reported in the same way to prevent embarrassment for company personnel, or loss of consumer confidence.

- Internal conflicts exist – Who is responsible for the VoIP system? That question opens up myriad choices but in many cases it also points to the fact that several different departments may have some ownership. It opens the way for internal conflict if two (or more) different reporting structures are involved with managing and operating the system. One has to be sure that this is part of clean reporting line and addressed if any conflicts exist.

With these issues as being some of the key risks that must be dealt with, it is also imperative that a documented policy is necessary. Several years ago, the IETF *Site Security Handbook* addressed the need for a data processing security policy because of the nature of the TCP/IP protocol suite. Recall in Chapter 1 that IP was never developed to be secure; in fact, it was designed to be an "open system" that would allow data sharing between organizations, departments, and different computer operating systems. Thus, the handbook stated that:

> *A computer security policy is a formal statement of the rules by which people who are given access to an organization's technology and information assets must abide.*

IETF *Site Security Handbook*

Wise words suggesting that a formal document is needed for the VoIP portion of the business. Moreover, security pundits throughout the years have suggested that the policy must address the crime triangle. As seen in Figure 2.14, the crime triangle

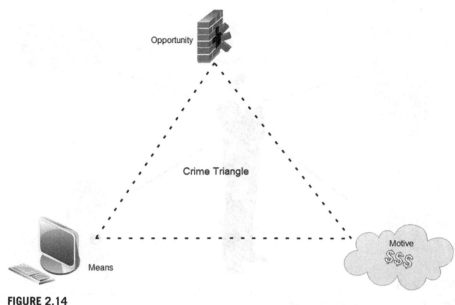

FIGURE 2.14

The crime triangle.

has three sides. In order for a crime to occur (as outlined in this book and others) there are three components: means, motive, and opportunity. If any one of the three components is missing, then a crime will not be committed.

1. If we have a means and an opportunity, but no motive, then there should be no incentive for a perpetrator to attempt a breach of the VoIP system.
2. If we have the means and the motive, but not the opportunity, then a crime cannot be committed.
3. If we have the opportunity and the motive, but not the means, then no crime can be committed.

Just evaluating the above three statements helps to understand that if there is any way to prevent the completion of the triangle, then the security of the VoIP system is assured (at least for now). The challenge is to make sure that one or more of the components are not available to a perpetrator so that the breach of security on the VoIP system and network will not be possible.

Following along the lines of keeping the triangle from being formed, there are many choices available to help in preventing penetration, breaches, and theft of the VoIP services. The list of possibilities to aid in securing the network includes some of the options shown in Figure 2.15. This graphic shows the pieces of the puzzle that can be put together to address the security needs. The more pieces used, the better, albeit the more overhead and expense. For example, the following pieces are included:

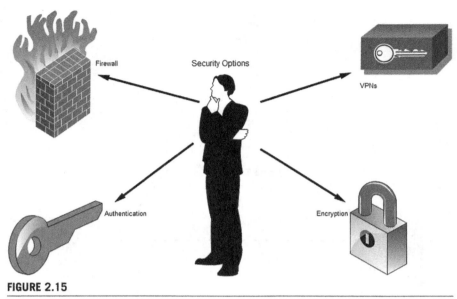

FIGURE 2.15

Security options to secure the VoIP.

1. Firewalls – These are typically the first targets from the internal and external networks. VoIP-aware firewalls are a requirement so that the firewalls do not prevent the VoIP from passing through. This also includes NAT boxes that work with the firewalls that stop the VoIP from happening due to the way that the protocols work. Session Traversal of UDP over NAT (STUN) allows the use of the VoIP protocols across the firewall and NAT combination.
2. Authentication – It is imperative that the users attempting to access the VoIP services are who they say they are. Authentication of the handset (or softphone) and the actual user is a solid way to secure the network. Unfortunately, not all authentication procedures are the same. The preferred method is port-based authentication for the handset and identity-based authentication for the individual. Identity-based networking can be built on certificates and PKI infrastructure (more on that later). Many of the VoIP system manufacturers are experimenting with installing certificates in their sets.
3. Encryption – Regardless of the overhead, which can be significant, the secure protocols allowing secure VoIP are a must. To prevent eavesdropping, manipulation, and insertion as well as replay, the secure protocols such as SRTP, SIPS, and other encrypted schemes are a must.
4. VPN – A virtual private network is also a very good bet when dealing with remote sites, remote employees (telecommuters), and branch offices. The VPN allows the mix and match of encryption, authentication, and the necessary hardware devices to protect the VoIP as well as data traversing the public or private Internets.

VULNERABILITY DETECTION AND AUDITING

To protect the network and close down the openings, it is a good idea to follow some general guidelines. The following is a list (not exhaustive) of things that can be done to aid in securing the VoIP service and network:

1. *Decide on a basic philosophy.* There are probably many options here but the possible two that should at least be considered are as follows:
   a. Protect and proceed – Many organizations choose to do whatever they can to protect the assets of the network and proceed with business as usual.
   b. The alternative is pursue and prosecute. This takes a different attitude that usually needs higher management approvals. Many organizations choose not to "air their dirty laundry" by publicizing that an event has occurred and that they are going to prosecute to the fullest extent of the law. This lets the whole world know that they were attacked and caught in the breach. This can be embarrassing and could lead to further complications.

2. *Match the level of response with the severity of the incident.* It is not prudent to spend more than the risk of an event is. For example, it is not wise to spend $1 million to protect $1000. Conversely, it is unwise to spend only $1000 to protect $1 million or more. This requires a clear assessment of the risk and the possible losses.

3. *Scan for security holes.* Decide what systems should be scanned for possible breaches and potential openings. Determine how often these systems should be scanned, whether it is weekly, monthly, or ongoing. Finally decide what corrective action needs to be taken.

4. *Audits.* Security audits have been an integral part of the IT departments for years. The VoIP system should be no different. Decide what to audit and how often to do the audits. Shake up the routine so that an audit trail will not be detected and usurped.

5. *Reduce the attack surface.* Take an active approach that monitors more than malware, including threats such as vulnerabilities, applications, websites, and spam. Ensure that the software in use, including applications, browsers, and plug-ins, is up to date, minimizing the risk from exploit-based attacks. Using the plug-in on-demand feature available in some browsers can also help reduce attacks from exploit kits using hidden content on websites.

6. *Protect everywhere.* Make sure users are protected wherever they are and whatever device they're using and combine endpoint (including mobile), gateway, and cloud technologies to share data and work together to provide better protection without impacting users and performance.

7. *Stop malware attacks.* Move beyond simply relying on antivirus signatures and look at layers of detection that stop threats at different stages of their execution. Ensure protection also looks at risky user behavior, not just for malicious code.

8. *Back up data.* Many forms of "ransomware" use encryption that is effectively unbreakable. Given the untrustworthy nature of "ransomware" authors the

only way to guarantee the return of your files is to restore them from your own backups.

9. *Stop data leaks and breaches.* There are three components of an information security strategy: the things required by law, the operational processes and procedures put into place, and the technology tools in use to get the job done.

10. *Keep people working.* Complexity is the enemy of security. Operational efficiency needs to be prioritized for both users and the IT staff. Consider workflows – what things get in the way or slow users down? By focusing on removing these barriers or problems, security improves and the staff and users will be efficient and happier too.

11. *Establish incident response teams.* This has been done by many departments but particularly the IT departments. Use the same feature of what the teams are to investigate and what the teams' plan is to respond to a breach or a suspected breach. Incident handling is a vast topic, but the following are a few tips to consider in the incident response:

   - Have an incident response plan in as much detail as possible.
   - Least privilege granted to users: do not give out unlimited privilege or access.
   - Defense in depth: create many layers of defense.
   - Diversity of defense: use different tools and techniques.
   - The choke point: find where everything stops if the choke point is closed.
   - The weakest link: try to find the weakest link and start shoring it up. One link at a time and soon the chain is stronger and secure.
   - Take a fail-safe stance: determine when to pull the plug and sound the alarm.
   - Ensure universal participation from all levels of management and users.
   - Simplicity: use the old KISS[2] routine.
   - Predefine the incident response team: perhaps members from various departments (i.e., Finance, Management, Real Estate, IT, Purchasing, Legal).
   - Define your approach: protect and proceed or pursue and prosecute.
   - Predistribute call cards: these are cards with the team members' names and numbers to be reached at any time.
   - Get users on the team: A little recruitment here and the odds are many users will want to be part of the response team.
   - Know how to report crimes and engage law enforcement.
   - Practice, practice, practice: practice makes perfect.

IS THE SYSTEM VULNERABLE?

The main problem is that the users of VoIP systems do not generally understand the technology they are using. Users see a phone on their desk, or occasionally a "softphone" on their computer. As a user, it is sometimes best to know what to do, but the chances are unlikely to really know how the whole solution works.

---

[2]Keep it short and simple.

The question of how much vulnerability exists is something that no author can answer for sure. This book's goal is to raise awareness of the risks. While VoIP servers are an amazing technology, they're also exposed to hackers from around the world. How vulnerable the VoIP system is depends on many factors. Have a conversation with the IT staff and VoIP providers about the examples described above. The rule is simple: demand accountability.

Ask a lot of questions from those who install the servers and solutions – and the VoIP providers. They should have anomaly detection systems in place to notice if usage and spending goes up dramatically in a relatively short period of time. They should also block expensive destinations unless asked for them to be unblocked. Later on in this book, several risky area codes and calling zones will be discussed. Target them to be blocked unless there is a vital business reason not to block them.

VoIP hacking is like most other forms of hacking – if there is not enough attention to security details, then the "bad guys" will get in and the onus is not on them. The Internet can still be considered the Wild West, and only with due diligence and awareness will the VoIP system and the organization be safe.

It is estimated that the worldwide cost of telecommunications fraud over the past year (2013) is $13 billion. VoIP fraud is bringing that number up significantly, and it's still growing. Interestingly, it's probably the cleanest form of money laundering possible – the telephone companies are a key part of it.

VoIP hacking isn't like having your web page defaced, or having a server hacked that needs to be rebuilt. It is the loss of real money straight from the organization's bottom line. The tools available to the hackers showing how easily VoIP systems can be hacked are readily available and typically shown on YouTube. Some of the tools that are commonly used and displayed on the web are (to name only a few)[3]:

- Viproy
- SIPDump
- SIPCrack
- SIPAutohack
- SIPVicious

The best rule of thumb is to prepare for the worst and hope for the best!

---

[3]All of these are available in Kali Linux, a wonderful live DVD package that has dozens and dozens of penetration and testing tools. Previously called BackTrack.

VoIP virtual private networks (VPNs)

VIRTUAL PRIVATE NETWORKS (VPNs) AND ENCRYPTION

In this chapter, the discussion will cover the use of VPN and encryption techniques as possible means for securing VoIP. Attempting to use any security method has its drawbacks such as the added overhead of handling the data transfer. Remember that voice is data and data is too! So when voice is tunneled inside a VPN, there is a price to pay, that being less data and more overhead. Additionally, when using a tunnel, the normal procedure is to use a form of encryption.

Thus, there are several choices available to secure the voice, albeit overhead notwithstanding. The choices addressed here will include:

- VPNs as one solution
- Typical end-to-end path
- Types of VPNs depending on the layer of the OSI model being implemented
- What a VPN offers
- Dealing with the needs and wants of the users of VoIP
- How much is enough; what are the consequences of a voice packet being dropped or lost?
- The five types of VPN that might be deployed

This coverage will then lead to a discussion on encryption, including the options of encryption technologies. Further, it will also discuss what the data scrambling brings to the overall performance and where it is used today. In addition, this chapter will address the use of public key infrastructure from an overview basis along with the use of 802.1X protocols to provide security on the network. Finally, it will address use of IP Security (IPSec) as a means of securing the VoIP calls as they traverse the LAN and WAN.

WHAT IS A VPN?

Before going into the actual solution it is prudent to do a quick tutorial on what a VPN actually is. There are many definitions of a VPN in the marketplace and each one has its own benefits and/or losses. So the first and foremost goal is to try to place a model with which the industry can live. The short version of a VPN is as follows:

A virtual private network (VPN) is an overlay network built on top of the public network through the use of a tunneling protocol, in which the tunnels provide for encryption, authentication and non-repudiation.

So another way of summarizing what a VPN is would be to state it as follows:

1. An extension of a private intranet
2. Used across the public networks (i.e., PSTN or Internet)
3. Proving a secure connection
4. Using a tunnel that makes it a virtual network
5. Normally owned by the carriers – although a private network can also be used
6. Used by an organization as though it is privately owned
7. Intended to eliminate the hassle of private ownership

That summary may well be subject to differences of opinion but it does convey what the industry is looking for in their networking strategies.

The definition above begs for more of a picture than just text. Shown in Figure 3.1 is a typical end-to-end path for a VPN. Note that firewalling is used on the ends between the public Internet and the intranet. Using the remote user as an example, perhaps with a softphone on the laptop computer, a connection is made with an xDSL or cable modem or, in the least likely mode, a dial-up link. The ISP connection uses the public Internet to provide the path across the public domain, and then passes the connection off to the firewall front-ending the private network (i.e., the LAN or CAN). This creates an end-to-end connection from the remote host to the corporate intranet.

However, cases have been reported in the past where an imposter creates a redirection to a false tunnel and thus to the wrong gateway. This can apply in a VoIP environment using a phone or a softphone and a laptop for data access. When a remote user accesses an unsecured network and particularly an unsecured Wi-Fi network, they expose themselves to a man-in-the-middle (MITM) attack. Yet many travelers (road warriors) still use unsecured networks if they have a VPN client. The risk is that a user's Wi-Fi connection (as in a coffee shop, free airport Wi-Fi access, Internet café, etc.) will be intercepted via an attacker on the network who executes a MiM attack. In Figure 3.2 one can see that across the Internet a false tunnel is built.

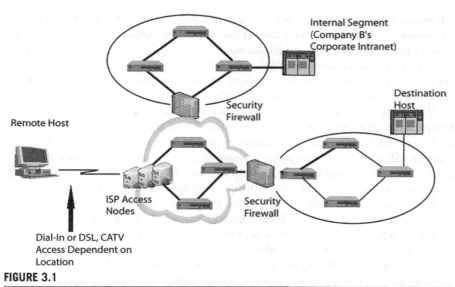

FIGURE 3.1

Typical end-to-end VPN path.

Still another risk is on a wired network (such as a hotel LAN or a remote rental office) an attacker can spoof ARP. The attacker's machine can advertise on the wire that it is the default gateway to the Internet and perform a MiM attack, causing a false tunnel to the imposter gateway. Users rarely notice anything amiss. Even if the imposter sets up a different form of user logon, the user will likely be oblivious to the

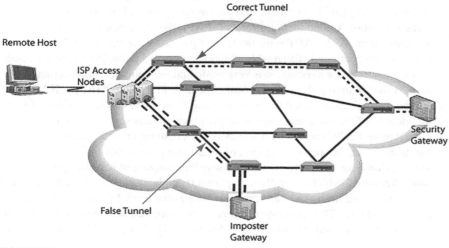

FIGURE 3.2

A false tunnel on a VPN.

difference. Once the user logs on to the imposter gateway (with the attacker capturing the username and password) they can get knocked off the connection. On retrying they connect to the correct tunnel and get through the VPN to the server. However, the correct logon on screen is now presented to the user who logs on as normal. The user will not recognize that something was different between the two logon screens that were presented and thus will not report any possible compromise to the security department.

Whenever a user's VPN credentials are sent in the clear, the attacker can sniff them and record them using one of many tools (Wireshark,[1] e.g.). If it's Secure Sockets Layer (SSL)–encrypted, the attacker can present a bogus certificate to try to intercept the SSL connection. The purpose is that the attackers will use the credentials to get access to the network or get free phone service. Moreover, attackers will typically save those stolen credentials and sell them. Educating the user is a must in this scenario as the user is the front line of defense in a situation like this.

The underlying assumption is that regardless of some of the risks, we are trying to provide a private network access over the public Internet. And, yes, risks still exist. Another risk is a "tailgater," who captures a set of credentials and gets onto the network by following the legitimate user onto the network using the same logon connection. This is particularly easier when dealing with a wireless connection.

THE POSSIBLE VPN SOLUTIONS

When looking at Figure 3.3 one can see that various layers of the OSI model can be employed to provide different forms of security. For example, stacked on top of each other, the layers can create a secure environment, but again at a great price in costs and overhead. Let's look at these one at a time:

- In the equivalent of layer 2 (data link) there are some very minimal security levels that can provide username and password sign-ons. For example, there is the Password Authentication Protocol (PAP), the older basic form of authentication. With PAP the username and password are transmitted over a network and compared with a table of name–password pairs. PAP is transmitted in the clear over the network; it is very basic and unsophisticated. Alternatively, there is the Challenge-Handshake Authentication Protocol (CHAP). CHAP is an authentication scheme used by Point-to-Point Protocol (PPP) servers to validate the identity of remote clients. An encrypted challenge is sent over the network. CHAP periodically verifies the identity of the client by using a three-way handshake. This happens at the time of establishing the initial link; the server sends a Challenge message. This three-way handshake can happen again at any time afterwards, which is totally transparent from the user. The client responds with a password hash. The verification is based on a shared secret (such as the user's password). The server then compares the received hash with a stored hash table of challenge and password pairs. Alternatively, there is a Microsoft version

---

[1]Formerly Ethereal.

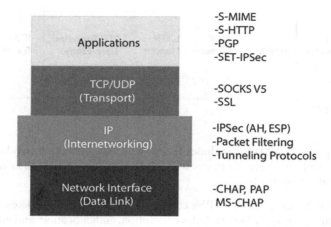

FIGURE 3.3

VPN solutions.

of CHAP called MS-CHAP. MS-CHAP v2 is more secure; it provides mutual authentication, stronger initial data encryption keys, and different encryption keys for sending and receiving. With MS-CHAP v2, the cryptographic key is always based on the user's password and a random challenge string. Each time it authenticates, a new string is used. MS-CHAP v1 was mainly used in windows 2000 and only provided one-way authentication; newer versions of Windows do not support v1, as v2 is much more secure. It uses a 40-bit encryption key based on the user's password. MS-CHAP v2 authentication is an exchange of three messages:

- The remote access server sends an MS-CHAP v2 Challenge message to the remote access client that consists of a session identifier and an arbitrary challenge string.
- The remote access client sends an MS-CHAP v2 Response message that contains:
  - The username
  - An arbitrary peer challenge string
  - A Secure Hash Algorithm (SHA) hash of the received challenge string, the peer challenge string, the session identifier, and the MD4-hashed version of the user's password
- The remote access server checks the MS-CHAP v2 Response message from the client and sends back an MS-CHAP v2 Response message containing:
  - An indication of the success or failure of the connection attempt
  - An authenticated response based on the sent challenge string, the peer challenge string, the client's encrypted response, and the user's password
- The remote access client verifies the authentication response and if it is correct, uses the connection. If the authentication response is not correct, the remote access client terminates the connection.

IP Header	IPSec Header	UDP Header	L2TP Header	L2TP Tunneled Data Frame	IPSec Trailer

FIGURE 3.4

L2TP over IPSec.

- Next, layer 3, the IP layer, includes IPSec [with Authentication Header (AH) and Encapsulating Security Payload (ESP) header], also packet filtering tools and tunneling protocols.

Whenever the discussion of VPNs comes up IPSec becomes the latest and greatest topic in the industry.[2] IPSec includes encryption, authentication, and other services in layer 3. Using IPSec alone provides the encryption and authentication; however, L2TP (which is not really a VPN technology but an access technology) combined with IPSec brings much more security to the forefront. An example of L2TP over IPSec is shown in Figure 3.4. The combination of L2TP and IPSec becomes a highly reliable VPN and is the most flexible for remote access.

- If one compares the layer 2 with layer 3 solutions, it can be thought of as follows:

Layer 2	Layer 3
Connection oriented	Connectionless oriented
Works similar to FR/ATM networks	Transport independent
Uses permanent virtual circuits	Uses Internet Protocol
Not directly connected to Internet	Inherently less secure
	Allows easy creation of extranets via the Internet

Packet filtering tools are also used in layer 3 that are used in firewalls. The packet filter either allows or denies packets from getting onto the network. Typical packet filters will be the firewall and/or the proxy server in a VoIP network. Packets are allowed to pass based on the policies that are established on the network. The two types of packet filters are:

- Stateful – A stateful filter remembers information about previous packets that have been forwarded. Dynamic filtering takes place because the filter inspects the packet header for source IP, destination IP, IP Protocol, TCP/UDP

---

[2]Recall from Chapter 1 the discussion of the NSA and Snowden, where an insider (albeit a contract employee) penetrated areas of the network and sensitive data that he had no rights to see. It is because of incidents like these that the standards-based IPSec should be carefully implemented.

Data Link Header	IP Header	GRE Header	PPP Header	Encrypted PPP Payload (IP Datagram, IPX Datagram, NetBEUI Frame)	Data Link Trailer

FIGURE 3.5

PPTP packet.

port number, ICMP messages, flags, and any options. This way there is a relationship to the packets being forwarded.

- Stateless – A stateless filter passes allowable packets along but maintains no memory of the packet or connection being used. Stateless filters can be easily overridden by hackers, thus becoming very susceptible to attack. SIP protocols use stateless filtering and use UDP as the means of transport. This is dangerous to use in VoIP but is the preferred method used by many vendors.

Other tunneling protocols include the Point-to-Point Tunneling Protocol (PPTP) as seen in Figure 3.5 in which a PPTP packet is shown. Users consider PPTP as a VPN technology in their pursuit for secure communications. However, PPTP messages typically do not deal with encryption or authentication. As a result, it is not really a VPN but merely a tunneling protocol. PPTP must have some other protocol to handle the encryption and authentication process. What one would see if using PPP to do this. PPP includes using Microsoft Point-to-Point Encryption (MPPE) and MS-CHAP v2. As discussed above, MS-CHAP has significant problems supplying the security that is needed. This is particularly true when MPPE uses MS-CHAP v1.

Looking back at Figure 3.3, the next layer is layer 4 solutions. At this layer one can see that the transport layer can support Secure Sockets (SOCKS) V5 or SSL VPN capabilities. Once again the use of any form of security at any layer adds to the depth of security at the cost of overhead and management.

SOCKS is an Internet protocol that handles the routing of packets between a client and a server, through a proxy. SOCKS5 adds authentication to ensure only authorized users have access to the server. Technically SOCKS operates at the session layer (layer5) of OSI and rides on other layer 4 technologies. In SOCKS a proxy server (used in VoIP systems, e.g.) handles the connection requests from the client device (a phone or a softphone) inside the firewall and either allows or disallows the connection based on the user credentials. SOCKS is used in a lot of the application layer gateways (ALGs) on a company's network. These ALGs supplement the firewall through the use of the proxy devices.

SSL is one of the most commonly used tunneling protocols as a robust and multipurpose protocol. Working at layer 4, the SSL protocol has been renamed as the Transport Layer Security (TLS). An SSL VPN is one of the three most commonly

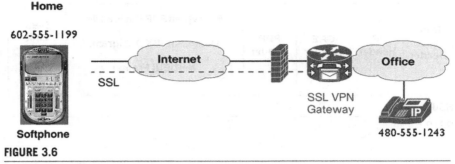

FIGURE 3.6

An SSL VPN gateway is used for connection.

used (along with PPTP and IPSec) but not compatible with IPSec, L2TP, or PPTP. What separates SSL VPNs from the others is that SSL can be used with a standard web browser, whereas the others require special client software on the user's computer. Moreover, the use of the SSL VPN brings less overhead to the overall performance (and in some cases has been said to improve the quality of the connection). In the past, the use of a VPN (regardless of the type) was not used on a handset; however, newer model phones from several vendors do provide this capability. This is also used as a softphone tool. Using a web browser on the laptop, for example, a user can use the SSL VPN to open a browser session and then connect to a SSL VPN gateway that allows the connection to or through the network at corporate. Alternatively, an SSL VPN can be used to log on and connect with the softphone to connect to any dial-up service from the corporate office. This scenario can be used for softphone to any phone (depending on the gateways available). Figure 3.6 is an example of a softphone on a laptop being used to connect to another IP phone by using the SSL VPN gateway.

WHAT A VPN CAN OFFER

A VPN (regardless of the type used) but specifically an SSL VPN is a good choice for making calls on a softphone when in a public area such as a coffee shop, airport, or Internet café. In this regard, the VPN tunnel will provide encrypted traffic to the far end. However, if the Wi-Fi connection is wide open, one must be careful that the initial sign-on/logon credentials may be sent in the clear and be exposed to eavesdropping. Moreover, a reconnaissance attack is possible when using public Wi-Fi access.

In general, the use of a VPN (regardless of the type) provides encrypted and authenticated connections to provide secure voice and minimizes, if not eliminates, MIM attacks and replay attacks. One should be sure to consider using such a tool when roaming or travelling anywhere away from the office.

The rationale for using a VPN is that an organization or individual looks for secure voice communications, however, with the connectivity and cost benefits of

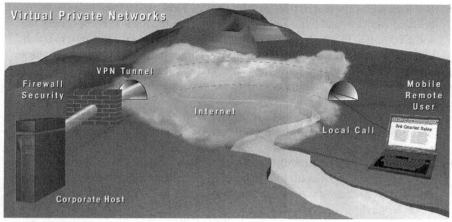

FIGURE 3.7

The steel pipe.

an Internet connection. So by handling the issues of a VoIP connection, a VPN provides:

- Encryption that will offer secure communications. Normally a VPN will use 128- or 256-bit encryption using AES.
- Authentication so that the systems will only allow authorized users to connect and use the network.
- Tunnels that hide the data, encrypt the data, authenticate the user, and hide the address of the parties.
- Virtually a steel pipe is created to let voice and data coexist on the Internet but keeps the rogue packets from penetrating the tunnels. Others' packets merely bounce off the steel pipe!

Figure 3.7 is an example of the VPN designated as the steel pipe.

Thinking of the VPN as a tool then it can be summed up as providing the following as a benefit of the VPN:

- Data integrity – The ideal situation is that the data (voice) cannot be manipulated by a replay or an insertion.
- Add-on security – By connecting to the Internet through a VPN tunnel, the network data are all well encrypted and secured by the VPN standard; all information is very safe from an attacker's eyes.
- Message privacy – The one thing that is crucial is that an eavesdropping attack can be prevented.
- Network anonymity – Through a VPN people can surf the websites in complete anonymity. Comparing this with the web proxy method, the VPN allows users to access Internet 100% anonymously.

- Unblock web sites and bypass web filters – A VPN can be used to access blocked websites and bypass network filters from the local ISP, especially in some countries in which Internet censorship is applied to web browsers (such as Far East and Middle Eastern countries). This is particularly true where these countries block VoIP (e.g., Skype is blocked in China).
- Authentication – The ability to ensure that the speaker is who he/she says he/she is and not an imposter.
- Access controls – As the tools develop the control of access will be seen later, but suffice it to say for now, only authorized persons are allowed to access the network for voice purposes.
- Audit and logging – The ability to check usage of specific VoIP trunks and services creates a powerful tool to manage and secure the network. Logging any failed and/or successful access attempts provides an indicator that an attack may be underway.
- Class of service and QoS – Using the SSL VPN as seen above may in fact improve the quality of a VoIP call. Moreover, with the VPN calls can be tunneled inside a steel pipe, meaning that an impersonator cannot see what is being carried inside the pipe. Finally on this point, if there are any blocks to specific ports (5060, 5061, 1720, etc.), then the call is carried in the outer pipe using either TCP or UDP standard ports. The blocked ports are hidden inside the pipe. This rings true whenever a government is blocking the VoIP calls. So class of service and quality of service are attainable through the use of the VPN.
- Reduce costs – Businesses like to use VPNs to set up multiple remote locations as a virtual local network to save the cost of renting dedicated Internet connections. The maintenance of establishing LAN connection through Internet VPN is very low compared with traditional dedicated line solutions.
- Remote work – Enterprises like to provide VPN connections to employees who work from home (telecommuters) or from remote sites during business travel.

WHAT EVERYONE EXPECTS FROM SECURING VoIP

Interestingly, this is not the only time the issue of wants and desires will arise. Whenever a network needs to be secured, the perceptions of the people involved will come into account as the policies and procedures are put in place. Let's be honest; if management, users, and the IT staff cannot all come to a compromise of what is expected, there will be problems enforcing the rules. Too many times, IT management puts policies in place that users do not accept or because of which they cannot accomplish their missions, thus impairing their performance. Overall what happens next is the end users begin complaining to their management resulting in demands of IT to start opening holes in the policies that ultimately lead to a nonworking solution. From historical perspective, it has been shown that anytime an enforcement of rules must apply to all (not just individual departments, individual users, or categories of users) or else the system will fail. Securing VoIP is not a trivial matter; there are always penetration and challenges that test the system. Thus, if the rules are not strong and enforceable, they will not achieve the end result of security.

Let's take a look at some generic wishes that can and will arise when trying to get to a secure VoIP (or a data network for that matter):

- Network managers/IT managers want to be able to provide the most secure network they can with as much strength in the rules as possible. Let's face it; their jobs depend on the ability to secure the voice. If they fail, then they will likely lose the confidence of management, lose the trust of users, and jeopardize their jobs. This is an unenviable position to be in for anyone, but it is a reality. Many an IT staff that attacks the problem becomes the brunt of the staff, seen as the enemy rather than a teammate. Thankless as it may sound, it is necessary for the IT management to push the security banner and be the champion for the company. The network managers also know that the network must be flexible as they pursue their security agenda. What this means is that the network vendors must be able to adjust and stick to the needs of the customer. Recall from Chapter 1 that many a vendor has produced changes in code or hardware that have opened up security holes, or the changes have caused other network tools and programs to be incompatible. There is no one solution, so flexibility in the network and the systems installed is a must.
- Users want everything! That is the usual response that management will offer. But, in reality, users want and need the network to be reliable, accessible, and secure. Their input often is seen as negative, but they also have the issue of having to conduct their day-to-day activities. If a system security policy or procedure changes the way they do business in a way that impairs their performance, they will be most vocal about it. Many a system in the past has floundered because the management could not get user buy-in. Thus, they may have a tendency to look for and find holes in the system that they will exploit to their advantage. Notwithstanding, it has always been said that 80% of the security breaches occur from in-house personnel. This is not a condemnation on the user population. Often times, it is the internal user who has more knowledge and opportunity to exploit the security of a security program. If a user is looking for a way to bypass some of the security, it may well lead to that person becoming a potential "internal hacker, cracker, or salami attacker." It is better to get the allies internally rather than encourage them to be potential probers that may open doors in our security systems and firewalls.

Beyond the potential hacker problem internally, if the end users are vocal enough to their management, then they can also create a scenario that is unworkable. As an example, if a department is responsible for premarketing or, for example, customer service, and the users in these groups complain long and hard enough to their management chain of command, then they may create enough discomfort for the department head to warrant the department head to request senior management to force a hole in the policies. This may come in the form of opening a pinhole in a firewall, or opening a bypass to a VPN to allow easier "nonrestrictive" access to the users in the department. Enough pinholes created in the firewalls or the access control lists leads to gaping holes that keep spreading, thus opening the door for a security breach. Consequently, a compromise must be reached with the users and management that meets the business needs while still ensuring the security of the VoIP systems (or any systems for that matter).

- Management – Having looked at IT and users, the next likely discussion leads to the wishes and desires of management. They want it to be the best system possible, secure in every way, but they also want it to be "inexpensive." What can be said is that management does not want the costs of securing a system (VoIP) to exceed the derived benefit. They also do not want or need the human capital costs to be jeopardized. They do not want complaints from their subordinates nor do they want the productivity of these employees to be limited. So it becomes a two-way street. They want cost efficiencies that do not impact employee performance. Rather they want it to be simple, agreeable, and revenue producing. However, management is also placed in a position that mandates they do not openly negate the intended security. There are laws such as Sarbanes–Oxley, a law passed in 2002 and known as SOX that requires companies to implement extensive procedures that prevent illegal activities internally within the company and to respond to any illegal activity investigations without delay. This particular act was put in place because of financial scandals and is designed to protect the shareholders and the public from fraudulent practices by an organization. Some of the requirements in publicly held companies[3] include:

- Ensure full financial disclosure
- Create consistent standards for internal policies[4]
- Require mandatory transparency of all corporate activities
- Increase the rights and protection of whistleblowers
- Requires corporations to report to independent external auditing committees

If an organization is in the medical practice, then it must also adhere to the Health Insurance Portability and Accountability Act (HIPAA/HITECH).[5] The HIPAA Privacy Rule provides federal protections for individually identifiable health information held by covered entities and their business associates and

---

[3]Parts of the law also apply to some privately held organizations and nonprofit organizations.
[4]Highlighted is one of the issues to which management must adhere.
[5]The HITECH Act is the Health Information Technology for Economic and Clinical Health Act, Title XIII of Division A and Title IV of Division B of the American Recovery and Reinvestment Act of 2009, Pub. L. No. 111-5, 123 Stat. 226, codified at 42 U.S.C. §§ 300jj et seq.; §§17901 et seq. It is transformational legislation that anticipates a massive expansion in the exchange of electronic protected health information (ePHI). The HITECH Act widens the scope of privacy and security protections available under HIPAA, increases potential legal liability for noncompliance, and provides more enforcement of HIPAA rules.

gives patients an array of rights with respect to that information. The Security Rule specifies a series of:

- Administrative
- Physical
- Technical

safeguards for covered entities and their business associates to use to assure the confidentiality, integrity, and availability of ePHI.[6] What this means is that more security is required for the protection of health care information, including that which can be obtained from a VoIP call or a transmitted data file. Securing VoIP is critical to protect the personal health information of consumers. Recall from Chapter 1 also that the targets of extortion and eavesdropping have included many health care facilities. Management faces some peculiar challenges if their systems do not provide sufficient protection of this information.

Additionally, an organization that deals in the retail industry will be influenced by the Payment Card Industry Data Security Standard (PCI DSS).[7] This compliance guide is designed to ensure that *all* companies that process, store, or transmit credit card information maintain a secure environment. The processing, storing, or transmission of this information typically involves data transmission facilities; however, with VoIP systems, the information can be equally transmitted verbally and must be protected. A number of situations have occurred in the industry where eavesdropping has produced information such as credit cards and security codes on those cards, or ATM cards and PINs have been disclosed. Moreover, the use of a combined voice and data information stored or transmitted can be manipulated, captured, and replayed causing a violation to payment card information, placing the organization and its management at risk of significant fines, loss of business, and loss of confidence for the organization's customers, bankers, insurers, and shareholders.[8,9] Not all breaches were attacks on stored data as opposed to data transmitted in real time (e.g., the wardriver gang seen in the section "What is the Impact?").

Management in these companies faces risks such as fines, lawsuits, and possible loss of position. Thus, hopefully these scenarios indicate the conflicts between what everyone wants and what everyone actually gets. It is necessarily a compromise between forcing the policies and procedures and getting buy-in from all groups.

---

[6]This information came directly from www.HHS.gov.

[7]PCI DSS 3.0 is the most recent. This is a guide that is used to assist organizations. The criticism is that it does not stop any form of attack. The companies that have been publicized regarding security breaches were all PCI compliant and yet they were still penetrated.

[8]In 2007 T.J. Maxx reported that hackers may have installed malicious software on their computers through the Wi-Fi system that caused the disclosure of 45.7 million credit and debit card accounts. The losses are estimated to amount to somewhere around £800 million. Other reports indicate the losses were projected at $4.5 billion.

[9]In December 2013 Target stores reported that hackers had breached their security systems and exposed 40 million credit and debit cards to potential fraud.

WHAT IS THE IMPACT?

The biggest question is one that has many answers. What is the impact if something happens to the VoIP packets? Although this may sound self-serving, every person involved with securing VoIP has to ask the question. For example, some of the breaches seen in security over the years have had varying impact. The T.J. Maxx credit card breach caused by wardrivers led to tens of millions of dollars in lawsuits for the company by the bankers associations representing approximately 300 banking organizations. There were significantly higher losses due to pushback by the retail creditors who brought approximately $256 (estimated) in losses to the store chain and the significant loss in branding confidence caused by the breach led to a significant loss. Yet at the same time, there were other security breaches that surfaced and barely got any interest. Look at some of the cases such as the breaches to Facebook and LinkedIn, Twitter accounts, and personal information being leaked. Although there may have been a first splash in the media (mostly the social media outlets), little follow-up occurred in the ensuing months. So, what this means is that although there is a loss of confidential information (private details such as social security numbers, names, addresses, telephone numbers, profile information) and/or financial data (PIN numbers, card numbers, ATM information, account information, etc.), there may be little reaction by the organization if there are no rules in place or some self-administered guidelines. So, back to the question that must be answered:

1. What is the impact if VoIP packets are lost? Lost might mean they are dropped or they are delivered to the wrong place. In this scenario, a few packets dropped might cause some degradation of the conversation. Depending on the packet loss (no greater than 10%, e.g.) there may be some inconvenience but not a likely breach to security. The user may complain about the quality of the connection, but that again will not jeopardize the security of the conversation. The packets are simply lost! There is no damage. Yet, this form of inconvenience if it consistently occurs will force the user to look for an alternate means of transmitting their voice (i.e., PSTN, a less secure network, a public Wi-Fi, etc.). If the packets are delivered to the wrong place due to corruption of a link or other type issue, then again it will not likely be a big problem as the less than 10% packets will not produce a stream that is intelligible, albeit they are probably random, not consecutive packets being dropped.

2. What is the impact if the VoIP packets (conversation) are heard by someone else and specifically not a competitor? Although this is not a desirable case, it probably isn't a very big deal for the most part. Surely, no one wants someone to listen into our conversations, but most of our conversations aren't confidential. For those that are confidential or discussions regarding personnel information, financial data, research and development (R&D) information, and pre-advertising information we certainly want to minimize the occurrence. A noncompetitor would probably just ignore the conversation or listen in curiosity. It is the information that one hears and thinks that they can benefit from with which we must be concerned. Thus, if a call can be listened into, we must protect against that.

3. What is the impact if the VoIP packets (conversation) are heard by a competitor? This is far more serious because the competitor will definitely use that as intelligence against our organization. For this reason whenever confidential material is discussed, encryption is a must. Competitors will go to special effort to gain a competitive edge. For example, if a retail company is planning a big advertising campaign and is discussing the details of the campaign (dates, prices, products, etc.) and a competitor learns of it in advance, that competitor might come out with a countercampaign either soon before the campaign or at the same time but with a better offer. This means that the competitor might draw the business to them rather than to the original retail organization. The losses in dollars for advertising, business opportunity, special pricing, and even extra shipments can be significant. What if a pharmaceutical company was discussing R&D efforts for a new drug and a competitor could listen in on the conversation? The competitor might gain a timing advantage or a counterdrug that could cost millions or even billions of dollars to the original company in losses. Finally, if a financial institution were discussing a possible shift in currency rates or in IPO stock offerings that a competitor eavesdropped, the competitor could change direction quickly and gain a financial advantage of unheard proportions. So one must be cautious that the VoIP cannot be eavesdropped whether by external means or from industrial espionage internally. Encryption and VPN tunnels along with authentication to ensure only the right persons are allowed on the conversation are a must.

4. What if the VoIP packets are being actively pursued by a competitor or an enemy (foreign government, terrorist group, etc.)? One cannot say enough about these risks and the potential need for secure communications. This includes the VoIP as well as data. An enemy or foreign government can do this on a regular basis and actively probe and attempt to penetrate our networks. One only needs to read the newspapers or read the information on the Internet to learn about the unrest in the world. The espionage and cracking of computer codes is done on a regular basis. What if a military application were attempting a raid on a terrorist group to prevent some other attack, and the terrorist group learned of the raid? The effort could be disastrous for the military organization orchestrating the raid. They could be wiped out through ambush, or the terrorist group could move their activities to a different place leaving the military organization orchestrating an embarrassment.

There are too many possibilities to enumerate the risk to life and limb or even financial risk or embarrassment in this chapter. Thus, one planning to secure VoIP must look at the likelihood of the risks shown above and base the planning and protection on their own assessment of the risks. At that point adding VPN technology to the picture brings increased security by inhibiting or denying:

1. Intermediate interference to the calls
2. Eavesdropping and sniffing, and MiM attacks
3. Forgery, replay, or data manipulation

CREATING THE VPN

Creating the VPN can be done in different ways. The user can choose between these differences based on the technologies used in the VoIP network, the degree of security needed, and the budget that is afforded to the organization for the security of VoIP. The ways that are typical include:

1. Desk to desk (phone to phone)
2. Router to router
3. Firewall to firewall
4. Between VPN devices (gateways)
5. Integrated devices (firewalls, ALGs, etc.)

In Figure 3.8 is shown a typical remote desk-to-desk–type connection. Note that the use of the laptop and softphone can pass through a gateway device or an integrated VPN device to provide this service. For a phone-to-phone scenario, there will always be something in the middles.

An alternative is to create a site-to-site VPN that is potentially a little bit easier, because this can be done between two routers as seen in Figure 3.9, or it can be done between two VPN gateway devices as seen in Figure 3.10. Regardless of how we do this the ultimate goal is the same. One must take into account, however, that using a site-to-site VPN will be more consistent when trying to communicate between

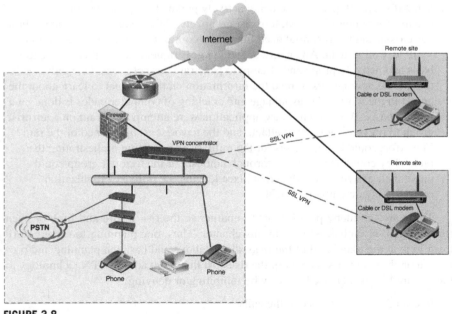

FIGURE 3.8

VPN from desk to VPN concentrator.

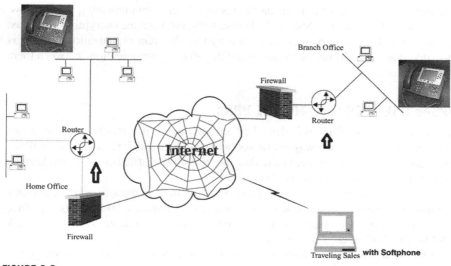

FIGURE 3.9

Site-to-site VPN between two routers.

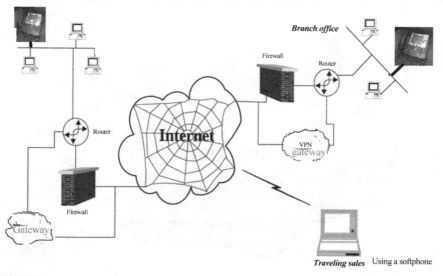

FIGURE 3.10

Site-to-site VPN between two VPN devices.

the different devices. What is meant here is that when communicating between two phones the VPN type (i.e., SSL VPN, IPSec, VPN, etc.) and the encryption type must be the same. If the two phones are owned by two different organizations, then it is possible that they will not be the same and therefore communications between them may not work.

IPSec USED FOR SITE-TO-SITE VPNs

In earlier sections, IPSec was described and discussed. It might be prudent at this point in time to circle the wagons (if you will) and do a quick review of what IPSec is all about. IPSec is a protocol suite that encrypts all IP traffic before the packets are sent from the source node to the destination.

In terms of computer networking and VPN, a site is geographically located in a portion of the organization's network. It can be a campus, a building, or an office where two nodes are connected to each other and communicate over the network (ATM, FR, MPLS, etc.) at high speeds.

Organizations with multiple branches scattered across the globe normally use VPNs to connect one branch office to another, or to enable communication between the branch offices and the head office/datacenter. An example of such a diverse network can be seen in Figure 3.11 where different access technologies are used at each site depending on availability and cost and the Internet (or other network) is the primary carrying capacity.

Earlier it was also stated that IPSec had the AH and the ESP header. IPSec is responsible for authenticating the identities of the two nodes before the actual communication takes place between them. In other words, IPSec makes sure that the

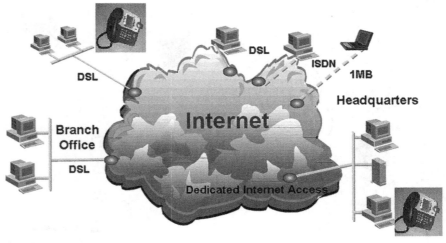

FIGURE 3.11

VPN connections at various sites.

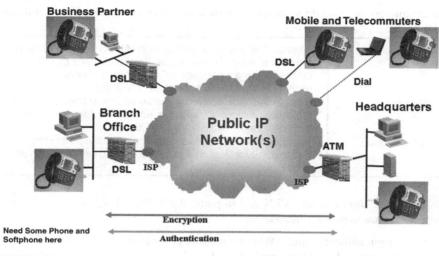

FIGURE 3.12

Authentication and encryption are used in IPSec VPNs.

two parties are who they say they are. This prevents an impersonation attack. IPSec can be configured to use any of the available algorithms to encrypt and decrypt the network traffic. In Figure 3.12 the idea of authentication and encryption can be seen using an IPSec VPN.

Of course, the primary goal to be achieved with IPSec or any other VPN is security that includes the following three elements (jokingly referred to as the CIA). Moreover, as seen in Figure 3.13 the intent is that the IPSec VPN can be used for

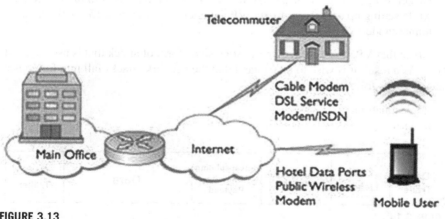

FIGURE 3.13

IPSec VPN used for telecommuters and mobile (dual) devices.

telecommuters and mobile users (perhaps on a dual phone such as a Wi-Fi and cellular device).

Confidentiality	Ensures that only the intended recipient can read the transmitted data while, at the same time, thwarting efforts by other parties that might intercept it. Confidentiality is provided by encryption algorithms, such as DES or 3DES
Integrity	Ensures the data received is exactly what was transmitted from the source without alterations or additions. Integrity is provided by hashing algorithms, such as MD5 or SHA
Authentication	Verification of the identity of a person or process that sent the data. Authentication is provided by mechanisms, such as exchanging digital certificates

When one thinks of any VPN and in particular IPSec VPN, the functions that these VPNs are to provide include:

- Data origin authentication – Who did it really come from?
- Data integrity – Has it been manipulated?
- Data confidentiality – Can anyone else hear the conversation?
- Replay protection – Can we be sure the data is original and not replayed?
- Automated management of encryption – Key management between the two communicating devices

IPSec can be configured to work in either of the following two available modes:

Transport mode – In transport mode, IPSec only encrypts and/or authenticates the actual payload of the packet, leaving the header information intact. See Figure 3.14 for transport mode.
Tunnel mode – In tunnel mode, IPSec encrypts and/or authenticates the entire packet. After encryption, the packet is then encapsulated to form a new IP packet using a different header. IPSec is configured to be used in tunnel mode while setting up secure site-to-site VPN tunnels. See Figure 3.15 for IPSec in tunnel mode.

Given that VPNs are used, there must be some form of attack that is used against them. As a result it is wise to understand that the network attacks fall into four basic categories, as follows:

- Impersonation
- Integrity

Data Trailer	IP Header	Authentication Header	Encapsulating Security Payload	Data	Data Trailer

FIGURE 3.14

Transport mode packet.

Data Trailer	IP Header	Authentication Header	Encapsulating Security Payload	IP Header	Data	Data Trailer

FIGURE 3.15

IPSec in tunnel mode uses a new IP header.

- Disclosure
- Denial of service

DISADVANTAGES OF IPSec VPN SITE-TO-SITE TUNNELS

To prevent the discussion from being one-sided in favor of site-to-site VPNs and especially with IPSec, it should be noted that there are very few vendors who even offer the use of VPNs on an IP phone. Although they may support SSL VPNs, which is still debatable, the use of an IPSec client has not materialized. As a result a few of the disadvantages of using IPSec VPN site-to-site tunnels are:

- An expensive router is required at each site to play the role of the VPN server. Although some organizations may already have such a router, it would not likely have the routers at telecommuter sites or small branch offices. This will limit the total availability of the VPN to the rest of the organization without significant cost.
- Because encapsulation, decapsulation, encryption, and decryption take place at the router, these devices incur processing overhead and increased CPU utilization. Thus, throughput and speed may likely be diminished.
- Configuring a site-to-site IPSec VPN can be quite complex and require highly skilled IT staff to do the configuration and maintenance. Hiring qualified IT professionals to perform the job can be expensive, especially for a smaller organization.
- The VPN client software is required at the routers, but may also be required in the telephone set, which makes it a compatibility and availability issue. For a softphone it is easier to install the VPN client software (application) on the laptop/desktop but for an IP phone, this is not realistic at this time.
- One needs to check with the vendor to be sure that a VPN can be used and that it will be vendor neutral in case a call is necessary between two phones that are not from the same organization. Also, if a call is going to a non-IP phone (i.e., a POTS phone), then the VPN does not work.

SUMMARY

Regardless of the type of VPN used, the design of the network is critical to prevent eavesdropping at public locations, manipulation if data can be captured, replaying the same portion of a call over and over, loss of confidentiality to prevent someone from arbitrarily listing in on a conversation, widespread divulging of personal and confidential information (nondisclosure), and the denial of service that can render the network totally inaccessible. For these reasons the need of a good plan must include some form of encryption and authentication as well as mitigating systems to prevent the hacker from getting into the network or launching a DoS or a DDoS attack.

The price that must be paid for this is in the amount of overhead and the cost of administering the network. However, there may be issues with compatibility, with availability, and with the expertise needed to handle the secure needs with a VPN.

Cryptography solutions

4

CHAPTER OUTLINE

CRYPTOGRAPHY SOLUTIONS

In Chapter 3, the discussion covered the use of virtual private networking (VPN) and firewall techniques as possible means for securing Voice over Internet Protocol (VoIP). Recall in Chapter 2 the puzzle included two other pieces as shown in Figure 2.15. What was not covered is the use of cryptography to scramble the VoIP so that it would be unintelligible to a listener. Although cryptography was mentioned in the previous chapter, and the use of the Advanced Encryption Standard (AES), there was little discussion on them. Thus, in order to be sure that enough discussion is provided, this section will address cryptography (encryption) in its historical and a high level of its current state. One can imagine that there are many books out in the marketplace dealing solely with encryption techniques and algorithms. It is not the intent here to cover anything to that level of depth. Instead a high-level look at options without the gory details is provided below.

Further, once the issue of encryption is addressed at least at a high level, the rest of this chapter will address different approaches to authentication and VoIP-specific encryption. By no means is this chapter designed to make the reader an expert on the use of encryption and authentication. Instead it is the intent to give a reader an understanding of the choices available and a working knowledge so that discussions with the vendors offering VoIP solutions can be challenged as to the security tools they also offer. Too often the vendor tends to try to get out of these discussions by claiming that they are the sales people and not the security folks, or that they are sales people and not the engineers who design the product. Nevertheless, it is imperative to not let the vendor off the hook with these casual statements. Rather, if they are truly interested in providing the necessary solutions, then they should bring the designers or the engineers in to have a meaningful discussion.

WHAT IS CRYPTOGRAPHY AND ENCRYPTION?

In every discussion anyone has about securing data, voice, or VoIP, the common thread that arises is the need to encrypt the information. The reason is that too often our data is kept in a storage system for current and future use. Look at the issues that faced Target stores at the end of 2013. Sometime between the day after Thanksgiving (Black Friday) and Christmas in 2013, Target stores had a data loss that exposed somewhere around 40 million customers.[1] Moreover, Neiman Marcus indicated that they had a security breach that exposed 20 million customer files (name, SSAN, address, e-mail, etc.) in January 2014.

Just the few issues that have been highlighted in the preceding discussions should be enough for anyone to realize that there is no really secure system out there. Whether it is a voice call, a voice store and forward system (voice mail), or data storage and/or data transactions, the risk is always present that someone is listening in, copying, stealing, or otherwise manipulating our information. Thus, it is incumbent on all organizations and individuals to protect the security of their own information, be it voice, data, or video. This is done through a strong encryption process. The reverse process is called decryption. By employing strong encryption techniques our sensitive and valuable information can be protected against cyber hackers, commercial espionage mercenaries, or spies from a foreign government/military organization, including terrorist groups. One has to understand that although our data may not seem valuable at the time, if it is compromised and divulged to others, the consequences can be significant. Remember in Chapters 1 and 2, examples were provided on how a hacker can get at the information.

So to best describe it, encryption is a process of converting information to a nonreadable or nonusable form to an eavesdropper in order to send it across any unsecure channel, but this also can apply to what is thought to be a safe transmission link. There are four desirable features that can be provided by various cryptographic functions:

1. Confidentiality
2. Integrity
3. Authentication
4. Nonrepudiation

Confidentiality means keeping privileged information a secret. Sometimes confidentiality is compared with privacy and, as might be expected, confidentiality is an important concept in online communications. If you want to keep voice or data a secret while transmitting it over the Internet, or any other network for that matter,

---

[1]And after the initial reports in January 2014 the number has been escalated to almost 70 million.

you should encrypt the voice data with a secret key, to make sure that the intended recipient is the only one who knows the key and can decrypt the information.

Integrity of the voice or data is the assurance that the voice or data information has not been changed, inserted, or replayed from the originally sent information. A one-way hash can be used to create what is known as message digests that can be used by a recipient device to be sure that no such tampering has taken place to the voice or data.

Authentication is the process of verifying one's identity. It is important to ensure that the person sending the voice or data is who they say they are. This is important for many types of transactions. Because of the Internet and the ability to communicate with anyone, anywhere, and at any time, whenever two parties are involved in a conversation or a transaction and they are not close to each other, it is much more difficult to be sure that the information is coming from the correct person. This is especially true with casual communications such as a VoIP phone call. One can never be sure who is on the other end of the call just from the sound quality of the connection. As already seen in the preceding discussions, it is possible for VoIP to be captured and manipulated, thus changing the whole meanings conveyed in a conversation.

A means of authenticating the caller and the message he/she is sending is to use a public key encryption. More will be seen below on the use of a public key infrastructure (PKI).

If we take a combination of integrity checking and authentication, then we have what we can consider nonrepudiation. A combined public-key cryptography and one-way hash can be used to generate a digital signature. The digital signature can tie together a calling party with the voice information that will just about guarantee we are speaking with the party to whom we think we are speaking and that the voice has not been manipulated.

This is a juncture that must have the average person wondering why encrypting voice is so important. We can never be sure that there is not a "listener" eavesdropping on our calls. If there is an incentive for a hacker to attempt to penetrate a conversation, then there is a high probability that it will be attempted. The goal is to make that impossible to achieve by using encryption and authentication. For now let's just stick with the encryption.

At one time, cryptography was just about the exclusive tool for the military and diplomatic agencies. Although most people have never really given it much thought, the military was securing voice for decades. In the 1960s and 1970s, for example, automatic secure voice communications (AUTOSEVOCOM) was a specialty tool for the military to communicate. Special phones, for example, the secure telephone units (STU), were developed by NSA for the military and manufactured by partners (Nortel, General Dynamics, and Motorola, to name a few). Later, after improvements were made the STU-IIs appeared with better encryption and compression techniques. In the mid-1970s AUTOSEVOCOM II incorporated technological advances and furnished higher-quality communications for the several thousand subscribers who were expected to use it when put into operation during the years 1980–1985. The US Army Communications Command acted as program manager for AUTOSEVOCOM II. This was form of encryption used electronically during the Vietnam Conflict. It was imperative when commanders in the field were discussing troop movement, resupply routes, and strategic plans to combat an enemy, the information had to be kept confidential. It would not do to have an enemy listening in on a radiotelephone conversation and preparing a counteroffensive move. Thus, the voice had to be kept secure. If one thinks about this, hacking (as we now know it) was taking place whenever someone could listen in on a conversation or intercept a data message with specific strategic information on it. Back then it was a "life and death" situation, where intercepted voice or data could lead to adverse results for an organization. Today, it happens to be more of a challenge to break into conversations and data transmissions, but the rewards are more financially oriented rather than militarily oriented.

Unfortunately, in the 1960–1970 time period because the technology was limited, voice quality suffered significantly. In fact, if two people were speaking with each other using encrypted voice, both of them sounded like Donald Duck because the voice quality was so poor. Although the voice was understandable, the quality and tone of the voice was horrible.[2] Later the AUTOSEVOCOM Network was replaced by the Defense Red Switch Network (DRSN) and the introduction of the Secure Telephone Unit – Third Generation (STU-III) secure phones. The STU-III was a lower-cost, user-friendly, secure telephone device. The terminals were designed to operate reliably, with high voice quality. It was used both on ordinary telephone networks (PSTN) in a nonsecure mode and as a secure instrument over the dial-up PSTN when needed. Obviously, in order to communicate securely, both ends of the call required a STU-III. The STU-III operated in full-duplex over a single telephone circuit using echo-canceling modem technology. STU-IIIs come equipped with 2.4 and 4.8 kbps code-excited linear prediction (CELP) secure voice. These features may sound reasonably familiar with today's technologies. The last AUTOSEVOCOM secure voice switch in the world was deactivated at the Pentagon in 1994. Now, what goes around comes around. The industry realizes that securing voice packets across the networks has become so much more necessary because the environment of hacking has proliferated so widely.

Therefore, in moving into an information society, the value of cryptography in everyday life in such areas as privacy, trust, electronic payments, and access control has become evident. In this way, the field of cryptography has broadened from classical military encryption techniques into areas such as authentication, data integrity, and nonrepudiation of voice and data transfer.

We use encryption all the time, but most folks don't even think about it. For example, we use an encryption tool when we:

1. Check e-mail
2. Withdraw money from an ATM
3. Pay a bill over the web
4. Make a cellular call
5. Charge a purchase on the web

---

[2]The author used the AUTOSEVOCOM system in Vietnam and can attest to the quality of voice being subpar.

These everyday activities are taken for granted, and in many cases, we don't even realize that encryption is occurring because it is transparent to us. However, taking the next step is a natural event to secure voice on the Internet for the very same reasons described herein. We do not want someone picking off our account numbers, PINs, and other financial information while we speak on the phone. We rely on encryption to ensure the validity of our financial transactions, prove our identity, and safeguard our privacy. Although some people hesitate to conduct business over the Internet, most of us engage in online transactions with confidence that encryption will protect our data. Now we must also rely on encryption to protect our VoIP.

EARLY CIPHERS USED

The history of encryption has been to try to devise an uncrackable code – and equal effort to crack them. For every measure created there is a countermeasure developed. For example, when radar guns were created for the police departments to catch speeders, soon after radar detectors were developed for the consumer to avoid being caught. Manufacturers were quick to respond to the need because of the potential financial rewards. So too with encryption ciphers. Whenever there is a new cipher developed, the challenge is to immediately find a way of breaking that code.

Early ciphers were relatively simple systems, easy for both sender and receiver to use. As children we used a code that was developed by Julius Caesar. The messages were encoded with a "substitution cipher" used by Caesar. In this substitution method each letter is replaced by the third letter after it in the alphabet: A is replaced by D, B by E, etc. At the end of the alphabet, the pattern wraps around to the beginning: X becomes A, Y becomes B, and Z becomes C. As one might expect, such simplicity works both ways. The coded text is easily decoded, especially when we think about the more sophisticated codes in use today. Caesar's cipher can be cracked simply by moving each letter in the encoded message back three spaces in the alphabet. OK, so what if I move the letter out four or five letters. The same patterns can be easily determined with today's technology. So substitution methods make for a far less reliable coding technique.

More sophisticated substitution ciphers, in which the alphabet is thoroughly scrambled, are nevertheless easy enough to break, even for a novice. Quotes and word puzzles in the local newspapers are examples of this type of scrambling. The English language is very repetitive; for example, the most common letter is usually "E," the second most common is "T," and a three-letter word that appears repeatedly is probably "The." By applying this type of "frequency analysis," an eavesdropper can easily guess which letters in the ciphertext represent "E," "T," and so on.[3] Voice is also very repetitive, in that sounds and vowels are readily replicated due to sampling.

---

[3]Jokingly one can watch the TV show *Wheel of Fortune* and recognize the more commonly used letters are R–S–T–L–N–E.

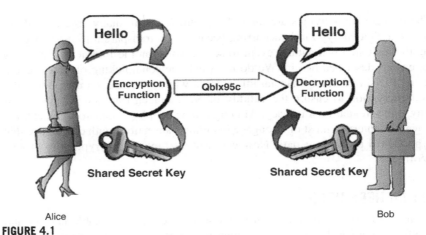

FIGURE 4.1

Symmetrical key encryption.

A VoIP call may have 50 samples/s using 160 bytes of voice. Using this scenario, an eavesdropper can begin to get the syllabic content of a word or sentence by capturing a few packets. However, if one has access to the network, and a packet capture tool (such as Wireshark), then a stream of packets can be captured and a stream analysis run, and then the actual two-way conversation can be played out. It doesn't take a lot of guesswork to determine the two Internet Protocol (IP) addresses communicating and then capturing the RTP packets for a period of time. The rest is just to let the application put the conversation together and play it out. Now, with unsecured VoIP the eavesdropper can understand what is being said, or can actually use another program to manipulate the voice packets and create different sentences, or replay the same voice as they see fit. One such program is Audacity that allows the manipulation of words or sentences. So encryption must be sufficient to keep this from happening. Complexity is no guarantee of security, however, so a detailed understanding of the risk and reward is a must.

Incidentally, it is helpful to know that prior to 1970 all encryption systems were symmetrical key encryption. This means that the keys for encryption and decryption were the same. A person in possession of *the key* could either send or receive messages. Some examples of a symmetrical key encryption/decryption include 3DES, IDEA, RC4, and AES.[4] This can be seen in Figure 4.1, which shows use of a symmetrical key. When Alice sends information to Bob, they use the same key to encrypt and decrypt the data.

In the early 1970s, Whitfield Diffie teamed up with Martin Hellman reasoned that for some applications this two-way symmetrical key capability was unnecessary. In a

---

[4]3DES or triple data encryption standard, IDEA is the International Data Encryption Algorithm, the RC4 is ARCFOUR or ARC4 is RSA code, and AES is the Advanced Encryption Standard.

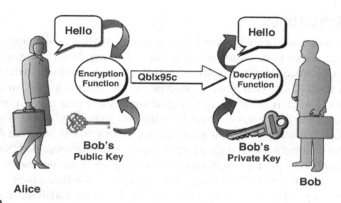

FIGURE 4.2

Public and private keys.

communications system with a different sender and receiver, each sending their own data one way, the encryption and decryption keys need not be the same. And, if two different one-way keys are used, then security can be enhanced. This added security helps when dealing with a VoIP system, for example. Together Diffie and Hellman created such a system. The real magic of their system is the use of a one-way key. Each message recipient (Bob) chooses a "private key" that he will use to decode messages. There should be enough possibilities, so that Bob can pick a key "more or less" at random. Then he uses the "one-way function" to work out the corresponding encoding key. This is a "public key," which he can share with Alice or anyone else, and anyone can use it to send an encrypted message to him.

Only Bob has the private key, so he and he alone can decrypt the message. No one else can figure out the private key because that would require them to reverse the one-way function. What is encrypted with the public key can only be decrypted by the private key. This understanding, that cryptosystems did not have to be symmetrical, opened the door to more intense use of cryptography. It simplifies the process considerably and makes way for a PKI. Anyone can use this PKI and public key system. It is used quite extensively in websites, online shopping services, bank transfers, and the like. The public key system allows far more flexibility in dealing with transactional processing. This is shown in Figure 4.2. The normal public-key encryption algorithms use either Diffie–Hellman or RSA software.

Alice, a customer using Bob's banking service, wants to tell Bob to move funds from her account to her mortgage company account, paying her monthly mortgage. She uses Bob's public key to encrypt the information before sending it to him. Bob is the only person with the private key, so he is the only one who can decrypt the message. Because of the private key limitation, Alice knows that no eavesdropper can capture and decode the information; thus, she feels safe in conducting the funds transfer. So what is locked with a public key can only be unlocked with the private key. Conversely, what is locked with the private key can only be unlocked with the public key.

DIGITAL SIGNATURES

Well, the dialog that just took place between Bob and Alice seems pretty straightforward. But another issue crops up that needs addressing. What if someone else is pretending to be Alice? How can Bob be sure that the instructions to transfer the funds are actually from Alice? Here is the second part of the process to prevent an impersonation attack. Alice is going to add a "digital signature" to her transactions using a hash function. Now the hash is different from the encryption key, so this is why there are two pieces. A hash function is another cipher code that no one, not even Alice, can decode. After creating the digital signature, Alice encrypts the scrambled "hash" message using her "own" private key. So now when Alice sends the message to Bob, she adds the digital signature to the message and encrypts it with Bob's public key. Bob will then use his private key to decrypt the message. But at the end of the message the leftover scrambled text is there. Because Bob has a copy of Alice's public key, he can reverse the signature with Alice's public key. Once he has that reversed, he can then hash Alice's message using the same hash and then get a string of scrambled text. If the two copies agree, then Bob can be sure it came from Alice. This process can be used for ATM cards and computer systems alike. Moreover, if a symmetrical key is needed, a symmetrical key can be created and sent it via encoded public key encryption to set up a secure communications using symmetrical key after the initial public key is used. This process of digitally signing messages provides two of the features of secure communications: authentication and nonrepudiation. As long as the sender has kept their private key safe, we can be sure that they sent that specific message.

This feature is crucial to e-commerce as well as other banking and finance activities.

Digital signatures can be used by anyone who wants to authenticate themselves to a recipient, but can also be used by the recipient to provide assurances to customers that they are who they say they are. This means that they can be used in a two-way dialog to authenticate both parties. Some of the public-key algorithms can be used to generate digital signatures. A digital signature is a small amount of information that was created using some private key, and there is a public key that can be used to verify that the signature was really generated by the sender using the corresponding private key. The algorithm used to generate the signature works the same way as any public and private key algorithm; without knowing the private key it is not possible to create a signature that would verify as valid. Digital signatures can also be used to certify that a public key belongs to a particular device/user. This is done by signing the combination of the public key and the information about its owner by a trusted key. The resulting data structure is often called a public-key certificate (or simply, a certificate). Certificates can be thought of as analogous to passports or driver licenses that verify the identity of the holder. A digital signature is seen in Figure 4.3.

LEADS TO A PUBLIC KEY INFRASTRUCTURE

As mentioned above, the use of public and private asymmetrical keys leads to a PKI. A hierarchy of authorities (as they are called) exists. These take the following types of structure:

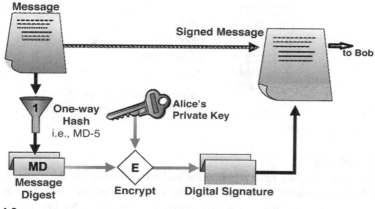

FIGURE 4.3

A digital signature that is appended to the data to authenticate the sender.

- The trusted party who issues certificates to the identified entities is called a certification authority (CA). CAs can be thought of as being analogous to governments issuing passports for their citizens.
- A CA can be operated by an external certification service provider, or even by a government, or the CA can belong to the same organization as the entities. CAs can also issue certificates to other (sub-)CAs. This leads to a tree-like certification hierarchy. The highest trusted CA in the tree is called a root CA. The hierarchy of trust formed by end entities, sub-CAs, and root CA is called a PKI.

Figure 4.4 is an example of the hierarchy of authorities.

FIGURE 4.4

Hierarchy of authorities.

Name

Public Key

CA Signature

Expiration Date

Other Information as Desired

FIGURE 4.5

A sample digital certificate.

X.509 certificates

When you start a cryptographic application and create your keys, the plan is to make your public key available to anyone who wants to communicate with you. But how can they be sure that a public key is your public key? What if a hacker intercepts the transmission of your public key and substitutes their own? There has to be a way for someone to verify your public key. Taking this one step further, what if someone uses his or her private key to "sign" your public key? A certificate is a signature verifying your public key. The certificate usually contains the person's name, their public key, the signer's signature of the key, and an expiration date. A standard exists for these certificates called X.509. As part of the ITU X.500 (formerly called the CCITT X.500) directory services specification, the X.509 standard specification spells out a structure for certificates that contains the following information (Fig. 4.5 shows a certificate with some minimal information):

- Version
- Serial number
- Signature algorithm
- Issuer name (signer or CA)
- Validity period
- Subject name (user)
- Subject's public key
- Issuer unique identifier (v2 and v3)
- Subject unique identifier (v2 and v3)
- Extensions (v3 only)
- Signature on the above fields

Some of the items above have only been defined in more recent versions of the X.509 specification. The current latest version of X.509 standard is Version 3. X.509 certificates are used in most web browsers and servers as the standard certificate to identify the server (and optionally the user), when using the Secure Sockets Layer (SSL) protocol. Some certificates can be self-signed by the organization that is issuing the certificate. For example, to get a certificate issued costs a lot of money. Many organizations do not want to spend the money to get certificates for their products or their websites because of the enormous cost. As a result, they create their own certificates and issue them as self-signed certificates instead of having one of the very large

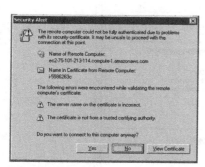 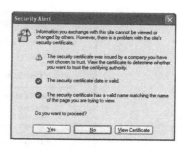

FIGURE 4.6

Windows certificate warnings.

CAs issue the certificate (such as Thwate, Equifax, VeriSign, and others). As a matter of fact, many times when accessing a website, a "pop-up" may appear on the screen that says something to the effect, "the server you are trying to access is attempting to issue you a certificate, do you want to view the certificate?" Another two messages propped by Windows are seen in Figure 4.6.

A point that has always been drummed into the industry is that if you are going to accept a certificate, you had better know who the issuer is and be sure that it is really that entity. Once you accept the certificate you have it on your computer (or laptop, phone, etc.). This can lead to a breach in the security if you received a bogus certificate. An example of a certificate is seen in Figures 4.7–4.9. This is a real certificate taken from a laptop, so it is valid. This particular one is from Equifax. If you open your cache of certificates on your computer and select a certificate, you can look at the details. The certificate has three tabs in this case: General, Details, and Certification Path. Clicking on the General tab the certificate information is displayed such as its (see Figure 4.7 for this basic information):

- *Supported uses of the certificate.* Summary information, such as the applications, signing, encryption, or authentication, for which the certificate can be used. This section also explains if a certificate has expired or is not valid.
- *Entity to which the certificate was issued.* The name of recipient of the certificate. Recipients can include end users, computers, or entities such as CAs.
- *The issuer of the certificate.* The name of the CA that issued the certificate.
- *Validity period of the certificate.* This includes the date the certificate becomes valid to the date that the certificate expires.
- *Issuer statement.* Clicking the *Issuer Statement* button opens a separate window that contains additional information about the certificate or a URL where additional information can be obtained.

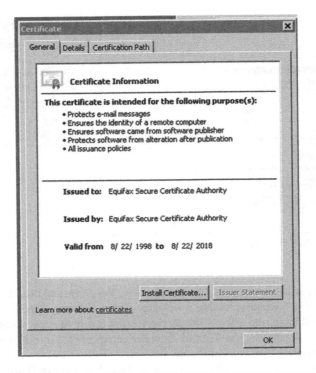

FIGURE 4.7

The General tab of a certificate.

The *Details* tab provides the following information about the certificate (in Fig. 4.8 the Details tab is shown in two parts):

- *Version*. The X.509 version number.
- *Serial number*. The unique serial number that the issuing CA assigns to the certificate. The serial number is unique for all certificates issued by a given CA.

Upper Portion   **Lower Portion**

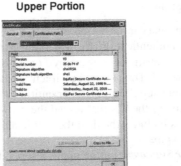 

FIGURE 4.8

The Details tab of a certificate.

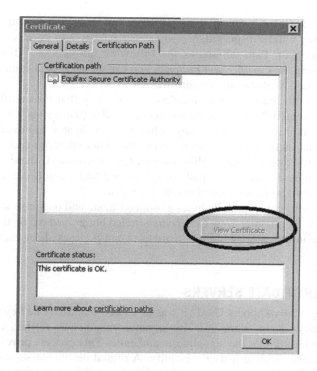

FIGURE 4.9

Certification Path tab.

- *Signature algorithm.* The hash algorithm that the CA uses to digitally sign the certificate.
- *Issuer.* Information regarding the CA that issued the certificate.
- *Valid from.* The beginning date for the period in which the certificate is valid.
- *Valid to.* The final date for the period in which the certificate is valid.
- *Subject.* The name of the individual, computer, device, or CA to whom the certificate is issued. If the issuing CA exists on a domain member server in your enterprise, this will be a distinguished name within the enterprise. Otherwise, this may be a full name and e-mail name or other personal identifier.
- *Public key.* The public key type and length associated with the certificate.
- *Thumbprint algorithm.* The hash algorithm that generates a digest of data (or thumbprint) for digital signatures.
- *Thumbprint.* The digest (or thumbprint) of the certificate data.
- *Friendly name.* (Optional) A display name to use instead of the name in the subject field.
- *Enhanced key usage.* (Optional) The purposes for which this certificate can be used.

There are additional X.509 v3 extensions that can be used in a certificate. If they are present, they will be displayed.

The Certification Path tab shows the following information. This is seen in Figure 4.9. Using the *Certification Path* tab, you can view the path from the selected certificate to the CAs that issue the certificate.

Before a certificate is trusted, Windows must verify that the certificate comes from a trusted source. This verification process is called path validation.

Path validation involves processing public key certificates and their issuer certificates in a hierarchical fashion until the certification path terminates at a trusted, self-signed certificate. Typically, this is a root CA certificate. If there is a problem with one of the certificates in the path, or if it cannot find a certificate, the certification path is considered a nontrusted certification path.

A typical certification path includes a root certificate and one or more intermediate certificates. By clicking *View Certificate* (circled but grayed out on the certificate shown), more information about the certificates can be learned for each CA in the path.

DIGITAL CERTIFICATE SERVERS

In the section "Early Ciphers Used" it was described that a private key can be used to create a unique digital signature. This signature can then be verified later with the public key to ensure that the signature is authentic. This process provides a strong method for authenticating a user's identity. A digital certificate server provides a central point of management for multiple public keys. This prevents every user from having to maintain and manage copies of every other user's public cipher key because managing these certificates and keys can be an administrative challenge.

Digital certificate servers, also known as CAs, provide verification of digital signatures. For example, if Bob receives a digitally signed message from Alice but does not have a copy of Alice's public cipher key, Bob can get a copy of Alice's public key from the CA to verify that the message is authentic. Also, let's assume that Bob wants to respond to Alice's message but wants to encrypt the message to protect it from prying eyes. Bob can again get a copy of Alice's public key from the CA so that the message can be encrypted using Alice's public key. This places everything in perspective so that the certificates can be managed at a certificate server and allows the central storage so that Bob and Alice do not have to have so many keys individually.

You can map certificates to access control lists for files stored on a server in order to restrict access. When a user attempts to access a file, the server verifies that the user's certificate has been granted access. This approach allows a CA to manage nearly all document security for an organization.

A huge benefit is had from using a CA that supports the X.509 standard for digital certificates. By using an X.509 certificate server an organization reaps the benefit that allows certificates to be verified and information to be encrypted between organizations. Assuming that the primary means of exchanging information between two organizations is e-mail or voice, for example, a CA could be far more cost-effective than investing in VPN because of the firewalls and VPN gateways needed as well as the client software for every client device. Moreover, managing this is much easier than configuring each device with a VPN client, setting up individual passwords and shared secrets for every client, and then maintaining that list. Thus, the X.509 PKI makes more sense. As for certificate management there are issues that must be addressed such as:

- How do you distribute the cryptography keys?
- How do you keep all the keys valid and active?
- How does anyone know that the key is valid?
- How do you manage the keys and how do you handle lost keys?
- If a private key gets lost, how does one restore their files that are encrypted (remember that anything encrypted with a public key can only be decrypted by the private key and anything encrypted with the private key can only be decrypted by the public key)?

As you can see, managing keys is no simple task. It is probably the main reason that organizations shy away from using cryptography. This is particularly true when dealing with novices and non-IT folks. Organizations that wish to use VoIP and data transfers may not have the expertise in-house to handle the use of cryptography keys and managing the user population. Thus, the use of PKI is seen as the salvation for organizations in this position. Cryptography can be implemented in many places; for example, in the Transmission Control Protocol (TCP)/IP stack, encryption can be done at any layer. At the application layer we can use Secure Real-Time Transport Protocol (SRTP), but there are other solutions that will be seen later. At the session layer the encryption is done using SSL as described above (now SSL is also called Transport Layer Security [TLS]). Normally the implementation of SSL or TLS is done within the application (i.e., a web browser or a server, etc.). At the networking layer (layer 3 solution) is the VPN already discussed in Chapter 3. Now that IP Security (IPSec) is more popular, this protocol is used for encrypting the data or voice to carry across the public Internet or any other unsecure network. At the data link and physical layers the encryption is done typically with a hardware solution and/or a software and hardware combination. It should be noted that hardware encryption is usually less overhead intensive. When using a software encryption (especially when using the AES encryption standard), it is processor intensive and battery unfriendly. This means that if using VPNs, IPSec, and a host of other software solutions, the older/some current handsets (wireless phones, softphones, etc.) will be challenged by the battery use and require a charging tool be on hand. Newer handsets are improving and will last a lot longer.

INSTALLING CERTIFICATES ON THE DEVICES

Earlier, in describing the PKI the need for a certificate exists that the user has to have on the device. In general, if an IP phone is provided by the vendor (of the IP PBX), then they will most likely already install the certificates on their system (the server and the client device). However, if a third-party phone, a smartphone (cellular), a smart tablet, or a softphone on a laptop is used, then the certificates for a specific system will probably have to be installed.

Now when discussing these certificates and looking at them from the notebook computer, if a vendor website offers a certificate, once it is accepted the same type of information will appear on the certificate in the computer's cache. These can be seen through the Microsoft console commands for the computer. Thus, if using a softphone, it is likely that some form of certificate is going to be used. When using an IP phone from the various vendors (i.e., Cisco, Avaya, ShoreTel, Siemens, etc.) there will be a certificate that can be installed for the client to validate the server (PBX, IPPBX, etc.). Just about all vendors have an installation procedure that lists how to import or install the certificates. An example of this is as follows (this is a generic installation of a certificate for a softphone):

1. On the computer where the softphone is installed, open a browser (Internet Explorer); click on Tools → Internet Options → the Content tab → certificates and the Certificate Manager tab is displayed. Click on the Import button and the Import Certificate wizard will open.
   a. On Firefox the sequence is similar; click on
      Tools → Options → Advanced → Certificates → View Certificates and the Certificate Manager will be displayed. Select the Server or Authorities tab and then select the Import button that will launch the wizard.
2. Next select the file where the certificate is located and import the certificate.
3. Import the certificate that the vendor has given you or if you are using a self-signed certificate that you created, select that certificate.
4. The wizard will ask where you want to store the certificate on your computer, so you must select the certificate store. Normally this is a trusted Root Certification Authority where the certificate is to be stored. Once you have selected the store, then click on OK and finish the import of the certificate.
5. Now you can launch the softphone and follow the manufacturers' instructions on configuring the softphone for the use of TLS.
6. Let's try a hard phone (IP phone) using TLS. Each IP phone has a web interface to configure it, so you will go to the web interface and log in.
7. Go to Security → Trusted Certificates. Click on the "Browse" button and upload the client certificate (if it is not already there).
8. Next go to Account. In the label that says Display Name and User Name, enter the extension number in the Register Name field (e.g., 2001); enter Authentication ID [whatever you want to call it: "your name" or "your extension number (2001)"]. In the field labeled Password enter the authentication password for the extension number (e.g., PW2001) and the IP address of the Session Initiation Protocol (SIP) server (IP PBX, e.g., 192.168.50.128). Next set the UDP port to 5061. Set the transport field to TLS. At the bottom of the page press "Confirm," Submit, or Save (whichever displays on your IP Phone).

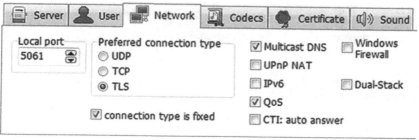

FIGURE 4.10

PhonerLite menu, part 1.

9. Another area is to use SRTP. In this case, go to the Account tab and select Advanced. If you need to select the protocol, select RTP. The option of Voice Encryption (or RTP Encryption) is set to "On." Press Confirm, Save, or Submit at the bottom of the page.[5]

Another word about the soft phones. There is a free application called "Phoner-Lite." PhonerLite is a clearly arranged application for Windows. It enables you to use your PC for Internet telephony (VoIP). PC requirements are a full-duplex sound card, a microphone and speakers (alternatively a headset), an Internet connection, and an account from a provider supporting the SIP protocol. PhonerLite supports several SIP profiles, each independently configurable. It supports state-of-the-art encryption methods such as TLS, SRTP, and ZRTP.

To configure PhonerLite:

1. Configure the SIP account you previously created in PhonerLite as usual. See Figure 4.10 for screenshot of PhonerLite.
2. Click the "Configuration" tab.
3. Click the "Network" tab and then specify the following settings:
   a. Local port: 5061
   b. Preferred connection type: TLS
4. Click the "Certificate" tab and then specify the following settings (see Fig. 4.11 for the screenshot):
   a. Client certificate – Click the ellipsis button (…). Browse to the certificate you are installing.
   b. Check certificate from the remote site – If you want PhonerLite to verify the validity of the certificates, select this check box.
   c. Select "Load Windows CA" by checking the box.
5. Click "Save." PhonerLite should now be able to register successfully.

---

[5]Every phone manufacturer does this a little differently. If these steps don't match your particular phone, look for the help button or play with the phone until you find the fields similar to what is described above.

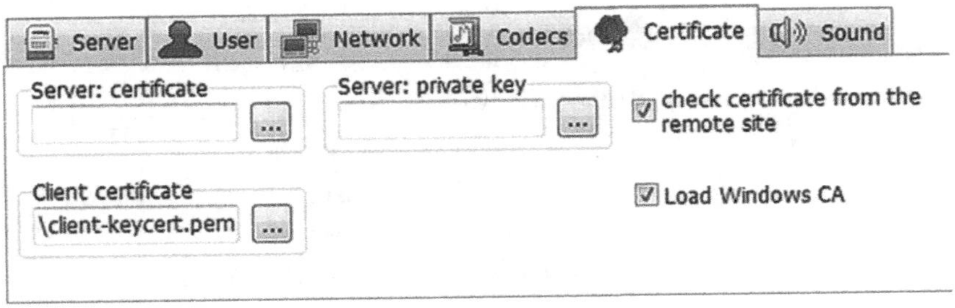

FIGURE 4.11

PhonerLite menu, part 2.

Another softphone alternative is Zoiper.[6] To use Zoiper you need a computer, a smartphone, or a tablet, an Internet connection, and a VoIP provider account or a PBX. Because you don't like it when people eavesdrop on your conversations, Zoiper offers free encryption for all your text, voice, and video communications with TLS/SRTP and ZRTP. Zoiper runs on a multitude of different platforms. No matter the platform such as Mac, Linux or Windows, iPhone, Android, or a web browser (Internet Explorer, Firefox, Safari, Chrome, etc.), Zoiper handles full Unified VoIP Communications that includes audio, video, fax, presence, and instant messaging all from a single interface.

Cisco uses different security tools for the Cisco Unified Communications Manager (CUCM). The following secure transport protocols are used for the signaling channels (Source: Cisco IP Phone Certificates and Secure Communications):

- *TLS:* Provides secure and reliable data transfer between two systems or devices, by using secure ports and certificate exchange. CUCM utilizes TLS to secure the control channel of SIP or Skinny Client Control Protocol (SCCP) end points to prevent access to the voice domain.
- *SSL VPN*: This client can be used in current model Cisco IP phones (7942, 7962, 7945, 7965, and 7975) to secure communications between the phones and devices that are located behind SSL VPN headends.
- *IPSec*: This provides secure and reliable data transfer between CUCM and voice gateways. This is the same technology that is used for VPNs that provides signaling authentication and encryption to MGCP and H.323 gateways.

To increase security, many devices support SRTP. SRTP authenticates and encrypts the media stream (voice packets) to ensure that the voice conversations, which originate or terminate on supported end points, are protected from eavesdroppers who may have gained access to the voice domain. Moreover, SRTP includes protection against replay attacks. The following sections will explain security best practices by detailing strong encryption and secure communications. The reader should note

---

[6]Just about every manufacturer has a softphone application for PCs, MACs, smartphones, and tablets. The operating systems include windows, MAC OS, Android, or Linux.

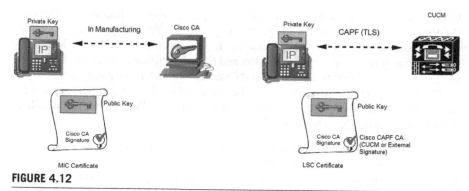

FIGURE 4.12

Cisco certificates for phones.

that Cisco will not provide an exhaustive description of the configuration options. The goal, by stressing security, is to offer a general understanding of the available options and provide administrators options for their infrastructure.

Cisco uses different certificates on their phones as follows (see Fig. 4.12 for a graphic representation of the certificates for a Cisco phone):

- *Manufacturer Installed Certificate (MIC)*: MICs are included on all 7941, 7961, and newer model Cisco IP phones. MICs are 2048-bit key certificates that are signed by the Cisco CA. When a MIC is present it is not necessary to install a Locally Significant Certificate (LSC). In order for the CUCM to trust the MIC certificate, it utilizes the preinstalled CA certificates CAP-RTP-001, CAP-RTP-002, and Cisco_Manufacturing_CA in its certificate trust store.
- *LSC*: A LSC must be installed on the Cisco IP phone utilizing USB tokens and the certificate trust list (CTL) client (illustrated below). The LSC possesses the public key for the Cisco IP phone, which is signed by the CUCM Certificate Authority Proxy Function (CAPF) private key (illustrated below). This is the preferred method (as opposed to using MICs) because only Cisco IP phones that are manually provisioned by an administrator will be allowed to download and verify the CTL file (illustrated below). Older Cisco IP phones, such as the 7940 and 7960, do not contain MICs. Cisco IP phones require an LSC to operate in secure mode.

However, Cisco further recommends that "due to the increased security risk, Cisco recommends using MICs solely for LSC installation and not for continued use. Customers who configure Cisco IP phones to use MICs for TLS authentication or for any other purpose do so at their own risk. Cisco assumes no liability if MICs are compromised."

Avaya also installs certificates for their 9600 phones through a Cisco ASA box as follows: the 9600 Series IP telephones support Media Encryption (SRTP) and use built-in Avaya certificates for trust management. Trust management involves downloading certificates for additional trusted CAs and the policy management of those

CAs. Identity management is handled by Simple Certificate Enrollment Protocol (SCEP) with phone certificates and private keys. SCEP applies to the VPN operation or to standard enterprise network operation. It is the protocol used by the Microsoft CA to securely transport key information and digital certificates to network devices, such as the Avaya 9600 IP telephone and Cisco Adaptive Security Appliance.

ShoreTel also has a paper that describes some of the X.509 certificates for their phones as they integrate with many other manufacturers. "With ShoreTel Mobility, security for mobile UC is built-in.

- Enterprise UC data is not stored on the mobile device mitigating the risk associated with lost/stolen devices.
- All transmissions between the RoamAnywhere Client on the mobile device, and the Mobility Router which is integrated with the PBX/UC infrastructure are authenticated and encrypted. While this creates a secure container for enterprise communications, a user's personal applications continue to flow normally outside the container. Certificate-based authentication (X.509) and AES-128/256 encryption, along with enterprise directory (AD, LDAP, RADIUS) integration ensure robust user and device level authentication and encryption.
- A high level of end-to-end and over-the-air (OTA) security is consistently maintained whether the mobile device is inside or outside the corporate firewall.
  - When the user is connecting from home or a hotspot, the RoamAnywhere Client automatically detects that the device is outside the enterprise firewall, and launches an application-layer SSL session, securing the connection. This eliminates the need for a user to manually launch a VPN client to secure communications.
  - When the user is in the office connected to the enterprise LAN, the solution takes advantage of Wi-Fi security standards such as WPA2 Personal and WPA2 Enterprise. #2 – Managing multiple platforms. With BYOD comes a wide variety of smartphones and tablets. While the sheer increase in the number of devices can be intimidating, it is delivering a consistent user-experience over a medley of platforms that is more daunting. IT managers are not only challenged with finding a solution that extends UC to these devices seamlessly from their existing infrastructure, but also having to provide on-going support to the application on all these devices. Imagine having to manage three separate mobile UC applications for supporting Android, BlackBerry and iOS devices. It means time and resources required for initial deployment and support are at least tripled. Now the magnitude of complexity can get exponential with large enterprises running multiple PBX/UC systems. Features and capabilities from different PBX/UC systems will need to be extended to a potpourri of devices. With ShoreTel Mobility, IT administrators have a single point of control and visibility. They manage a single solution irrespective of their PBX/UC vendor, and the mobile device OSes they support.

- Multiple Smartphones, One Solution. ShoreTel Mobility supports a wide variety of smartphones and tablets from Android, Apple iOS, BlackBerry OS and Symbian S60.
- Multiple PBX/UC Systems, One Solution. ShoreTel Mobility provides heterogeneous PBX support. It supports PBX/UC systems from Cisco, Avaya, Nortel, ShoreTel, and Microsoft. PBX and UC capabilities from any of these leading systems can be extended to any leading mobile device platform with a single solution. Even organizations with multiple PBXs or a mix of PBX vendors can deploy a single Mobility Router."

SUMMARY

Just about all manufacturers recognize that a certificate-based system is what they need to install for their phones, PBXs, and peripheral equipment. One of the more common ways to do this is with an asymmetrical key (public and private keys) X.509 PKI. Through the use of the public and private keys certificates and encryption keys are far easier to manage. Many of the manufacturers support SSL VPN clients, IPSec clients, and TLS clients in a mix and match as needed. This allows greater support for the end-user devices and gives a user much more flexibility in setting the security strategies for their organization. Regardless of the choice taken, encryption is a necessary portion of any VoIP system because there are too many opportunities for the evil hackers to penetrate through the systems.

Authentication

5

CHAPTER OUTLINE

AUTHENTICATION DEFINED

As already stated several times before, authentication is the process of making sure that someone is who he/she claims to be. For example, when using an account such as online banking or funds transfer, the user needs to ensure that the remote computer is actually the bank's computer, and not a man-in-the-middle acting as and responding as your bank. Whenever the topic of authentication arises, it is natural to also say the words 802.1X, which is the standard for authentication using a form of Extensible Authentication Protocol (EAP). 802.1X is used to allow or deny users access to a network. Moreover, it is a security protocol that also works with both wired and 802.11 wireless networks such as 802.11 a/b/g/n/ac. One would not use a wireless enterprise solution without some form of 802.1X EAP because of the risks posed with wireless connectivity.

DETAILS OF 802.1X AUTHENTICATION

For the purposes of the next discussion, wireless connectivity will be used, so long as it is understood that wired networks also use 802.1X. The main parts of 802.1X authentication are as follows (see Fig. 5.1 for the three components described below):

- A supplicant – A client end user, which wants to be authenticated. This is usually a wireless computer, tablet, smartphone, or wireless VoIP phone.
- An authenticator – An access point or a layer 2/3 switch. The authenticator acts as an intermediary for the end-user device, which limits the user device from communication with the authentication server.
- An authentication server – The authenticating device is typically a Remote Authentication Dial-In User Service (RADIUS) server (but can integrate with an

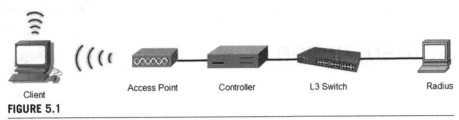

FIGURE 5.1

The components of 802.1X.

AD server or a LDAP server). The RADIUS server verifies that the user is who he/she says they are and allows or denies access depending on the successful exchange of credentials (username and password or certificate).

In a wireless network, 802.1X is used by an access point to implement WPA. In order to connect to the access point, a wireless client must first be authenticated using WPA or WPA2. The controller will not allow layer 2 traffic onto the Ethernet until the authentication is granted by the RADIUS server.

In a wired network, layer 2/3 switches use of 802.1X to implement port-based authentication. Before a switch forwards packets through a port, the attached devices must be authenticated. After the end user logs off, the virtual port being used is changed back to the unauthorized state.

The good news when using 802.1X is that the layer 2/3 switches and the access points do not need to know how to authenticate the client. In fact, they only pass the authentication information between the client and the authentication server (RADIUS). The authentication server handles the actual verification of the client's credentials.

802.1X uses EAP to handle and control all communication from the supplicant to the authenticator and from the authenticator to the authentication server.

EAP was considered to be one of the underlying protocols to allow different systems and methods to be used. This way a user is not relegated to a single security authentication protocol. Instead, EAP supports several authentication methods. The most prominent of the methods in use include the following:

1. EAP-Transport Layer Security (TLS) is widely supported. It uses PKI as discussed in earlier chapters. With EAP and TLS two certificates are used, a server certificate and a client certificate, to authenticate the supplicant (client) and authentication server. As part of TLS handshake mode (i.e., public key operation), TLS selects a symmetrical cipher to use for TLS record mode:
   a. It also creates and securely exchanges a *shared secret key* for the symmetrical cipher.
   b. The supplicant already knows it from the authentication process.
   c. And the authentication server passes it securely – usually as a RADIUS attribute to the authenticator.
   See Figure 5.2 for an example of the EAP-TLS. This is a mutual authentication of the client and the server.

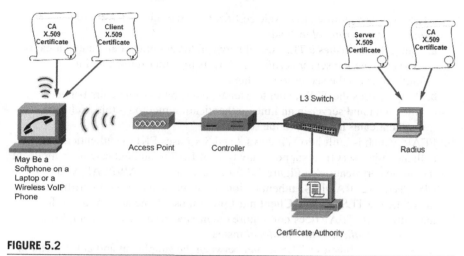

FIGURE 5.2

EAP-TLS.

2. EAP-Message Digest 5 (MD5) uses a username and password as standard. Recall the discussion on hash and digital signatures in earlier chapters. Actually what happens is the supplicant's password is hashed with MD5 and the hash value is used to authenticate the supplicant. The server sends the client a random challenge value, and the client proves its identity by hashing the challenge and its password with MD5. Normally this method is not used in public networks because of its vulnerabilities. Typically this is a one-way authentication of the client. This is very prone to man-in-the-middle attacks.

3. LEAP is Cisco's Lightweight EAP. It works mainly with Cisco products. It also uses MD5 hash, but both the supplicant and authentication server are authenticated. LEAP has been compromised in the past, so it is not the preferred means of authenticating.

4. EAP-TTLS – EAP with TTLS is Protected EAP (PEAP) and Tunneled TLS uses PKI to authenticate the authentication server. This was originally developed by Funk Software (later acquired by Juniper) and Certicom Corporation. Nearly any type of inner authentication method can be used by TTLS to authenticate the supplicant:

   a. Password Authentication Protocol (PAP)
   b. Challenge Handshake Authentication Protocol (CHAP)
   c. Microsoft CHAP (MS-CHAP)
   d. Microsoft CHAP version 2 (MS-CHAP v2)
   e. EAP-MD5
   f. EAP-TLS
   g. EAP Generic Token Card (EAP-GTC)

TTLS does not require client-side certificates – it employs a *two-stage authentication protocol* instead:

a. Stage 1 establishes a TLS tunnel between the supplicant and authentication server using the server certificate – this is the outer tunnel, and it authenticates the server to the client.

b. Stage 2 uses the TLS tunnel to exchange attribute–value pairs between the client and server in an inner authentication method – this exchange authenticates the client to the server.

5. PEAP, which is built into Windows 7 and 8.x,[1] uses PKI to authenticate the authentication server. It supports any type of EAP to authenticate the supplicant including certificate. See Figure 5.3 for an example of EAP-PEAP with MS-CHAP v2. RADIUS authentication server presents a server certificate to negotiate the TLS session. Client must present username and password for authentication. PEAP does not require client-side certificates – it employs a *two-stage authentication protocol* instead:

a. Stage 1 establishes a TLS tunnel between the supplicant and authentication server using the server certificate – this is the outer tunnel, and it authenticates the server to the client.

b. Stage 2 uses the TLS tunnel to protect a second EAP exchange, called the inner EAP exchange – this exchange authenticates the client to the server.

A summary of the different types of EAP is shown in Table 5.1. This is not all inclusive but does cover the primary ones. This table shows that for the strongest security a mutual certificate swap is preferred.

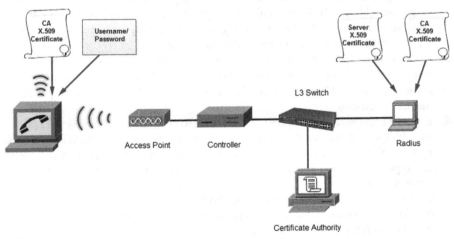

FIGURE 5.3

PEAP with MS-CHAP v2.

---

[1]Initially it was built into Windows XP, which may still be in use in some organizations. Now it is built into the successors of XP.

Table 5.1 A Summary of EAP Types

	EAP-MD5	LEAP (Cisco)	EAP-TLS (MS)	PEAP (MS/Cisco)	EAP-TTLS (Funk)
Security Solution	Standards-based	Proprietary (supported by many vendors)	Standards-based	Standards-based	Standards-based
Certificates – client	N/A	N/A	Yes	No	No
Certificates – server	N/A	N/A	Yes	Yes	Yes
Client password authentication	Yes	Yes	N/A	Yes	Yes
Credential security	Weak	Moderate (depends on password strength)	Strong	Strong	Strong
Dynamic key exchange	No	Yes	Yes	Yes	Yes
Mutual authentication	No	Yes	Yes	Yes	Yes
Support for legacy authentication methods	N/A	N/A	N/A	No	Yes

Because the IEEE standard for 802.1X covers port-based access control for devices (phones, PCs, terminals, etc.) one must understand that when rolling out VoIP using 802.1X, a potential problem is the use of the Ethernet port. In a wireless world the 802.1X authentication takes place after the AP association stage for the client. However, in the wired world most VoIP phones provide an Ethernet port so that a client PC can connect to the network. If you're using 802.1X, it is important to ensure that the layer 2/3 switch is configured to allow multiple devices on the same port. Otherwise, only the first device to establish a connection – the phone or the PC – will be able to access the network. Recall in the beginning chapters, the VoIP phone actually has a three (or more)–port switch that allows the phone and the PC to bridge across the port connected to the LAN. So if the switch is configured to allow only a single device to authenticate, the first device (most likely the phone) will be allowed to authenticate and the second device (the PC) will not. More on that a little later in this chapter.

It is also necessary to protect against a different form of eavesdropping. If you set the network up so that your voice traffic is on the same network as your data traffic, a risk to confidentiality is introduced that was not an issue on a traditional voice network. In fact, if you miss this part of the connectivity and confidentiality issues, any computing device on your LAN can become an eavesdropping device. Of course, the solution and the prevention are to place VoIP traffic on a separate VLAN and the data on its own VLAN. Not everything is secure, so you must be cognizant of the VLAN security practices. Make sure that the VLANs are secure and that a computer device cannot "jump" across the VLAN to get on the Voice VLAN. This is a particular problem when using a softphone on a PC because the same device is used for both types of traffic. Remember that authentication is essential for VoIP. Authentication as described above allows you to verify that the users and equipment on the network are who they say they are. It is imperative that you provide authentication (preferably using the 802.1X standard). This is also true for remote users; you can use secure tunnels and authentication to be sure that the access is authorized. If a user fails to authenticate, then deny access.

Along with the authentication and the secure tunnels make sure that you are encrypting as best you can. Encryption varies from vendor to vendor and how your network is set up [e.g., using a VPN connection and particularly an IP Security (IPSec) tunnel].

Initially security in VoIP was a very low priority. With the move toward VoIP in enterprises, Wi-Fi hot spots, cellular networks, and residential uses, securing VoIP was raised up several notches on the security priority list. As already discussed in the early chapters of this book, the number of threats to VoIP security is dramatically increasing. Three things can be done to make VoIP possibly more secure:

1. Use a VoIP-enabled firewall.
2. Use 802.1X authentication.
3. Encrypt the traffic and the control information.

Use a VoIP-enabled firewall

A firewall is a device or a program that establishes a shield between your computer or network and the sources of security threats (i.e., hackers, malware, and viruses). This shield filters and inspects data going in and out of the network. If a network is controlled by a central server, firewall software can be installed on that server, thus protecting all machines and devices on that network. Firewalls can also be embedded into hardware. For example, routers may have firewalls built-in to filter VoIP packets in and out of your VoIP network. See Figure 5.4 for the firewall configuration in a corporate and telecommuter environment.

Firewalls and Network Address Translation (NAT) can produce a problem to VoIP implementers. As most know, the firewall's job is to block traffic considered invasive, intrusive, or just plain malicious from flowing through them. The firewall provides a central location for implementing security policies on the network. The dynamic port setting and call setup procedures of both H.323 and SIP protocols make traditional firewalls unusable.

Today many of the devices connected on the Internet use a NAT function present in the border router. While the NAT prevents the Internet from initiating connections to the device (bad for IP telephony or other forms of peer-to-peer communications), it protects the users against malicious attacks. Using NAT, one may also connect

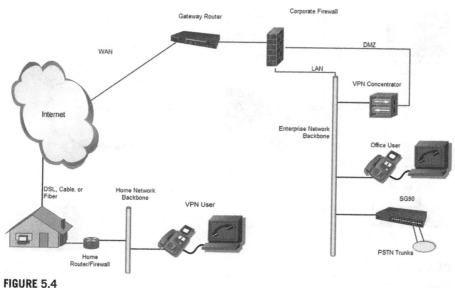

FIGURE 5.4

Firewalls can be a device or a program running on a PC.

multiple devices to the Internet by only using one public IP address. So NAT has both advantages and disadvantages. A firewall's NAT is an extremely effective tool that hides internal network addresses and allows any device on a LAN to share the same external IP address. NATs also indirectly secure the LAN, by making internal IP addresses inaccessible from the public Internet.

However, NAT has significant implications for VoIP calls. First, an attempt to make a call into the network becomes very complex when a NAT is present. The reason is that many of the communication parameters in SIP are transmitted within the SIP message; such parameters include the IP and port numbers used for signaling and media. A SIP device behind NAT does not know much about how it will be seen from the Internet; it only knows its own IP address and the ports where the SIP application runs. Once communication with the Internet starts, the NAT device translates the private IP:port combination of the SIP device connected on the private NAT interface to a temporary mapping of a public IP:port on the interface connected to the Internet. The scenario is shown in Figure 5.5.

When Alice tries to call Bob whose internal IP address is 172.16.0.97, she only knows Bob's public IP address: 79.1.6.6. There is no way to tell whether the call is for Bob or Tim who is also located on the same LAN subnet. One possible solution is to assign a static port for each internal IP address. Say Bob's address is 79.1.6.6:13864 and Tim's address is 79.1.6.6:13865. Unfortunately, dynamic port allocation like this for voice communication in H.323 and SIP won't allow this approach to work.

For a SIP device with a private address to be reachable from the network, it must first initiate a connection to the Internet. The SIP REGISTER function can handle

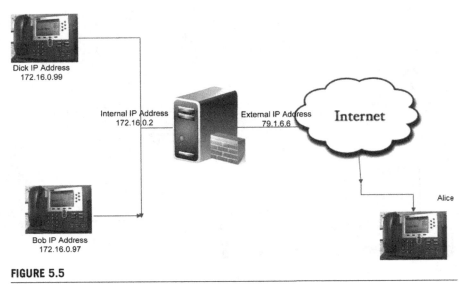

FIGURE 5.5

Firewall and NAT.

this situation. It is a function that maps the current location of the SIP device into the SIP registrar. When a SIP call is attempted, the SIP registrar is contacted to find the actual Internet address of the IP phone. Session Traversal Utilities for NAT or Simple Traversal of UDP Through NAT (STUN) is a standard[2] designed to help SIP devices figure out how they are seen from the Internet. The SIP device might use the values presented by a STUN server (reachable on the public Internet) in the SIP signaling. Unfortunately, depending on the type of NAT different mappings are opened in the NAT device for each new IP address:port combination. This renders the information provided by the STUN server useless for initiating communication to addresses other than the STUN server address. So STUN cannot provide a 100% safe solution to traverse the NAT.

A commercial solution to the firewall and NAT problem is the use of application-level gateways (ALGs). An ALG is software included on a firewall or NAT box, which allows for port/address configuration dynamically, based on the application. A VoIP-enabled firewall with the ALG software can understand the H.323 or SIP protocol information and opens dynamic ports only when necessary. This prevents us from opening up fixed ports that are punching permanent holes in the firewall. A VoIP-enabled NAT device combined with the ALG software functionality can open up VOIP packets and reconfigure internal IP address or external (routable) IP addresses.

VoIP-enabled firewalls and other appropriate protection mechanisms should be employed on any network that allows internal and external calls to be made. Because of the inherent risks presented by operating telephony across the Internet, VoIP

---

[2]See RFC 5389 for STUN.

systems incorporate an array of security features and protocols. VoIP-enabled firewalls are necessary components in the VoIP network. If permitted, ALGs that offer state-of-the-art intrusion detection/prevention should also be installed. This really works out to a situation whereby if VoIP-enabled firewalls and NAT boxes are not used, the whole network is at risk for penetration and hacking. As the old saying goes, "Pay me now or pay me later."

Use 802.1X authentication for IP phones

As discussed above, authentication is simply asking for credentials (username and password or any other secret information) from any user who requests access to a network or service. The model used is to implement 802.1X EAP to authenticate every user and every device. This way only real and valid users are allowed to authenticate and false ones are denied. Any system administrator, user, or device must be authenticated and authorized, regardless of its location, before it is able to access any network resources. After all, the whole purpose of 802.1X authentication is to prevent unauthorized devices from plugging directly into the LAN. If authentication is not available, then anyone with access could plug a rogue phone directly into the network and totally trash the network or cause havoc on the entire network. When one looks at the VoIP protocols, it is a common event that they are open. As a result a rogue phone (from a different manufacturer) could plug in and register on the network, unless the phone *must* authenticate first. Authentication is the "make good" effort to prevent this.

Taking a closer look at this authentication process is important. First, IP phones must be authenticated! An IP phone is simply an Ethernet device as seen earlier in Chapter 1. This Ethernet device has added capabilities that enable it to handle VoIP as well as other functions. In some manufacturers' environments, the IP phone has been beefed up with additional processing power and other resources (memory, etc.) to support applications (IM, MMS, video, or other functions). As seen earlier, the IP phone is plugged directly into the LAN. Typically, traffic of any unoccupied access point to a network, such as a port on a wired or wireless Ethernet switch, is blocked until the 802.1X authentication process is complete. When a device plugs into a network and it is detected, the port on the switch is set as "unauthorized" and only 802.1X traffic is allowed. Should the supplicant log off or a user simply unplugs its network cable from the network, the authenticator is notified and the status of the port is returned to an unauthorized state, where only 802.1X traffic is allowed until another 802.1X authorization process has been completed. This helps to prevent the arbitrary unplugging of one phone and plugging in a different phone. Figure 5.6 is an example of the dialog that takes place using the supplicant, authenticator, and authenticating server.

A significant benefit of the IP phone is that an IP phone has a second port for the data access to be plugged in. This way only a single cable needs to be installed to every office, the single cable being capable of supporting simultaneous voice and data. So the two ports on the phone allow for the phone and a PC to be plugged. See Figure 5.7 for a summary of the IP phone being plugged into the network.

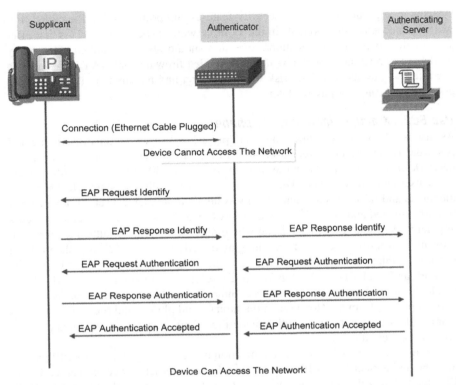

FIGURE 5.6

802.1X process.

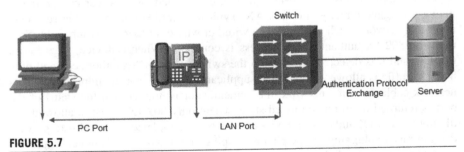

FIGURE 5.7

An IP phone connected to the network.

Attacking VoIP Authentication

When a new or existing VoIP phone is connected to the network, it sends a REGISTER request to the IP-PBX server for registering the associated user ID/extension number. This REGISTER request contains important details (such as user information, authentication data, etc.) that could be interesting and useful to an attacker.

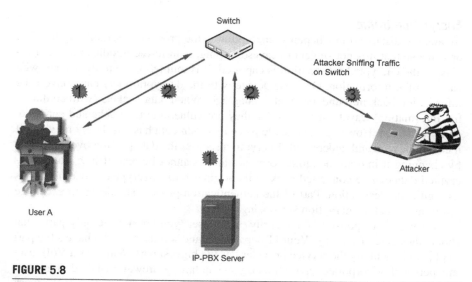

FIGURE 5.8

A hacker can capture all the authentication details with simple tools

Looking at Figure 5.8 one can see where a hacker with packet capture tools (Wireshark, SIPCrack, VOMIT, etc.) can actually catch all the information.

Assume that we have physical access to the VoIP network. Using the tools and techniques described in previous chapters scanning and enumeration tests can be performed to obtain the following details:

- IP address of SIP server
- Existing user IDs/extensions

If this was a perfect world, the authentication process would work without flaw. However, there is a gap in 802.1X protection. For example, if a hacker has physical access and if an Ethernet hub is inserted between an authenticated supplicant and the network, other devices connected to the hub can access the network. To help solve this potential problem, Ethernet switch suppliers have taken steps by blocking traffic on a port if the media access control (MAC) address of the supplicant changes. 802.1X went through revisions to facilitate secure communication over publicly accessible LANs/MANs. In fairness, the 802.1X standard was never really intended to offer security beyond authenticating and authorizing physical connections to a network. As a result, once a device has been authenticated and communication commences, 802.1X does not offer security on any of the ensuing data traffic. It is incumbent on the architects of the network carrying VoIP (or data for that matter) that supplemental security techniques be used with 802.1X, such as the IPSec standard for authenticating and/or encrypting packets. Also, 802.1AE (MAC Security) together with 802.1af (Authenticated Key Agreement for MACSec[3]) can also be used for data encapsulation, encryption, and authenticity with key management.

---

[3]Can also be referred to as Linksec.

Encrypt the traffic

As already discussed in Chapter 4 encryption is the process of scrambling the data or voice so that it is not subject to eavesdropping, man-in-the-middle attacks, or replay. If the encrypted information is captured, it is unintelligible to the hacker who captured the information. Only the device with the decryption key can convert the information back into understandable language. When data packets (with confidential information) travel over networks, they are vulnerable to attacks and can quite easily be stolen. However, a valuable piece of stolen data has absolutely no value if it cannot be read and understood! Encryption secures the data passing over networks by changing it into an ineligible form, so that it cannot be read if it is stolen. Encrypted data can be converted back to its original form (decrypted) once it reaches its legitimate destination. Part of the authentication process should be to exchange information on the encryption keys being used.

Just who is responsible for security? As a user, you are not the only party that should take care of security. Your IT department and service provider have a big part to play in it; actually the service provider has the biggest part. While, as a VoIP user in a personal or corporate environment, you can have a firewall installed, it is commonly out of your reach to enforce authentication and encryption. This is the work of your VoIP service provider.

SIP uses a stateless, challenge-based mechanism for authentication that is based on authentication in HTTP. This flow uses HTTP Digest for authentication using TLS transport. TLS transport is used because of the lack of integrity protection in HTTP Digest and the danger of registration hijacking without it. Any time that a proxy server or user agent (UA) receives a request, it *may* challenge the initiator of the request to provide assurance of its identity. Once the originator has been identified, the recipient of the request *should* ascertain whether or not this user is authorized to make the request in question. The SIP server provides a challenge to the initiator (let's use Bob for this example). Bob enters his valid user ID and password. Bob's SIP client encrypts the user information according to the challenge issued by the SIP server and sends the response to the SIP server. The SIP server validates the user's credentials. It registers the user in its contact database and returns a response (200 OK) to Bob's SIP client.

The "Digest" authentication mechanism provides message authentication and replay protection only, without message integrity or confidentiality. Protective measures above and beyond those provided by Digest need to be taken to prevent active attackers from modifying SIP requests and responses. Note that due to its weak security, the usage of "Basic" authentication has been deprecated. Servers *must not* accept credentials using the "Basic" authorization scheme, and servers also *must not* challenge with "Basic."[4]

When using encryption (and authentication for that matter) the goal is to stop the hacker. Below is a different summary of many of the risks associated with VoIP and specifically the SIP protocol. Encryption helps and there are many forms that

---

[4]This is a change from RFC 2543.

can be used. Primarily most people use AES encryption (AES 128 or AES 256) to keep the VoIP secure. For registration and authentication purposes, it is a good idea to use encryption. Another alternative is to use PGP for the authentication. Although some of the risks have already been addressed in earlier chapters, the following are the key risks:

- *Eavesdropping* – Most hackers steal credentials and other information through the eavesdropping mechanism. Through eavesdropping, a hacker can obtain names, password, and phone numbers, which gives them access to:
  - Takeover voice mail, as was the case in Florida when a group of hackers took over a voice mail system in the evening hours and used it as voice mail boxes for callers to a group of prostitutes. In the mornings, they reset the mailboxes back to their normal use and the hacked company did not know about it for 3 months until customers calling after hours could not leave voice messages for their company contacts.
  - Change expensive calling plans; this is not uncommon where the hacker group calls the carrier and opens up new calling patterns. Because they have the appropriate credentials (username and passwords) the carrier assumes that they are speaking with the appropriate company representative. The costs for this can skyrocket and the sticker shock at the first billing cycle is a rude awakening.
  - Set up call forwarding – Hackers and internal employees are guilty of this. Externally hackers will set up a call forwarding arrangement on an extension. The hacker then tells all the friends to call the company's "toll-free" number and ask for extension xxxx, which is the forwarded number. This happened when hackers and employees had forwarded their calls to a resort in a foreign country. Once the hacker has the credentials, the subsequent step leads to service theft. This is toll theft and runs into hundreds of thousands of dollars.

Stealing credentials to make calls without paying is not the only reason behind identity theft. Many people do it to get important information such as business data – if one can break into a voice mail system and listen to confidential messages, and then, by the way, set the message as "unheard" or "new" so that the intended recipient doesn't even suspect someone has listened to their voice mail.

A phreaker can change calling plans and packages and add more credit or make calls using the victim's account. Using VoIP, an attacker can create a virtual number for any country. He/she can then use a local number and forward the calls overseas, thereby giving one the impression of being a popular Fortune 500 organization anywhere in the world.

- *Viruses and malware* – VoIP using softphones (tablets, laptops, and smartphones) and software are vulnerable to worms, viruses, and malware, just like any Internet application. Since these softphone applications run on user systems such as PCs and PDAs, they are exposed and vulnerable to malicious code attacks in voice applications. Softphones create a greater risk to the VoIP network than a hard phone (IP phone) because the softphone is just a piece of software that runs on the computing device. As a result, the emphasis should be to ensure that virus scanners, personal firewalls, and malware detection/removal software are up to date. Many organizations do not allow the use of softphones, whereas others minimize their use.

- *Denial of Service/Distributed Denial of Service (DoS/DDoS)* – As described earlier a DoS attack is an attack on a network or device denying it of a service or connectivity. It can be done by consuming its bandwidth or overloading the network or the device's internal resources causing systems to crash and restart. In VoIP, DoS/DDoS attacks can be carried out by flooding a target with unnecessary SIP call-signaling messages, thereby degrading the service. This causes calls to drop prematurely and halts call processing.

  Many organizations do not truly understand the risk. Their initial reaction is to ask why someone would launch a DoS attack. Once the target is denied of the service and ceases operating, the attacker can get remote control of the administrative facilities of the system. Additionally, as already described, there is the possibility of extortion where the hackers threaten to take a phone system out of service with a DoS attack unless the organization pays a ransom.

- *Spam over Internet Telephony (SPIT)* – Anyone who uses e-mail regularly knows what spamming is (and phishing for that matter). Simply stated, spamming is actually sending many e-mails to people against their will. These e-mails consist mainly of online sales calls, opportunities to make a fortune, drug sales, stock market sales, pornographic materials, and the like. Spamming in VoIP is equally common now, and is starting to get more sophisticated, especially with the emergence of VoIP as an industrial tool. The more an organization relies on VoIP, the greater the risks of these attacks.

  Understand that every external VoIP account has an associated public IP address. It is easy for spammers to send their messages (voice mails) to thousands of IP addresses. Voice mail systems as a result will suffer and in particular the spam is a form of DoS. With spamming, voice mail systems will become clogged and more disk storage space will become necessary. Moreover, spam messages can easily carry viruses and spyware along with them if they are software based.

- *Call tampering* – Call tampering is an attack that involves tampering a phone call in progress. For example, the attacker can simply spoil the quality of the call by injecting noise packets in the communication stream. He/she can also withhold the delivery of packets so that the communication becomes spotty and the participants encounter long periods of silence during the call. This creates frustration causing the two parties to abandon the call. Replay attacks are a form of tampering whereby a portion of the call can be manipulated and resent, causing confusion, miscommunication, and the like. Tampering is not to be taken lightly.

- *Man-in-the-middle attacks* – Once again this was discussed earlier, but stated again to make sure that the point is well taken: VoIP is particularly vulnerable to man-in-the-middle attacks, in which the attacker intercepts call-signaling SIP message traffic and masquerades as the calling party to the called party, or vice versa. Once the attacker has gained this position, he/she can hijack calls via a redirection server. The other alternative is to gain the credentials by initiating a MITM attack and then posing as the server whereby the credentials (username and password) are presented by the caller, thinking that they are connected to the correct server.

- *Vishing* – Another form of SPIT (as covered above) is phishing over VoIP. Vishing is another word for VoIP phishing. Vishing attacks consist of sending a voice mail to a person, masquerading it with information from a party trustworthy to the receiver, such as a bank or online paying service, making him/her think he/she is safe. The voice mail usually asks for confidential data such as passwords or credit card numbers. You can imagine the rest! This is also equated to social engineering where similar attacks take place between two humans.

Phishing is an attack against data privacy whereby the victim himself/herself gives out his/her personal data; after the ploy, the trap is set.

Phishing works like this: a data thief sends you an e-mail message or a voice mail making it seem like it is an official message from a company you have financial or other interests with, such as your bank, PayPal, eBay, etc. In the message, you are informed about a problem that puts you in alarm and are requested to go to a site or phone a number where you have to give your personal data such as credit card number, passwords, etc. In many cases this can also involve a person representing your credit card company and states that your card has been compromised. Review Chapter 1 and see how often this happens. Once you call or connect to the perpetrator of the phishing attack, they ask that you verify your information (account number, social security number, address, PIN number, etc.).

In today's world, it is hard to believe that this occurs; however, unfortunately it happens every day particularly among elderly people, who are not exposed to this cheat regularly, novices, and younger people just coming into the business arena. The results of a phishing attack can be financially devastating.

Some examples of phishing attacks include:

1. You get an email from PayPal, eBay, or companies of their like, informing you of some irregularity on your part, that your account is frozen. You are told that the only way to free your account and complete any transactions is to go to a given link and give your password and other personal information.
2. You get a voice mail from your Internet banking department saying that someone has tried to tamper with your password, and that something has to be done quickly to save your account. You are requested to phone a given number and give your credentials so that you can change your existing account credentials.
3. You get a phone call from your bank saying that they have noticed some suspicious or fraudulent activities on your bank account, and asking you to either phone back (because most of the time the voice is pre-recorded) or give your bank account number, credit card number, etc.

People also ask why phishers didn't use the PSTN before VoIP. The answer is obvious when you consider the way the telephone companies built the PSTN; it is maybe the most secure modern means of telecommunication and has the most secure network and infrastructure. As described in the first part of this book, VoIP is much more vulnerable than PSTN.

Phishing is easier for attackers using VoIP for the following reasons:

- VoIP is cheaper than PSTN and is now quite widely available.
- With VoIP, attackers can tamper with the caller ID (spoof the caller ID to any number they want). To the victim, the caller ID that shows up on the incoming call appears as if their bank or any other trusted party is calling. This sets the stage for the hook to be set.
- VoIP software for PBXs, like any open-source PBX, provides the programmer with limited skills the necessary tools to do so much more. Anybody with basic knowledge of VoIP can spoof the caller ID and imitate just about any organization.
- VoIP hardware, such as IP phones, ATAs, routers, and IP-PBXs, are extremely low cost now and the software that comes with these devices is web-based so that just about anyone can configure and inject them into a network. These devices are portable and can be hidden most anywhere.
- VoIP hardware and software (freeware) makes it easy for vishers to record phone calls of numerous victims who have been hooked, getting a copy of a voice call (can also use Wireshark, VOMIT, and Audacity to capture calls and manipulate the voice for a replay).
- Unlike for PSTN, VoIP numbers can be created and torn down in minutes, which makes tracking the vishers extremely tentative for the law agencies.
- With VoIP, vishers can create one generic message and propagate it to thousands, or they can use some of the old-fashioned tools such as war dialing.

A new issue is the single-ring phishing. In this case a caller calls your number and then hangs up after the first ring. Of course, there will be no voice message in this call attack. Now the called party sees that a missed call has occurred and instinctively calls the missed incoming caller back to see what the call was about. This is where the bite comes in, because the call could be to some "pay per call" service or to a fraudulent area code, etc., where the caller calling this number back gets charged some variable cost ($25.00 or $50.00 per call). It may also be to some toll-free number that forwards (because of VoIP the caller ID can be spoofed) but the called-back number may be to an answering machine that keeps you on hold for long periods of time by offering some prize, etc. The cost per minute to these numbers can be exorbitant.

AUTHENTICATION ON WIRELESS NETWORKS

When a VoIP solution is deployed in an enterprise network, network administrators may set up authentication of connected devices so that only the allowed devices gain access to the network. Several methods are available, depending on the supportability of connected devices. Two typical methods are IEEE 802.1X and MAC address–based authentication. Although the part does not describe all possible combinations of authentication methods on VoIP phones and endpoint hosts, some of the common scenarios are described. Using MAC address–based authentication to authenticate VoIP phone and 802.1X to authenticate endpoint host are the most common as addressed above.

Now that VoIP softphones, smartphones, and wireless sets can be used on a Wi-Fi network, things become a bit more complicated in some scenarios. One of the most common methods of authentication is to use MAC address–based authentication for the VoIP phone while 802.1X for the endpoint host, because each device must be authenticated separately. This configuration requires that the network administrator obtain the MAC address of the VoIP phone and populate the authentication server with appropriate credentials. Currently most endpoint hosts such as laptops and desktops support 802.1X. However, not all VoIP vendors and models support 802.1X and in particular the certificates described in this chapter. The managed L2/L3 switches support different authentication methods on a given interface, which allows each device or supplicant to be authenticated individually. MAC address–based authentication as well as 802.1X is implemented for a VoIP phone and endpoint host when different VLANs can be configured. Typically a VoIP profile is created for a specific VLAN (we can say VLAN 10 for voice) and we can use DSCP values that define the type of traffic (so a DSCP of 46 is voice). With different vendor products (an example of Cisco) the Cisco Discovery Protocol can be used to fingerprint the sets. A second VLAN is created on the switch for data traffic (VLAN 20 for data). By separating the two types of traffic with different VLANs the authentication and authorization can be applied differently and the two types of traffic will remain separate. In some cases we can use EAP (in various flavors described above) and in other cases we cannot. This varies depending on the vendor and the phone. Some switches can only support certain types of EAP but are not totally EAP agnostic. Some capabilities exist that allow authenticating the VoIP phone using MAC address–based authentication while using 802.1X for endpoint host centrally. Some VoIP phones do not support 802.1X. In such cases, the MAC address of the VoIP phone can be used to provide some level of security while 802.1X is used for the endpoint host. One such access switch is made by Aruba: "The Aruba Mobility Access Switch supports various methods to deploy VoIP in enterprise networks. These methods include different ways to connect VoIP phones and endpoint host devices physically as well as various types of configuration that can be implemented on the Mobility Access Switch. Furthermore, the VoIP solution can also provide security by adding an authentication mechanism such as IEEE 802.1X or MAC address–based authentication. In addition to a clear understanding of the various available options discussed, careful planning prior to actual deployment is highly recommended for successful VoIP deployment in enterprise networks" (Source: Aruba Networks).

Because the VoIP has moved to a wireless architecture, it is also important to recognize that users will attempt to use their wireless VoIP phone, smartphone, softphone, etc., in a hot spot. This can be tricky because the Internet cafés (hot spots) and public Wi-Fi networks remain unsecured. These are open connections to allow for the connectivity to as many people as possible and in most cases for no cost. There are many books that address how to protect your data in a public hot spot, but the best is to use a VPN. VPNs were already discussed earlier.

Remember when using an open access point the traffic going to the access point is in clear text and therefore can be captured (eavesdropped, MITM, replay, etc.). So the first thing to watch is the AP access, and then use a VPN client if at all possible (SSL-VPN, or a VPN client from the VoIP manufacturer, etc.).

SUMMARY

Authentication is a must; if possible, an EAP-TLS or EAP-TTLS technique should be chosen. Whenever the manufacturer offers a certificate-based authentication, use it. When 802.1X cannot be used for the authentication of a VoIP phone, MAC-based authentication may be the best choice. As part of the authentication process, understand the risks of the common attacks and address the needs appropriately; mainly train the users. Encryption keys are exchanged during the authentication process, so choose the best form of encryption that will work in your environment. Also keep in mind that softphones are unique exposure points in a VoIP network because they are more vulnerable (at least for now) to software-based attacks such as viruses, malware, and hacking. Keep the software up to date on the devices employing softphones. The good news with softphones is that these devices make authentication and authorization with 802.1X far easier. Finally keep in mind that wireless devices (laptops with softphones, wireless VoIP phones, tablets, and smartphones) are all exposed when being used in public Wi-Fi networks and must be protected differently.

Other protocols
SRTP, ZRTP, and SIPS

CHAPTER OUTLINE

OTHER PROTOCOLS

Up to now, several techniques for securing our data and voice have been addressed, including encryption, authentication, and VPNs. Each tool has its own merit as seen in the preceding chapters. However, when looking at the overall security of Voice over IP (VoIP), the tools are applied to make the VoIP secure. As a result, when using these tools there are different protocols that come into play at the highest levels of the OSI model to create the necessary security. These include Secure Real-Time Transport Protocol (SRTP), Zimmerman Real-Time Transport Protocol[1] (ZRTP), and Secure Session Initiation Protocol (SSIP or SIPS). While the concept of the Real-Time Transport Protocol (RTP) and Session Initiation Protocol (SIP) protocols was discussed in the early chapters of this book, a quick review of these protocols along with the enhancements to secure them will be addressed in this chapter.

It must be understood that an IP network might not be very reliable to carry voice calls. As discussed for the case of a circuit-switched network, there is a dedicated path built at the time of the call. All voice traffic goes across that path for the

---

[1]Philip R. ("Phil") Zimmermann, Jr. is the creator of Pretty Good Privacy. He is also known for his work in VoIP encryption protocols, notably ZRTP and Zfone.

duration of the call. No one else is on that path except the two parties[2] conversing. So there is less likelihood that the traffic will be interrupted/intercepted on the way or that someone will eavesdrop the call. Conversely, if the voice traffic is going over a packet-switched network such as the Internet, the traffic is sent in packets and it is possible that the packets can take different paths to reach the final destination. Along the way, the traffic packets can pass through many gateways (or other devices) over which the sender or receiver has no control. It becomes quite possible that someone is listening to the traffic and even potentially recording the voice. (This is actually not all that much different from today's voice networks that use fibers, switches, etc., belonging to others.) Thus, packet-switched networks for voice traffic are potentially more vulnerable and less secure. As mentioned earlier, SIP is especially designed for voice on IP networks, so it is important that SIP provides some level of security.

There are two important points that should be addressed here. First, SIP is a signaling protocol for VoIP and it carries the information about the following[3]:

- The identity of the calling party
- The identity of the called party
- The list of the calls
- The services (media capabilities, codec, etc.)

It is possible that the users involved in a conversation do not want this information to be disclosed to any third party. So, there must be some way to protect the SIP messages from being intercepted and decoded enroute to the destination. The second and more important issue is to protect the actual voice traffic from being tapped by an unwanted person or machine. To overcome these two issues, SIP messages as well as the RTP data, that is, voice content, should be both encrypted and secured on an end-to-end basis. Encrypting the RTP traffic can be done either at the application layer using SRTP or at the network layer using Encapsulating Security Payload (IP ESP). This was discussed as a part of the IPSec Protocol. At the same time, keeping the SIP messages and the media information both private and intact is crucial.

As already discussed, authentication is another very important factor in SIP. The user should be authenticated before being registered by registrar server, for example. Registrar should make sure that the user who is registering is actually the user and not someone else. Additionally, the authentication between client and server should be mutual, meaning that a client should authenticate to a server and the server should authenticate to the client. This is where the 802.1X protocols are applicable as described in Chapter 5.

---

[2]Unless there is a conference call.

[3]One could think of (and compare) this as analogous to an ISDN BRI. The signaling is done across the D channel and the talk is done on the two B channels. The bandwidth is shared on the primary circuit between the two voice paths and the signaling path. Because the signaling and control packets can take different routes instead of using a dedicated path, potential problems can exist. If a SIP (signaling) packet gets lost when a call is being terminated (torn down), the RTP channels could get locked up on that end of the connection. This would create certain problems for the network and users alike.

Thus, a client should be able to authenticate the registrar server. This will prevent registering with a fake server. A mutual certificate swap will allow this. Moreover, before sending the Invite message to a SIP proxy server, the proxy server should require the user agent (UA) to be authenticated and the UA should also authenticate the proxy server. Because there are myriad devices involved it becomes imperative that all clients and servers authenticate.

Other security issues in SIP exist, such as the need to reduce the risk of a denial-of-service (DoS) attack or distributed-denial-of-service (DDoS) attack as discussed in Chapter 2. If a proxy server is the subject of a DoS/DDoS attack, it could become unavailable for the legitimate SIP clients as already shown. The use of the application layer gateways and intelligent proxy servers aids in mitigating these DoS/DDoS attacks.

Earlier some of the security threats and how SIP can handle these concerns were shown. Make no mistake though, it is very important to note that if the SIP client is using a wireless network, then the security concerns are far more exponential. With wireless connectivity, the attacker does not need physical access to the network and the traffic can be sniffed in the air between the user and the access point. There are several good books that deal with Wi-Fi network security and how to ensure securing the client and the data from sniffing and man-in-the-middle attacks. Suffice it to say, be aware is the operative word.

OVERVIEW OF REAL-TIME TRANSPORT PROTOCOL AND REAL-TIME TRANSPORT CONTROL PROTOCOL (RTCP)

First, a quick review of the RTP is provided so that the enhanced secure version will be easier to understand. What then is RTP? The RTP provides end-to-end communications (network transport) functionality for VoIP. Basically, when thinking of RTP it would be safe to assume that the media is what is being addressed. VoIP encompasses real-time audio (voice) and real-time data (such as audio streams, video, or any form of simulated data). RTP has an inherent responsibility to provide the transport of application layer data (traffic) but does not ensure the resource reservation[4] nor does it guarantee any form of quality of service (QoS).[5] It should be understood that there can be significant packet loss in an RTP connection. Actually the packets can be:

- Lost
- Delayed
- Reordered (out of sequence)
- Duplicated
- Corrupted

---

[4]RSVP handles resource reservations and can be used hand in hand with RTP.
[5]QoS can be handled through any of the fair weighting and queuing protocols. However, the delivery of a RTP packet is not assured.

To solve some of the problems, a checksum is used to detect when an error occurs. However, there is more to the overall VoIP functionality in that there can be many causes of problems, such as:

- Congestion can cause a significant amount of packet loss. (At what level of packet loss does the conversation become unintelligible?)
- There can be corruption on the link (or network) that will cause significant packet loss due to timeouts.
- The amount of queuing delay can create problems on the VoIP (and specifically the RTP) network.
- Noise and erratic interference can cause significant problems. Noise includes static noise across the network, and also interference caused from adjacent electrical equipment that will create interference on the circuitry. The significant problems entail loss of packets due to the noise and static, loss of connections if the interference is high enough, and poor quality of the voice reception due to these issues. Static and fuzzy conversations are also possibilities with these issues.[6]
- The basic routing may cause different packets to take different routes[7] causing out-of-sequence delivery.[8]

RTP can be used on a unicast or a multicast transmission, although the more common form is unicast. In Figure 6.1 the RTP is shown as an application layer protocol. The RTP provides features for real-time applications, with the ability to reconstruct timing, loss detection, security, content delivery, and identification of encoding schemes. For each participant, a particular pair of destination IP addresses defines the session between the two end points, which translates into a single RTP session for each phone call in progress. RTP is an application service built on UDP, so it is connectionless, with best-effort delivery. Although RTP is connectionless, it does have a sequencing system that allows for the detection of missing packets. When packets are missing there is no mechanism to request a retransmission, but the systems will allow for the replay of an earlier packet to fill in for the missing packet(s).

In Figure 6.2 the packet structure for RTP is shown. This is a packet structure that is for UDP/IP and then the RTP. Note that if looking from left to right the IP header is used first for the routing information. Following the IP header is the UDP header that will define the port. The combined IP address and port number creates the socket for the VoIP traffic. Next in line is the RTP header that contains a significant amount

---

[6]It has been proven that when noisy and static-filled calls are made or received on a VoIP network, users have a tendency of avoiding the use of VoIP in favor of the older dial-up telephone network (POTS).

[7]This also includes packets sent from A to B that may have different routes than packets from B back to A, thus having different loss, delays, and jitter from each other.

[8]The fact is that if voice packets arrive early, they can be buffered and then played out at a later time; however, voice packets that arrive late have no value and should be discarded. This leads to a lot of packet loss and the potential of voice problems.

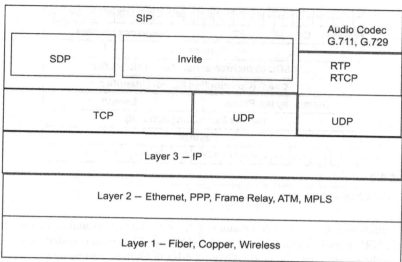

FIGURE 6.1

The RTP stack.

of information (see below). Finally comes the RTP payload (the actual traffic, be it voice, audio, or video).

In Figure 6.3 the RTP header is shown. As mentioned, a significant amount of information is represented here. Typically the RTP header will contain 12 bytes (however, an extended header may contain 16 bytes). These fields contain the following information:

- *Version (V)*: 2 bits. This field identifies the version of RTP. The current version is 2 based on RFC 3550.
- *Padding (P)*: 1 bit. If the padding bit is set, the packet contains one or more additional padding octets at the end that are not part of the payload. The last octet of the padding contains a count of how many padding octets should be ignored. Padding may be needed by some encryption algorithms with fixed block sizes or for carrying several RTP packets in a lower layer protocol data unit.
- *Extension (X)*: 1 bit. If the extension bit is set, the fixed header is followed by exactly one header extension.

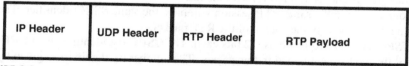

FIGURE 6.2

The RTP packet structure.

0	1	2	3	4	5	6	7	8	9	10	11	12	13	14	15	16	17	18	19	20	21	22	23	24	25	26	27	28	29	30	31
Ver		P	X	CC				M	PT							Sequence Number															
Timestamp																															
SSRC (Synchronization Source) Identifier																															
CSRC (Contributing Source) Identifier																															
Defined by the Profile																Length															
Header Extension (Optional)																															
Payload																															
x	x	x	x	x	x	x	x	0	0	0	0	0	0	0	0	0	0	0	0	0	0	0	0	0	0	0	0	0	0	1	0

FIGURE 6.3

RTP packet header format.

- *Contributing source (CSRC) count (CC)*: 4 bits. The CC contains the number of CSRC identifiers that follow the fixed header. This field is added by a mixer to indicate who the talkers are. Given a 4-bit field, there can be up to 15 CSRCs (talkers).
- *Marker (M)*: 1 bit. Marker bit is used by specific applications to serve a purpose of its own. The marker bit is usually dependent on the RTP profile. It is often used to mark the start of a burst of speech.
- *Payload type (PT)*: 7 bits. This field identifies the format (e.g., what Codec was used to create the payload) of the RTP payload and determines its interpretation by the application. This field is not intended for multiplexing separate media. The byte length of the payload is not indicated in the header; instead it is established in the RTP profile and its association with the PT (voice, audio, video, etc.).
- *Sequence number*: 16 bits. The sequence number increments by 1 for each RTP data packet sent, and may be used by the receiver to detect packet loss and to restore packet sequence. The initial value of the sequence number is random (unpredictable).
- *Timestamp*: 32 bits. The timestamp reflects the sampling instant of the first octet in the RTP data packet. The sampling instant must be derived from a clock that increments monotonically and linearly in time to allow synchronization and jitter calculations. The clock rate is determined by the profile, although it usually is 8000 ticks/s (based on an 8 kHz clocking system).
- *SSRC*: 32 bits. The SSRC field identifies the synchronization source. This identifier is chosen randomly, with the intent that no two synchronization sources within the same RTP session will have the same SSRC identifier. The intent is to identify the source of the RTP packet.
- *CSRC list*: Zero to 15 items, 32 bits each. The CSRC list identifies the CSRCs for the payload contained in this packet. The number of identifiers is given by the CC field. If there are more than 15 CSRCs, only 15 may be identified. CSRC identifiers are inserted by mixers, using the SSRC identifiers of CSRCs.

The receiver needs three pieces of key information for synchronization – the synchronization source, packets in order, and sampling instant of packets, which it gets from three header fields:

- Synchronization source (SSRC): The receiver may be receiving data from several sources. So for proper arrangement it needs to identify the source of individual packets, which is possible from the SSRC field.
- Sequence number: It is not enough to identify the source; the order is important too. The sequence number increments by 1 for each RTP data packet sent, and may be used by the receiver to detect packet loss and to restore packet sequence. The loss or out-of-order delivery occurs due to network problems.
- Timestamp: For media delivery not just the order of the packets but also the sampling instant of individual packets is important. Several consecutive RTP packets may have equal timestamps if they are (logically) generated at once, for example, belong to the same video frame. Consecutive RTP packets may contain timestamps that are not monotonic if the data is not transmitted in the order it was sampled, such as MPEG interpolated video frames. (The sequence numbers of the packets as transmitted will still be monotonic.) So the sequence number is not enough for synchronization.

In a(n) audio/video session audio and video data are transmitted using separate channels. The receiver matches the video data with corresponding audio data using timestamp.

As part of its specification, the RTP PT field includes the encoding scheme that the media gateway uses to digitize the voice content. This field identifies the RTP payload format and determines its interpretation by the Codec in the media gateway. A profile specifies a default static mapping of PT codes to payload formats.

With the different types of encoding schemes and packet creation rates, RTP packets can vary in size and interval. When planning voice services RTP parameters must be taken into account. All the combined parameters of the RTP sessions dictate how much bandwidth is consumed by the voice bearer traffic. RTP traffic that carries voice traffic is the single greatest contributor to the VoIP network load.

Note also that sitting right alongside of the RTP in Figure 6.4 is the RTCP. RTCP is designed to monitor (but not provide QoS) and report back to the sender the timing

FIGURE 6.4

The RTCP.

and control information. Both RTP and RTCP operate independently of the underlying transport and network layers, or if you will, they will run on just about any transport and network layer protocols. To be fair, however, the RTP and RTCP traditionally operate, as seen in this figure, on top of TCP or UDP and then IP. Earlier the discussion was that for running VoIP, the UDP and IP (UDP/IP) protocols are better and for signaling and control TCP/IP can be used.[9] Initially RTP was addressed in RFC 1889 that was later superseded by RFC 3550. It is not needed for RTP to work. The primary function of RTCP is to provide feedback on the quality of the data distribution being accomplished by RTP. This function is an integral part of RTP's role as a transport protocol and is related to the flow and congestion control functions of the network. Although the feedback reports from RTCP do not describe where problems are occurring (only that they are), they can be used as a tool to locate problems. With the information generated from different media gateways in the network, RTCP feedback reports enable an administrator to evaluate where network performance might be degrading.

RTCP

Looking at the RFC 3550, the RTCP is based on the periodic transmission of control packets to all participants in the session, using the same distribution mechanism as the data packets. The underlying protocol *must* provide multiplexing of the data and control packets, for example, using separate port numbers with UDP. RTCP performs four functions:

1. The primary function is to provide feedback on the quality of the data distribution. This is an integral part of the RTP's role as a transport protocol and is related to the flow and congestion control functions of other transport protocols. The feedback may be directly useful for control of adaptive encodings, but experiments with IP multicasting have shown that it is also critical to get feedback from the receivers to diagnose faults in the distribution. Sending reception feedback reports to all participants allows one who is observing problems to evaluate whether those problems are local or global. With a distribution mechanism such as IP multicast, it is also possible for an entity such as a network service provider who is not otherwise involved in the session to receive the feedback information and act as a third-party monitor to diagnose network problems. This feedback function is performed by the RTCP sender and receiver reports.

2. RTCP carries a persistent transport-level identifier for an RTP source called the canonical name (CNAME). Since the SSRC identifier may change if a conflict is discovered or a program is restarted, receivers require the CNAME to keep track of each participant. Receivers may also require the CNAME to associate multiple data streams from a given participant in a set of related RTP sessions, for example, to synchronize audio and video. Intermedia synchronization also requires the NTP and RTP timestamps included in RTCP packets by data senders.

---

[9]An example is for H.323 protocols the signaling is done on TCP port 1720. In SIP protocols the session is initiated on port 5060 for carrying the RTP and port 5061 for RTCP.

3. The first two functions require that all participants send RTCP packets; therefore, the rate must be controlled in order for RTP to scale up to a large number of participants. By having each participant send its control packets to all the others, each can independently observe the number of participants. This number is used to calculate the rate at which the packets are sent.
4. A fourth, *optional* function is to convey minimal session control information, for example, participant identification to be displayed in the user interface. This is most likely to be useful in "loosely controlled" sessions where participants enter and leave without membership control or parameter negotiation. RTCP serves as a convenient channel to reach all the participants, but it is not necessarily expected to support all the control communication requirements of an application. A higher-level session control protocol may be needed.

Functions 1–3 above *should* be used in all environments, but particularly in the IP multicast environment. RTP application designers *should* avoid mechanisms that can work in only unicast mode and will not scale to larger numbers. Transmission of RTCP *may* be controlled separately for senders and receivers, for cases such as unidirectional links where feedback from receivers is not possible.

Further the RFC describes the RTCP Packet Format as follows (this specification defines several RTCP packet types to carry a variety of control information):

- SR: Sender report, for transmission and reception statistics from participants that are active senders as seen in the sender report shown in Figure 6.5.
- RR: Receiver report, for reception statistics from participants that are not active senders and in combination with SR for active senders reporting on more than 31 sources as seen in the receiver report shown in Figure 6.6.
- SDES: Source description items, including CNAME, along with optional fields (e-mail, phone, address, etc.) as seen in Figures 6.7 and 6.8.
- BYE: Indicates end of participation when a user drops off a connection, along with the reason for leaving.
- APP: Application-specific functions are a packet that is application dependent.

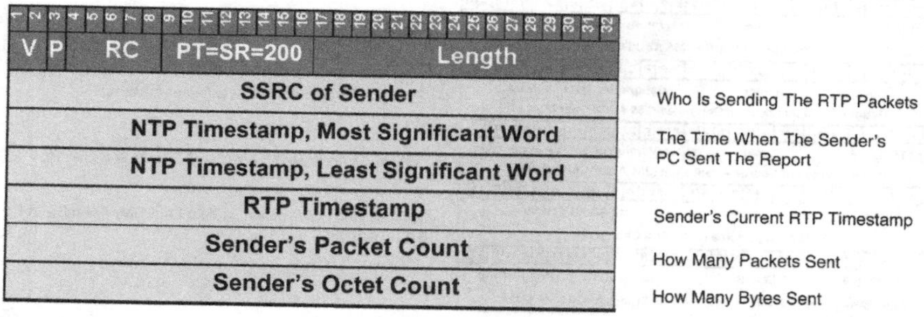

FIGURE 6.5

Sender report.

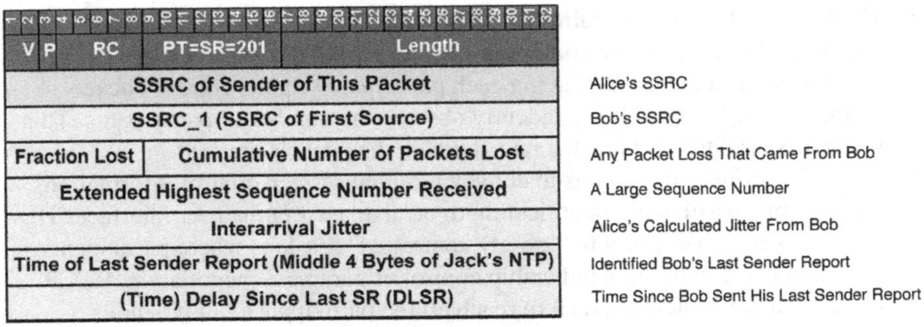

V
P
RC
PT=SR=201
Length
SSRC of Sender of This Packet
SSRC_1 (SSRC of First Source)
Fraction Lost
Cumulative Number of Packets Lost
Extended Highest Sequence Number Received
Interarrival Jitter
Time of Last Sender Report (Middle 4 Bytes of Jack's NTP)
(Time) Delay Since Last SR (DLSR)
Alice's SSRC
Bob's SSRC
Any Packet Loss That Came From Bob
A Large Sequence Number
Alice's Calculated Jitter From Bob
Identified Bob's Last Sender Report
Time Since Bob Sent His Last Sender Report

FIGURE 6.6

Receiver report.

V
P
RC
PT=SDES=202
Length
SSRC/CSRC_1 of Sender
SDES ITEMS
SSRC /CSRC_2 of Sender
SDES ITEMS
SDES Header
A Chunk Identifies The Sender; Each Chunk Is Sent to Identify One Sender

FIGURE 6.7

Source description items.

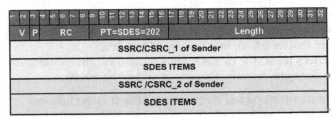

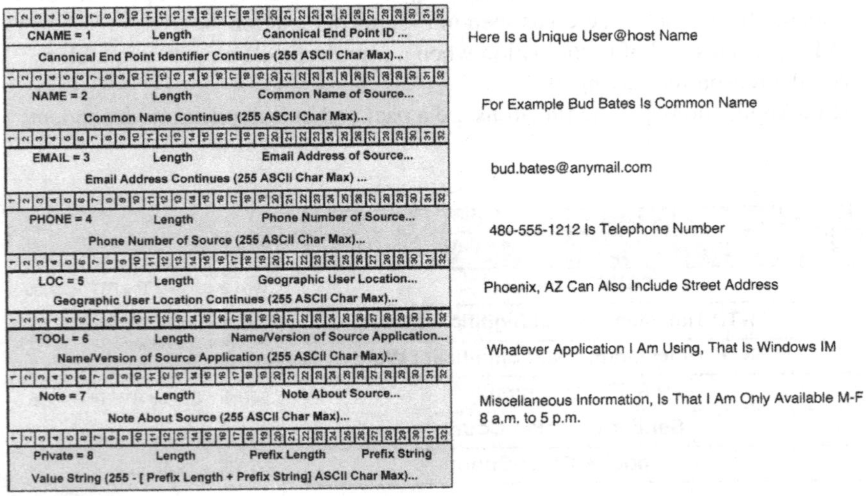

CNAME = 1
Length
Canonical End Point ID ...
Canonical End Point Identifier Continues (255 ASCII Char Max)...
NAME = 2
Length
Common Name of Source...
Common Name Continues (255 ASCII Char Max)...
EMAIL = 3
Length
Email Address of Source...
Email Address Continues (255 ASCII Char Max) ...
PHONE = 4
Length
Phone Number of Source...
Phone Number of Source (255 ASCII Char Max)...
LOC = 5
Length
Geographic User Location...
Geographic User Location Continues (255 ASCII Char Max)...
TOOL = 6
Length
Name/Version of Source Application...
Name/Version of Source Application (255 ASCII Char Max)...
Note = 7
Length
Note About Source...
Note About Source (255 ASCII Char Max)...
Private = 8
Length
Prefix Length
Prefix String
Value String (255 - [Prefix Length + Prefix String] ASCII Char Max)...
Here Is a Unique User@host Name
For Example Bud Bates Is Common Name
bud.bates@anymail.com
480-555-1212 Is Telephone Number
Phoenix, AZ Can Also Include Street Address
Whatever Application I Am Using, That Is Windows IM
Miscellaneous Information, Is That I Am Only Available M-F 8 a.m. to 5 p.m.

FIGURE 6.8

Optional information fields.

Each RTCP packet begins with a fixed part similar to that of RTP data packets, followed by structured elements that *may* be of variable length according to the packet type but *must* end on a 32-bit boundary. The alignment requirement and a length field in the fixed part of each packet are included to make RTCP packets "stackable." Multiple RTCP packets can be concatenated without any intervening separators to form a compound RTCP packet that is sent in a single packet of the lower layer protocol, for example, UDP. There is no explicit count of individual RTCP packets in the compound packet because the lower layer protocols are expected to provide an overall length to determine the end of the compound packet.

Each individual RTCP packet in the compound packet may be processed independently with no requirements on the order or combination of packets. However, in order to perform the functions of the protocol, the constraints given in the following are imposed.

RTCP enables administrators to monitor the quality of a call session by tracking packet loss, latency (delay), jitter, and other key VoIP concerns. This information is provided on a periodic basis to both ends and is processed per call by the media gateways. Some gateway devices might not employ RTCP because the facility to report such information is not applicable to the end user. For example, a single residential user (with an analog phone) might not have access to the gateway providing the service. Also, the media gateway vendor can use a more scalable approach of tracking call quality statistics. In this case, the storage, transport, and presentation of statistical information are device dependent.

So summarizing the above overview, RTP is the media carrying capacity; in other words, when setting up a voice or video call (conference) the media is created separately for voice and video. Moreover, while sending RTP packets, RTCP control information is also created using a UDP port. It may be a surprise to many people to know that despite the flexibility provided by the IP platform, VoIP calls might still be going in an unencrypted format! What this means, of course, is that VoIP is not totally secure and a determined hacker may gain access to the call. This is why SRTP is a recommended protocol to secure VoIP calls.

FUNCTION OF SECURE RTP

What most people do not understand is that RTP communications are transmitted in clear text. Ask yourself if that is OK? Most of the telephone communications in the analog world (as discussed in Chapter 1) were transmitted in their native form. Well, that's how calls were wiretapped! At least in the analog world, the intruder requires access to the particular phone line (the wire pair as discussed in Chapter 1) that is transmitting the voice physically in order to intercept the communications. However, in the IP world, a hacker might stay where he/she is, compromise the communicating device (or any device in the same network), and access the communications! So if the RTP (the actual data packets carrying the voice) is in clear text, then eavesdropping is simplified. Unless there is some form of encryption used, the VoIP is at risk. As voice communications (VoIP) have become more vulnerable to the same type of

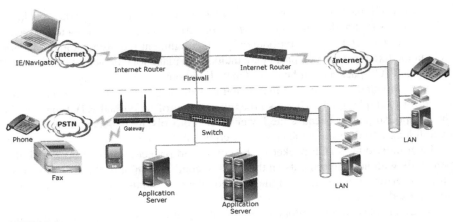

FIGURE 6.9

Two distinct networks.

attacks that data has endured over the past two decades, organizations are constantly trying to ensure that precautions are taken to ensure privacy and security in their communications. However, one cannot lose sight of the other forms of communications [Presence, Instant Messages (IMS), Multimedia Messages (MMS), fax, video, and data] when attempting to secure the RTP stream because VoIP networks are far more complex than an IP network alone. Moreover, when dealing with IP telephony there are two distinct networks that are usually interconnected as seen in Figure 6.9. The use of a telephone gateway provides the transition across a PSTN and an IP network. This gateway is responsible for the signaling between the different networks. The gateway and other devices (such as NAT devices and firewalls) add an additional degree of complexity to securing the RTP packets in VoIP.

Enter SRTP and SRTCP

SRTP defines a profile of RTP, which includes encryption, authentication, and integrity and protection from a replay attack. Through the efforts by Ericsson and Cisco engineers the SRTP was introduced in early 2004 and covered in RFC 3711. Besides SRTP, the introduction of Secure Real-Time Transport Control Protocol (SRTCP) included the protection and secure features for control signaling. A user can elect whether to use RTP/RTCP or SRTP/SRTCP independently. These are optional protocols that can be activated or deactivated, with a single exception of message authentication that requires that SRTCP is active. The RFC 3711 has specific goals in mind for the use of VoIP, including:

- Ensuring confidentiality of the payloads of RTP and RTCP packets
- Protecting the integrity of the entire packet(s) along with a replay protection
- Providing the framework for the upgrade of current and future cryptographic transforms

- Limiting the bandwidth needed to preserve the RTP header compression (and integrity)
- Controlling the overhead and costs associated with the additional headers and cryptographic algorithms
- Providing small code to reduce the overhead and reduced memory
- Developing independence from the underlying protocol layers (i.e., transport, network, link, and physical layers used for RTP)
- Developing the protocols that will be useful in protecting the RTP and RTCP on both wired and wireless networks

As one looks at RFC 3711, it begins with a description as follows: SRTP provides a framework for encryption and message authentication of RTP and RTCP streams. It defines a set of default cryptographic transforms, and it allows new transforms to be introduced in the future. With appropriate key management, SRTP is secure for unicast and multicast RTP applications.

SRTP can achieve high throughput and low packet expansion. It proves to be a suitable protection for heterogeneous environment (mix of wired and wireless networks). To get such features, default transforms are described, based on an additive stream cipher for encryption, a keyed-hash–based function for message authentication, and an "implicit" index for sequencing/synchronization based on the RTP sequence number for SRTP and an index number for SRTCP.

SRTP framework

SRTP is a profile of RTP that aims to provide confidentiality, message authentication, and replay protection to RTP data and control traffic. It uses a single master key to derive keying material via a cryptographically secure hash function. In SRTP, a cryptographic context refers to the cryptographic state information maintained by the sender and receiver for the media stream. This includes the master key, session keys, and identifiers for encryption and message authentication algorithms, lifetime of session keys, and a rollover counter (ROC).

Each RTP packet consists of a 16-bit sequence number (SEQ) that is monotonically increasing. The ROC is maintained by the receiver and is incremented by 1 every time the sequence number wraps around. For a multicast stream with multiple senders, a synchronization source identifier (SSRC) uniquely identifies a sender within a session. A cryptographic context for SRTP is identified by the triplet (SSRC, destination network address, destination port).

For data encryption, SRTP uses a single cipher, Advanced Encryption Standard (AES), in one of the following two modes:

1. Segmented Integer Counter mode
2. f-8 mode

The input to AES is the triplet (key, SSRC, SEQ), where "key" is the encryption key, SSRC is the synchronization source identifier, and SEQ is the sequence number of the packet. Instead of using AES as a block cipher, SRTP uses it as if it were a stream cipher and encrypts datagrams by exclusive-ORing (XORing) them with the output of AES applied to (key, SSRC, SEQ).

The encryption transforms defined in SRTP map the SRTP packet index and secret key into a pseudorandom keystream segment. Each keystream segment encrypts a single RTP packet. The process of encrypting a packet consists of generating the keystream segment corresponding to the packet, and then bitwise XORing that keystream segment onto the payload of the RTP packet to produce the encrypted portion of the SRTP packet. In case the payload size is not an integer multiple of n_b bits, the excess (least significant) bits of the keystream are simply discarded. Decryption is done the same way, but swapping the roles of the plaintext and ciphertext.

SRTP key derivation – SRTP – uses a cryptographically secure pseudorandom function (PRF) to generate encryption and authentication session keys from the master key, master salt, and the packet sequence number. The sequence number of the packet is chosen by the sender. Both master key and master salt are derived deterministically by applying HMAC, keyed with the material received during the key exchange protocol, to a known plaintext (as defined by the key exchange protocol). The determinism of key derivation is a fatal flaw since it makes an unwarranted assumption about the key exchange protocol used to create the master key.

The authors of the RFC described SRTP as a "bump in the stack" implementation that fits somewhere between the application and transport layers of the OSI model. The SRTP is designed to capture an RTP packet on the sending side and creates the SRTP packet, forwards the SRTP to the receiving end where the SRTP captures the SRTP packet, and strips off the overhead and submits the RTP packet to the receiver. Similarly, SRTCP provides the same services to RTCP that SRTP provides to RTP. Basically, the above excerpt from the RFC indicates that both authentication and encryption will be used to ensure secure VoIP. SRTCP message authentication is a mandatory feature that protects the RTCP fields and keeps track of the authenticated members, supplies the necessary feedback (QoS), and maintains the packet sequence counters.

SRTP is created as a packet as shown in Figure 6.10 and the packets are authenticated and encrypted as shown in Figure 6.11.

Secure RTP using ZRTP

What is ZRTP? ZRTP describes an extension header for RTP to establish a session key for SRTP sessions using authenticated Diffie–Hellman (DH) key exchange. An implementation of ZRTP is available as Zfone. The main distinguishing feature of ZRTP is that it does not require prior shared secrets or the existence of a separate public key infrastructure (PKI). This is an important consideration since it eliminates the need for a trusted certificate server.

Because DH key exchange is malleable and does not provide protection against man-in-the-middle attacks, ZRTP uses a Short Authentication String (SAS), which is essentially a cryptographic hash of two DH values, for key confirmation. The communicating parties confirm the established key verbally over the phone, by looking at

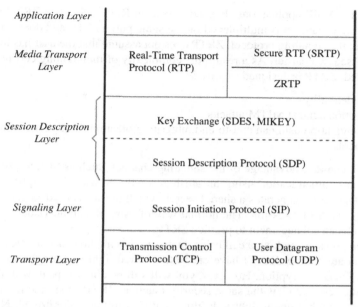

FIGURE 6.10

The SRTP packet framework.

their respective phone displays and reading the displayed SAS values to each other. After that, they rely on key chaining: the shared DH secrets cached from the previous sessions are used to authenticate the current session.

ZRTP is a protocol, developed by Phil Zimmerman and others, for media path DH exchange to agree on a session key and parameters for establishing unicast SRTP

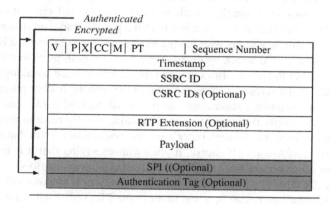

FIGURE 6.11

The authenticated and encrypted parts of the SRTP packet.

sessions for VoIP applications. It is addressed in RFC 6189. The ZRTP is media path keying because it is multiplexed on the same port as RTP and does not require support in the signaling protocol. ZRTP does not assume that the user has installed a PKI as discussed earlier. As a result, the complexity of maintaining certificates can be avoided. ZRTP is designed to provide:

- Confidentiality
- Protection against MITM attacks
- Authentication using an end-to-end integrity protection through the signaling protocols

ZRTP can take advantage of the signaling channel (such as SIP) to provide discovery and authentication using an attribute of the Session Description Protocol (SDP). The ZRTP generates a shared secret, which in turn is used to generate keys and salt for a SRTP session. The normal way of using the audio/visual profiles for RTP can be an enhancement to provide SRTP.

When you start making a call using an encryption method such as ZRTP and the party you are calling doesn't have encryption, a red light (warning) will alert you that there is no encryption. However, you will still be able to speak with the party. If the other end also has the same security (such as ZRTP), then the red light will be replaced with a green light indicating that encryption is confirmed. Now there is no guesswork in the call; you can be sure that the call is encrypted. But what if you suspect that there is a man-in-the-middle attack underway? How do you know that the MITM isn't receiving the data (possibly someone who has attached to your LAN or possibly even a telephone company person), capturing the packets, and then decoding them? Then being in the middle, the MITM creates a separate leg with the other end of your call using an encrypted message with the original intended called person.

That is the beauty of the ZRTP: it uses a DH key agreement to generate a random password for the call, without ever transmitting the password to the other person. Each phone creates an incomplete mathematical equation and sends it to the other phone. By solving the equations together, both the phones find the same result: a secure pair of passwords, without ever having to transmit the passwords. ZRTP allows the detection of a MITM attack by displaying a SAS for both users to read and verbally compare over the phone. Both you and the person you are speaking to will see the passwords on the screen. If there is a man in the middle, his/her phone will also have to solve the equations, generating four passwords instead of two: and you won't see the same passwords as the person you are speaking to. By reading the passwords to each other and recognizing each other's voices, you can be certain that the encryption is running *end-to-end*. Of course, it goes without saying that it is important to recognize the other person's voice when they read the passwords to you. This helps to ensure the ZRTP works. However, if you are calling a new person (with whom you have never spoken), there can be some flaws in the ZRTP that will guarantee that a MITM doesn't exist but it doesn't guarantee that you are speaking with the person you were expecting. The call may have been redirected without your knowledge.

ZRTP is an interactive session between two parties: the initiator and the responder. Using an agreed to run mechanism, the initiator is selected as the person who commits to the call (using the F5 key). Then the protocol works into basically four different phases:

1. *Discovery and protocol negotiation* (F1–F4). The parties start up a protocol transaction and agree on a supported ZRTP version and cipher suites.
2. *DH key establishment* (F5–F7). This is almost "missionary position" DH, with one exception (the F5 message: the commit message).
3. *Key confirmation* (F8–F10). Here the parties verify that they've agreed on the same key.
4. *Secure communication.* "SRTP begins."

In Figure 6.12 is shown a handshake that takes place to establish the secure session. Using the normal setup in SIP, the caller (Bob) sends an INVITE message to Alice. This goes through the proxy server in the middle of the picture. As normal SIP session is working the "trying (100)" message is sent back to Bob and then the "ringing (180)" message. Finally Alice's phone answers and an "OK (200)" message is sent to Bob's phone. Bob's phone then returns an ACK.

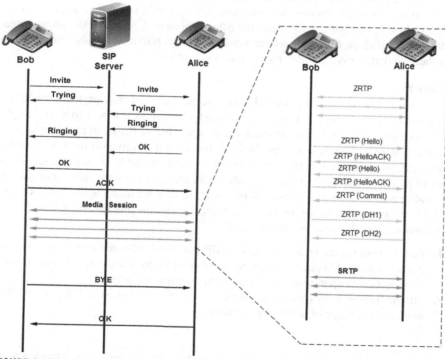

FIGURE 6.12

A SRTP session between Bob and Alice using ZRTP.

The next phase is the media session is being set up. On the same port as the media (in-band) the peers then communicate the key exchange shown in the ZRTP dialog. The ZRTP (Hello) message is sent from Bob to Alice. Alice now sends back a ZRTP (HelloACK) along with her own ZRTP (Hello). Bob then sends back a ZRTP (HelloACK) back to Alice. Alice now sends a ZRTP (Commit) by keying the F5. This makes Alice the initiator. Now the two devices send back their DH1 from Bob to Alice and DH2 from Alice to Bob. The key exchange has taken place and a SRTP session is conducted.

Figure 6.12 shows that after this, the SRTP concludes and Bob sends a BYE message and Alice sends an OK (200) message back.

Initially the ZRTP was designed to be used with Zfone[10]; however, Zfone has virtually disappeared and a new implementation is through a commercial entity from Phil Zimmerman called Silent Circle and the product is a softphone called Silent Phone. Silent Phone was based on the ZRTP and does similar things as the Zfone. For example, the Zfone started out the connection with an idle phone that then converts the color of the security to red meaning unsecure. As the devices begin the handshake, the coloration goes to orange[11] until the two phones finally get the shared secure words to verbally compare (and prevent the MITM attack). Note in Figure 6.13 the compare words are "clockwork and Pegasus." Once the two devices are synced up and the compare phrases are complete, the system's coloration goes to green. The right side of Figure 6.13 shows the Silent Phone and, although the image looks different, it is close where the secure word compare is provided and the confirmation is there so that the system now moves into a secure call.

MIKEY

Multimedia Internet KEYing (MIKEY) is another key exchange protocol for SRTP defined in RFC 3830.[12] It is mainly intended to be used for peer-to-peer, simple one-to-many, and small-size (interactive) groups. One of the main multimedia scenarios considered when designing MIKEY has been the conversational multimedia scenario, where users may interact and communicate in real time. In these scenarios it can be expected that peers set up multimedia sessions between each other, where a multimedia session may consist of one or more secured multimedia streams (e.g., SRTP streams). The following are some typical scenarios that involve the multimedia applications that may be encountered:

1. Peer-to-peer (unicast), for example, a SIP-based call between two parties, where it may be desirable either that the security is set up by mutual agreement or that each party sets up the security for its own outgoing streams.
2. Simple one-to-many (multicast), for example, real-time presentations, where the sender is in charge of setting up the security.

---

[10]Zfone was a product of Phil Zimmerman that was tested to work with many of the softphones at the time.

[11]On my desktop the color was orange; on others it may well look yellow.

[12]Additional variants in RFC 4650, RFC 4738, RFC 6043, RFC 6267, and RFC 6509.

These Are From Zfone

These Is the Silent Phone
From Silent Circle

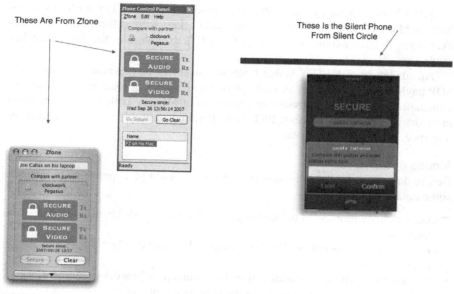

FIGURE 6.13

Silent Circle's softphone for use with ZRTP.

3. Many-to-many, without a centralized control unit, for example, for small-size interactive groups where each party may set up the security for its own outgoing media. Two basic models may be used here. In the first model, the initiator of the group acts as the group server (and is the only one authorized to include new members). In the second model, authorization information to include new members can be delegated to other participants.

4. Many-to-many, with a centralized control unit, for example, for larger groups with some kind of Group Controller that sets up the security.

The key management protocol is designed to have the following characteristics:

- End-to-end security. Only the participants involved in the communication have access to the generated key(s).
- Simplicity.
- Efficiency. Designed to have:
  - Low bandwidth consumption
  - Low computational workload
  - Small code size
  - A minimal number of round-trips
- Tunneling. Possibility to "tunnel"/integrate MIKEY in session establishment protocols (e.g., SDP and RTSP).
- Independence from any specific security functionality of the underlying transport.

MIKEY can operate in three different modes: preshared key with key transport, public key with key transport, and public key with authenticated DH key exchange. A later extension provides for a DH exchange in the preshared key mode.

An advantage of MIKEY is that it allows the key to be negotiated as part of the SDP payload during the session setup phase in SIP. Thus, it requires no extra communication overhead. An obvious disadvantage of MIKEY is that it requires either prior shared secrets or a separate PKI, with all attendant problems such as certificate dispersal, revocation, and so on.

Modes of MIKEY

Before describing the three modes of MIKEY it should be appropriate to describe some notation:

- Data security protocol is the security protocol, such as SRTP, used to protect the media session.
- Data security association (data SA) comprises the session key (TEK) and a set of parameters.
- Crypto session (CS) is a unidirectional or bidirectional media stream. A CS is protected by a unique instance of a data security protocol.
- Each CS has a unique identifier known as the CS ID.
- Crypto session bundle (CSB) is a set of CSs that derive their session keys (TEKs) from a common Traffic Generating Key (TGK) and a set of security parameters.
- CSB ID is a unique identifier for the CS bundle.
- TGK is a bitstring agreed upon by two or more parties associated with a CSB. One or more TEKs can be derived from the TGK and the unique CS ID.

Preshared key transfer

The preshared case is, by far, the most efficient way to handle the key transport due to the use of symmetrical cryptography only. This approach also has the advantage that only a small amount of data has to be exchanged. Of course, the problematic issue is scalability as it is not always feasible to share individual keys with a large group of peers. Therefore, this case mainly addresses scenarios such as server-to-client and also those cases where the public-key modes have already been used, thus allowing for the "cache" of a symmetrical key.

In this mode, the key is generated by the initiator and transferred to the responder. The message is integrity-protected using a keyed MAC and encrypted. The respective keys are derived from the shared secrets and a random value using a cryptographically secure hash function. MAC is a keyed message authentication code computed over the entire message using the authentication key. It is assumed that the TGK is chosen uniformly at random by the initiator. For mutual authentication, the initiator may request the responder to send a verification message that includes the message header, timestamp, the initiator and responder identities, and a MAC.

Public key transfer

Public-key cryptography can be used to create a scalable system. A disadvantage with this approach is that it is more resource consuming than the preshared key approach. Another disadvantage is that in most cases, a PKI is needed to handle the distribution of public keys. It is possible to use public keys as preshared keys (e.g., by using self-signed certificates). It should also be noted that, as mentioned above, this method may be used to establish a "cached" symmetrical key that later can be used to establish subsequent TGKs by using the preshared key method (hence, the subsequent request can be executed more efficiently).

As in the preshared key mode, the initiator's message transfers one or more TGKs and a set of media session security parameters to the responder. The initiator's message is CERT. Here CERT I stands for the initiator's certificate. In this mode, the encryption and authentication keys are derived from an envelope key chosen by the initiator at random.

PKE is the encryption of the envelope key under the responder's public key. Note that this requires prior knowledge of the responder's (properly certified) public key. A signature is used over the entire message using the initiator's private signing key. As in the preshared key mode, the initiator may request a verification message from the responder.

Public key with Diffie–Hellman exchange

In general, the DH key agreement method has a higher resource consumption (both computationally and in bandwidth) than the previous ones, and needs certificates as in the public-key case. However, it has the advantage of providing perfect forward secrecy (PFS) and flexibility by allowing implementation in several different finite groups.

Note that by using the DH method, the two involved parties will generate a unique unpredictable random key. Therefore, it is not possible to use this DH method to establish a group TEK (as the different parties in the group would end up with different TEKs). It is not the intention of the DH method to work in this scenario, but to be a good alternative in the special peer-to-peer case.

Let G denote a large cyclic multiplicative group with generator for a fixed cyclic group. This method creates a DH key that is used as the TGK. This method is only used for creation of single peer-to-peer keys, not a group key. The initiator sends a message to the responder that provides a secure way to give the responder the initiator's DH value. The DH value must be random/pseudorandom and secretly chosen according to the security protocol parameters. The signature covers the initiator's MIKEY message using the initiator's signature key. Then the responder returns a message, in a secure way, in order to pass along the responder DH value to the initiator. The DH value must also be random/pseudorandom and secretly chosen. A timestamp included in the original initiator message is the same as the timestamp in the responder's message. The responder's signature covers the responder's MIKEY message using the responder's signature key.

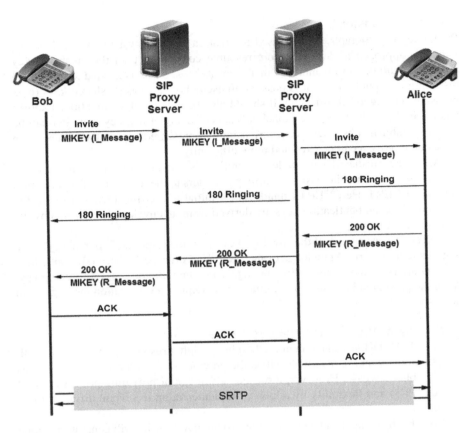

FIGURE 6.14

Call setup with MIKEY.

The DH group parameters (group and generator) are chosen by the initiator and sent to the responders. Then both parties calculate the TGK and generator for initiator and responder from the exchanged DH values.

Transport protocols

MIKEY *may* be integrated within session establishment protocols. Currently, integration of MIKEY within SIP/SDP and RTSP is defined in KMASDP.[13] MIKEY may use other transports, in which case how MIKEY is transported over such a transport protocol has to be defined.

Using the standard ladder diagram, a simple call setup with MIKEY is seen in Figure 6.14. Once again Bob and Alice wish to speak so the normal VoIP call setup takes place, albeit this time the SDK parameters are exchanged with MIKEY.

---

[13]Arkko, J., Carrara, E., Lindholm, F., Naslund, M., Norrman, K. Key Management Extensions for SDP and RTSP.

SIGNALING: SESSION INITIATION PROTOCOL

The SIP (RFC 2543 now obsolete and replaced by RFC 3261) is part of IETF's multimedia data and control protocol framework. It is a powerful client–server signaling protocol used in VoIP networks. SIP handles the setup and teardown of multimedia sessions between speakers; these sessions can include multimedia conferences, telephone calls, and multimedia distribution. It is used for IP telephony (which includes voice and video), Presence, Instant Messaging, conferencing, and more. It should also be understood that SIP has become the preferred signaling protocol[14] because of its openness and extensible nature. Left unprotected it is vulnerable to myriad attacks.

SIP is a text-based signaling protocol transported over either TCP or UDP, and is designed to be lightweight. It inherited some design philosophy and architecture from the Hypertext Transfer Protocol (HTTP) and Simple Mail Transfer Protocol (SMTP) to ensure its simplicity, efficiency, and extensibility.

SIP uses *invitations* to create SDP messages to carry out capability exchange (using profiles) and to set up call control channel use. These invitations allow participants to agree on a set of compatible media types based on the profiles. SIP supports user mobility by proxying and redirecting requests to the user's current location. Users can inform the server of their current location (IP address or URL) by sending a registration message to a *registrar*. This function is powerful and often needed for a highly mobile voice user base. The SIP client–server application has two modes of operation; SIP clients can signal through either a *proxy* or *redirect* server.

- Using proxy mode, SIP clients send requests to the proxy and the proxy either handles requests or forwards them on to other SIP servers. Proxy servers can insulate and hide SIP users by proxying the signaling messages; to the other users on the VoIP network, the signaling invitations look as if they are coming from the proxy SIP server.
- Under redirect operation, the signaling request is sent to a SIP server, which then looks up the destination address. The SIP server returns the destination address to the originator of the call, who then signals the SIP client.

A SIP network consists of the following entities:

1. End points
2. Proxy and/or redirect server
3. Location server
4. Registrar server

End points or UAs represent phone devices or software modems. SIP users are not bound to specific devices; they register themselves with the registrar and use a special form of address resolution to identify other users. SIP user identification is based on a special type of uniform resource identifier (URI) called SIP URI, similar to e-mail addresses.

---

[14]Initially the H.323 protocol suite with H.225 was preferred due to the semblance to Telco protocols; however, SIP became the winner as time wore on.

A location server stores the address bindings of users when they register themselves with the registrar. SIP servers can operate in a proxy mode or redirect mode:

- In the proxy mode, the server intercepts messages from the end points, inspects their To: field, contacts the location server to resolve the username into an address, and forwards the message to the appropriate end point or another server. SIP also supports forking proxies, which receive a single request and forward it to multiple recipients; this makes SIP potentially vulnerable to DoS attacks.
- In the redirect mode, the only difference is that instead of forwarding the packet along the actual route, the redirect server returns the address to the end points and the onus of transmitting the packets is placed on the end points.

SIP uses a HTTP-like request–response mechanism for initiating a two-way communication session. The protocol itself is modeled on the three-way TCP handshake. Media exchange takes place directly between respective UAs. From the network security point of view, this implies that both hops must be secured on a hop-by-hop basis and the direct path must be secured as well. Additionally when using SIP (or an H.323 protocol for signaling) the signaling protocol may also be carrying cryptographic keys (i.e., SDES). Therefore, it is imperative to watch out for the manipulation, snooping, or alteration of the signaling messages.

SIP messages can be transported over a TCP stream, provided the packet size is smaller than the maximum transmission unit (MTU), or embedded into UDP datagram packets. Therefore, security mechanisms used to encrypt and authenticate multimedia streams must support UDP as a transport layer protocol. This requirement excludes several popular security mechanisms such as the TCP-based Transport Layer Security (TLS).

Attacks on SIP
Denial of service

As seen earlier in this book, a DoS attack focuses on rendering a network of service unavailable, usually by directing a high volume of traffic toward the service thereby denying it to legitimate clients. A DDoS allows a single network user to cause multiple network hosts to flood the target host. If SIP is exposed to manipulation, then a hacker can redirect calls, fork calls to a different location, and parallel fork calls to multiple locations (all impersonation-type attacks).

The SIP architecture makes it particularly easy to launch a DDoS attack. An attacker can put the victim's IP address into a spoofed router header request, and send it to forking proxies, who will greatly amplify the number of messages returned to the victim.

Reflection is another way to stage a DoS attack. An attacker can send spoofed requests to a large number of SIP elements and proxies, putting the victim's IP address into the source field. Each of the recipients will generate a response, overwhelming the victim.

A limited protection against spoofed SIP requests can be provided by IPSec, but end-to-end IPSec is challenging to deploy in a typical VoIP environment where end points are dynamic, and it is not clear from the specification how SIP interoperates with IPSec.

BYE

Another important vulnerability in SIP is that BYE requests to terminate sessions are not authenticated since they are not acknowledged. Instead, a BYE request is implicitly authenticated if it is received from the same network element (on the same path) as a previous INVITE. A third-party attacker can thus observe the parameters of an eavesdropped INVITE message, and then insert a BYE request into the session. Once the BYE request is received by the target, the session would be torn down permanently. Similar attacks can be launched on re-INVITE messages used to change session parameters.

A wide variety of DoS attacks also become possible if registration requests are not properly authenticated and authorized by registrars. If a malicious user is able to deregister some or all other users in the network and register his/her own device on their behalf, he/she can easily deny access to any of those users/services. Attackers can also try to deplete storage resources of the registrar by creating a huge number of bindings.

Authentication

Authentication is particularly difficult to achieve in SIP, because there are a number of intermediate elements such as proxies that possibly modify the contents of a message before it reaches the desired destination. All such intermediate elements must be trusted. SIP registration does not require the From: field of a message to be the same as the To: header field of the request, allowing third parties to change address-of-record bindings on behalf of another user. If the attacker can successfully impersonate a party authorized to change contacts on behalf of a user, he/she can arbitrarily modify the address-of-record bindings for the associated To: address. Because SIP authentication relies implicitly on the authenticity of the server and intermediate proxies, the attacker who is able to successfully impersonate a server or a proxy can do arbitrary damage including denying service to the client or launching a (distributed) DoS attack. This requires the existence of some methodology for the client to authenticate the server and/or the proxy. Unfortunately, no such mechanism is specified in the SIP RFC.

Secure SIP

As the RFC describes it, SIP is not an easy protocol to secure. Its use of intermediaries, its multifaceted trust relationships, its expected usage between elements with no trust at all, and its user-to-user operation make security far from trivial. Security solutions are needed that are deployable today, without extensive coordination, in a wide variety of environments and usages. In order to meet these diverse needs, several distinct mechanisms applicable to different aspects and usages of SIP will be required.

Note that the security of SIP signaling itself has no bearing on the security of protocols used in concert with SIP such as RTP, or with the security implications of any specific bodies SIP might carry [although Multipurpose Internet Mail Extension (MIME) security plays a substantial role in securing SIP]. Any media associated with a session can be encrypted end-to-end independently of any associated SIP signaling.

The fundamental security services required for the SIP protocol are:

- Preserving the confidentiality and integrity of messaging
- Preventing replay attacks or message spoofing
- Providing for the authentication and privacy of the participants in a session
- Preventing DoS attacks

Bodies within SIP messages separately require the security services of confidentiality, integrity, and authentication.

Secure SIP is a security mechanism defined by SIP RFC 3261 for sending SIP messages over a TLS-encrypted channel. Originally used for securing HTTP sessions, TLS can be repurposed to protect SIP session communications from eavesdropping or tampering. By deploying SIP-based devices that support Secure SIP, network administrators benefit from these increased levels of security for their VoIP networks.

The most basic level of security, required to be implemented by all SIP UAs and SIP proxy servers, is Message Digest 5 (MD5) authentication. This provides a basic level of authentication challenge between a SIP proxy server and SIP UA. At the other end of the spectrum, Secure/Multipurpose Internet Mail Extensions (S/MIME) can be implemented to encrypt data directly within SIP messages. Support for S/MIME has not been as widely accepted as other methods because of the PKI support and the complexity of managing and distributing security certificates.

Full encryption of messages provides the best means to preserve the confidentiality of signaling – it can also guarantee that messages are not modified by any malicious intermediaries. Unfortunately, however, SIP requests and responses cannot be naively encrypted end-to-end in their entirety because message fields such as the Request-URI, Route, and Via need to be visible to proxies in most network architectures so that SIP requests are routed correctly. Note that proxy servers need to modify some features of messages as well (such as adding Via header field values) in order for SIP to function. Proxy servers must therefore be trusted, to some degree, by SIP UAs. Every step along the way the fields needed to handle the routing need to be visible to the devices.

SIP entities also have a need to identify one another in a secure fashion. When a SIP end point asserts the identity of its user to a peer UA or to a proxy server, that identity should in some way be verifiable. A cryptographic authentication mechanism is provided in SIP to address this requirement.

Transport and network layer security

Transport or network layer security encrypts signaling traffic, guaranteeing message confidentiality and integrity. Oftentimes, certificates are used in the establishment of lower layer security, and these certificates can also be used to provide a means of authentication in many architectures. Two popular alternatives for providing security at the transport and network layers are, respectively, TLS and IPSec.

In a Secure SIP session, the SIP UA client contacts the SIP proxy server requesting a TLS session. This SIP proxy server responds with a public certificate and the SIP UA then validates the certificate. Next, the SIP UA and the SIP proxy server exchange session keys to encrypt or decrypt data for a given session. From this point, the SIP proxy server contacts the next hop and similarly negotiates a TLS session, ensuring that SIP over TLS is used end-to-end.

One might ask why a security protocol such as IPSec is not used for a direct, secure, end-to-end connection between SIP end points. Because IPSec encrypts data end-to-end, the SIP proxy servers between the SIP end points would not be able to interpret and modify required information in the SIP messages. TLS is a lighter-weight and more easily managed protocol than IPSec, and thus more appropriate for SIP-based VoIP end points, which are often processing and resource constrained. The security mechanism between SIP proxy servers within a network may use TLS, IPSec, or other security mechanisms, as long as the information is decrypted at each hop.

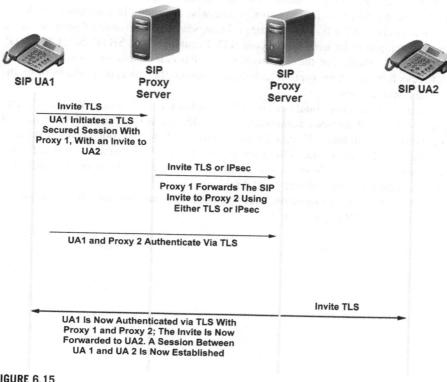

FIGURE 6.15

SSIP using TLS and IPSec.

The most commonly voiced concern about TLS is that it cannot run over UDP; TLS requires a connection-oriented underlying transport protocol, which means TCP. It may also be arduous for a local outbound proxy server and/or registrar to maintain many simultaneous long-lived TLS connections with numerous UAs. This introduces some valid scalability concerns, especially for intensive cipher suites. Maintaining redundancy of long-lived TLS connections, especially when a UA is solely responsible for their establishment, could also be cumbersome.

TLS only allows SIP entities to authenticate servers to which they are adjacent; it offers strictly hop-by-hop security. TLS does not allow clients to authenticate proxy servers to whom they cannot form a direct TCP connection.

A compromise might look like the graphic shown in Figure 6.15. The figure shows is basically how both TLS and IPSec can be combined to form a Secure SIP and prevent the threats as discussed above.

SUMMARY

Protocols are necessary to secure both the media channel and the control channel. Unfortunately there are far too many people who are attempting to penetrate (hack) VoIP networks and calls. To solve the problem, several media channel protocols have been developed to be used in a Secure RTP format, such as SRTP, SRTCP, ZRTP, MIKEY, etc. Moreover, these protocols use what is the basis for most secure data networks forming an encryption technique to secure the voice, data, video, or multimedia communications.

Secure SIP is an optional item for SIP UAs, but more SIP-based VoIP end points provide it. VoIP network administrators should take a look at implementing this technology within their SIP-based networks to gain from the added level of security that Secure SIP can provide. Using Secure SIP helps to keep the actual user information (not the voice but information regarding name, URI, address, etc.) confidential and prevents the DoS, redirects, and disconnects.

It is unfortunate that these protocols are necessary, but they are a fact of life when planning any VoIP implementation.

The business case for securing VoIP

7

CHAPTER OUTLINE

BEFORE WE START

Whenever one looks at a small business, it becomes obvious that both voice and data are the lifeblood of their business. Regardless if the voice calls are made to/from customers and clients, suppliers, or banking transactions, or if the data is going to the same places, any penetration of the security of either the voice or the data network can cause significant damage to the business. Several of the research houses continually study the impact of such a breach. In fact, these research houses estimate that organizations have lost in excess of $50 billion over the past 5–6 years due to security breaches. Other studies estimate that the annual losses in voice and data breaches exceed $13 billion per year and climbing. One only has to look at the examples used in Chapter 1 to get a feel for the types and frequency of security breaches. These breaches come from both internal and external sources.

It is not surprising that many surveys indicate that many small business owners do not make voice and data network security a priority. According to some of the vendors providing goods and services to industry, >80% of the incidents that result in data loss or theft could have been prevented if the business had a security plan in place. The reason many small businesses don't comply with these undertaking can vary, but some of the examples of why they are in this position are as follows:

1. They lack the expertise to secure their networks.
2. They have limited resources (people) to apply security rules and enforce them.
3. The security policies are restrictive; thus, they are ignored by employees and managers alike.
4. They assume that the vendors serving them will take care of security.
5. Voice and data departments are not under common administrative management and are disparate in their attempts to secure their networks.

One must understand that in the new world of telecommunications, voice is data and data is too! That said, every business needs to recognize that a breach of either side of the network exposes the other side. For example, if a data breach occurs (someone penetrates the data network), then bridging across to the voice network is a high possibility. The components installed in the network are similar if not the same. With this in mind, the business scenario is that the entire network must be globally protected and where applicable, specialized components (such as an application gateway) are added to protect specific applications.

Alternately, larger organizations potentially have rock-solid security to protect their data assets; for many organizations this is mandated by law (i.e., HIPAA, SOX, PCI) to maintain compliance. Using tried and true principles and a baseline security audit, the checklist can be extensive; yet once you get through the audit, there aren't too many stones left unturned.

More often than not, however, VoIP isn't part of that audit. There are two implications here, and both of them must be addressed. First is the fact that VoIP is barely, if at all, part of the security compliance envelope. The technology is relatively new and not well understood by the audit community in terms of the risks posed by VoIP-enabled security threats. As such, it's under the radar. Because VoIP isn't usually part of the audit checklist, the auditors don't go there. Ultimately, this means a change in attitude is necessary in compliance and understanding the technology that must be added to the audit checklist.

If internal/external audit was the only stakeholder group regarding network security, the solution would be simpler. However, IT is a significant key stakeholder – notwithstanding the most important one – and is as much a part of the problem as the solution. Regardless, the general consensus is that IT knows or believes that their network is protected from VoIP-enabled security threats; however, in most cases this simply is not the case. In fact, management in many organizations don't have a clue if the data and VoIP networks are actually secure. Worse, management may be told that the security is far better than it actually is. This doesn't mean that VoIP cannot be secured; it is just a matter of priorities. So let's think back a bit:

1. VoIP is still in its infancy – In telecommunications, any technology takes a while to flesh out and be fully accepted and implemented. VoIP was actually introduced in 1996, and as early innovators experimented with it, the masses sat back and watched. Now with less than 20 years in play, more organizations are finally accepting VoIP as a viable technology.
2. Security was not a primary concern when VoIP was initially deployed. Many organizations decided that they could isolate the VoIP from the data network. Moreover, they looked upon VoIP as they did the plain old telephone service (POTS) as was delivered by the telephone companies. Because the telephone companies secured their own networks, it was not a concern for the organization. Thus, organizations saw it as just an extension of an old trusted service.
3. VoIP has reached critical mass and is now a commodity. Telephone companies have been replaced with new Internet telephony service providers (ITSP) whose

principal goal is saving an organization money through consolidation of the voice and data networks.

4. Many organizations have adopted an "ostrich policy" by sticking their heads in the sands and ignoring the security risks associated with VoIP. They just assume that it is being taken care of, and do not want to hear anything to the contrary.

There are several areas where management has either ignored VoIP security or underfunded the security effort. For example, many of the IT departments have assured management that there is no risk because the IP network is secure and the VoIP portion is merely an extension of the IP network. Unfortunately as IP networks have become the common fabric for data transport, VoIP was in a position to become the weak link. Generally, VoIP security is voluntary, and if the associated threats are not viewed as either imminent or real, getting adequate resources for a solution becomes a real challenge. Departments in charge of VoIP (finance, IT, or other) seem to believe that they are immune from the data risks because they feel:

- The VoIP infrastructure is secure because the IP telephone system is connected directly to the PSTN and does not use SIP/H.323 trunking. Just locking up your IP PBX does not protect the system. As already seen in earlier chapters, more ways exist for an attack by hackers. In fact, newer ways are being developed every day. Just because you separate the telephone lines from IP (SIP/H.323) networks doesn't guarantee that VoIP is secure. As already discussed different layers are used by a VoIP device including VoIP applications whether on an individual telephone set, a softphone or a networking component, protocols that are common in various networking components, network servers that are jointly used by the data and the voice networks (e.g., DNS and DHCP), and the OS and other configuration databases. Just think of how complex the strategy becomes when including IP PBX, phones, softphones (various possibilities), gateways, routers, switches, servers, voice mail systems, interactive voice response systems, etc.[1] An attacker can access the VoIP infrastructure from remote through direct/indirect attacks on any of these applications or devices, or through indirect attacks on the data network. Just because the IP PBX is not

---

[1]One company that was brought to our attention tests and monitors contact centers, most of which are now fully VoIP (or hybrids and working toward full VoIP). The problem becomes even harder and larger for them as they often have multiple contact centers with normal agents, plus work-from-home agents, and then add disaster failover and failback, call recording, RAN, IVR, back-end systems, text to speech, speech recognition, SIP trunking, web services, mobile apps, text messaging, web chat, social media, e-mail, WebRTC, cloud services, and more, all running together. And then they have to keep all of it secure along with making it work, and hopefully robust.

A telling statistic – 95% of their first run tests on new/upgraded systems fail. Multiple best-of-breed subsystems that pass unit tests seldom work together out of the box. Getting a large system to work well can take weeks to months in some cases. Some companies and integrators get this and plan for it; others learn by experience.

There are now people in the industry building "cloud systems" that can source and terminate 100,000 or more concurrent calls. The question then becomes: "What happens if one of these gets hijacked?"

connected directly to the IP network, the likelihood that a common local area network (LAN) is in use makes this all a possibility.

- The VoIP infrastructure is secure because separate VLANs isolate the VoIP from the data network.[2] VLANs are used to address issues such as scalability, security, broadcast domains, and network management. A VLAN is composed of a group of devices that communicate as if they were attached to the same local network, regardless of their physical location. An IP PBX with PSTN trunking and several physical telephones (hard phones) attached to it is usually implemented on a dedicated VLAN. The VLAN provides some security by isolating your VoIP from data traffic. This is what many attempt to achieve, but tools exist to hack this configuration. There is no "one solution" that solves all the potential problems. Additionally, softphones running on a mobile device such as a laptop or smartphone (cell phone) introduce a complexity to the "isolation" because these devices operate on both data and voice networks to properly perform. The mobility allows these softphones to operate outside the IT core networks, so the VLAN cannot keep them secure. One should understand that softphones impose a major threat to VoIP infrastructure security. The increasing popularity of these devices and the proliferation of bring your own device (BYOD) to the office creates a bigger problem yet.

- The VoIP network is secure because it is part of a solid security infrastructure on the data network. Think again! Most enterprises already invested significant money and talent to secure their data network. VoIP can't be secured by just extending the data security infrastructure. VoIP is not just another data application; it works differently. Unlike data VoIP is real-time communication. Real-time communications needs various signaling protocols (e.g., SIP or H.323) to identify the calling parties, define call characteristics, and ring the phone. These are all critical pieces of information that also have to be protected. The signaling protocols use individual characteristics such as a dynamic assignment of ports for RTP traffic. Signaling protocols also wreak havoc on NAT devices as already seen. Moreover, after signaling is completed (i.e., the other party answers), the VoIP is carried on the IP network (e.g., the Internet) using packetized voice. Existing data security solutions are not designed to deal with the specific issues caused by the RTP. For example:
  - RTP traffic is a stream of packets with random, binary content created by digitizing human speech.
  - All VoIP phones, regardless of the vendor and/or location, use this protocol.
  - RTP traffic flows directly between phones without any centralized controllers.

- The VoIP infrastructure is secure because it has a VoIP aware firewall and/or session border controller (SBC). Both VoIP aware firewalls and SBCs are closely related applications with similar functionality. Firewalls (VoIP aware)

---

[2]Unless specific measures are taken (i.e., different certificates and authentication methods) a savvy person can "jump" across VLANs on the layer 3 switch.

are usually deployed in enterprises and SBCs are typically deployed in VoIP service providers' networks. The SBC manages SIP traffic and enables it to traverse NAT or a firewall perimeter in a service provider environment. Signaling protocols send information including IP addresses and UDP port numbers of the end devices. A normal firewall or NAT device cannot see this information. SBCs allow NAT and firewall traversal, normally by incorporating those elements with signaling controllers for the required signaling protocols. The SBC acts as a proxy that manipulates packets and is not transparent to the VoIP traffic. Security functions were added to SBC after the initial releases of SBCs. The security functions provided include protocol scrubbing and anomaly detections that are usually only offered by the most expensive SBC implementations. Moreover, these implementations have a number of weaknesses:

- False-positive ratios for exploitation detection are much higher for anomaly detection engines than for signature-based solutions. One will undoubtedly not want the false-positive errors.
- Only standard VoIP protocol anomalies (SIP, RTP) are recognized, and even for these vendors their "nonstandard" extensions are not recognized.
- Hundreds of vulnerabilities could still be exploited to harm VoIP infrastructure, as only a small number of the exploits are related to SIP and RTP.
- Any updates to the anomaly detection engine, or support for new protocol extension/changes, require new software loads/releases and long verification/testing cycles. This will likely change as the products mature, but they pose problems that must be addressed today.

SBC provides very little VoIP protection. Therefore other devices are needed such as VoIP Intrusion Prevention Systems (VIPS), VoIP Network Access Control (VNAC), and Anti-Spam over Internet Telephony (Anti-SPIT). A risk management approach to security requires VoIP vulnerability and compliance assessment tools.

- The VoIP infrastructure is secure because it uses proprietary protocols and applications from vendor (X) who assured fully secure VoIP. Can anyone really guarantee (assure) fully secure VoIP? Hundreds of known vulnerabilities exist and apply to all VoIP vendors. Most vendors ignore any reference to security until the contract is signed. Extensive research into the vendor's products is required. A common tool to use is a Data Security Audit checklist and vulnerability assessment (VA). These tools are effective to proactively find security problems and applying a fix before real problems occur.

So how is a VA performed?

- Identify vulnerable corporate assets because they are stored/transmitted over VoIP infrastructure.
- Identify processes in which business is relayed over unified communications.
- Define ways to minimize the risks associated with security breaches.

Once the VoIP system/service is installed, regular VAs should be a mandatory part of your overall proactive VoIP security process. When vulnerabilities are identified, they should be addressed immediately, particularly items such as patching, reconfigurations, or network tuning.

Within the VoIP network, various security solutions should be deployed to protect VoIP services from security threats, some of which were highlighted in Chapter 1. Any security architectures and solutions used (i.e., application layer gateways, firewalls, NAT, etc.) must be "VoIP aware" so they do not hinder QoS, serviceability, and availability. The preferred approach to this security is to build a multilayer security infrastructure. The layered approach should provide internal and external network protection. In most cases, this infrastructure will consist of a number of security devices and host-based applications. A comprehensive VoIP aware protection security infrastructure should include such items as:

1. VoIP aware firewalls
2. SBCs
3. VIPS
4. VoIP DoS defenses
5. VoIP network intrusion detection systems (IDS)
6. Host VoIP IPS (include DHCP and DNS hosts)
7. VNAC
8. VoIP Anti-SPIT [VoIP is also vulnerable to SPIT]

These components should be used to protect the network and provide a cohesive set of tools to protect the end-to-end VoIP infrastructure.

Some things that can be done immediately to create a more secure infrastructure include the following:

1. Review all security procedures.
2. Review the training materials (either vendor provided or self-created).
3. Work with IT and IT audit to review existing security-related processes.
4. After review, make any necessary changes to accommodate specific requirements of VoIP networks.
5. Add a compliance and auditing process that includes a VoIP component.
6. Ensure confidential phone conversations are carried out over encrypted links to prevent taps and eavesdropping.
7. Harden the network so that redirection and forking are prevented.
8. Perform VAs.
9. Fix what doesn't work.

OVERVIEW OF THE RFC 2196

Before planning the business case for VoIP security, one can look at the basics of RFC 2196. This RFC is generic when looking at any security program, thus can fit equally well for VoIP. The RFC addresses the planning process as a guide to any policies and procedures necessary for sites that have systems and networks connected to the Internet. It can also be used for non-Internet-attached systems and sites because as a realistic approach, all systems will ultimately be connected in some fashion. For example, in the beginning steps of this chapter, it was pointed out that even though the VoIP systems may be only connected through the PSTN, it is most likely that the LAN that the VoIP system is connected to has a router or gateway connected to the Internet. Therefore, even though the PSTN is the "only" connection for the IP PBX, it can be said that inevitably a thread can be woven between the PSTN and the Internet. The RFC provides the framework for setting the policies and procedures for securing the system. The guidelines include such statements as follows:

1. Identify what you are trying to protect.
2. Determine what you are trying to protect it from.
3. Determine how likely the threats are.
4. Implement measures that will protect your assets in a cost-effective manner.
5. Review the process continuously and make improvements each time a weakness is found.

As one can see, these are generic enough to address just about any system. However, looking at the threats already pointed out in this book, it becomes obvious that the same rules apply. It should be noted that many a research house and some vendors are rapidly prepping for the next generation hack. Although VoIP hacking has not hit the mainstream (albeit the examples already shown in earlier chapters), vendors are gearing up for more. One such representative of a vendor who makes SBCs has stated that, while VoIP hacking and IP PBX hacking aren't currently widespread, it is only a matter of time until the hacking community catches up. The more common threats today are voice tapping (eavesdropping), toll fraud, and identity fraud (theft).

Looking further at the RFC, and in particular Chapter 5 that deals with incident handling. Although written to minimize damages from a computer breach, it can easily be implemented to handle breaches in VoIP. The goal of any security plan, whether dealing with an external hacker or an internal breach (e.g., a disgruntled employee, a mole practicing industrial espionage), is to mitigate the damages by having a plan in place in advance. Traditional computer security has primarily dealt with protecting the system from attack and then monitoring the systems to detect when an attack is underway. This applies equally to VoIP systems because of the very nature of VoIP being a casual (conversational) transaction often without any rules. So the gist of the planning process will include the following steps:

1. Have a plan in place so if and when an incident occurs, there are defined procedures. This should go without saying, yet there are many organizations that have not even considered the risks of VoIP attacks. Because there could be different operating groups responsible for the data security versus VoIP security, consistence may not exist. The easiest plan is to add a VoIP section to the data contingency plan rather than reinventing the whole plan.

Another issue is to have a team in place upfront that will be the incident response team. These members will be trained on how to detect, mitigate, and respond to an incident. Further, the team members will be prepared to recover the systems and services after an incident occurs. The RFC states that the need for the team is inevitable. One issue that usually crops up is the fact that the planning with teams should have both technical and managerial members of the team. This requires management commitment due to the cost and the prioritization of efforts (management personnel may not always be available). Clearly, at least a champion needs to be a member of the team who can break down the political barriers within an organization.

Another area that will help in the planning process is to determine the degree of exposure to confidential or proprietary information, and how to protect and recover the information. Just look at the examples in Chapter 1 where Snowden whistleblowing created such a widespread embarrassment to the US government. Moreover, look at the issue with Target's loss of customer information (and then how soon it took the company to announce that the data breach occurred). When personal information is involved, the identity theft issue is paramount. Or if a government agency or contractor is involved and when classified information may be breached, then the incident response takes on far more sensitivity and legal issues that must be addressed.

One cannot forget the issue of media coverage. What is the extent of an organization's image, confidence from bankers and shareholders, etc.? A good rule of thumb is to have a media representative (public relations department) to aid in addressing these issues and allowing the technical and managerial personnel to deal with the VoIP breaches. Moreover, the media relations group can also deal with some of the legal issues that might arise. Documentation of what the organization did to prevent the breach is always a plus. The technical team can research the operating systems and flaws, patch the systems when necessary, work with the vendors to determine and create fixes, and finally determine any workaround solutions until fixes can occur. This combined with the media relations efforts helps to circumvent legal issues taken against the organization.

A rather interesting statistic of VoIP and network security stems from a survey[3] that had been conducted by one of the research houses that surveyed business managers and CIOs. Of the companies surveyed the following came out:

a. Ninety percent claimed that they had detected security breaches in the networks *or* their VoIP systems.

b. Eighty percent of those surveyed indicated that they suffered some financial loss.

c. Seventy percent stated that the breaches were serious including:
   - Theft of confidential or proprietary information
   - Financial fraud or ransomware
   - Sabotage of the networks or DoS attacks

---

[3]This was a limited survey. The total numbers were not revealed.

The average loss due to financial fraud, toll fraud, or loss of confidential information was over $2 million. There are other incidents where in a single day organizations lost in excess of $200k in toll fraud. The numbers can be staggering amounting to $40–50 billion losses for toll fraud annually. Domestically in United States it is approximately $13 billion.

Another interesting statistic is that 70–80% of the companies surveyed detected internal attacks (toll fraud, eavesdropping, and DoS attacks).

Other information is categorized in the type of losses suffered by organizations. In the following table is a summary of impact that must be taken into account:

Direct Losses	Indirect Losses
Loss of funds or economic theft Loss of proprietary information Theft of secrets (eavesdropping) Loss of customer information (credit card, PINs, health information, personal information such as social security numbers) Denial of service – loss of network access	Loss of sales and/or new orders Competitive advantage losses Branding damages Contractual losses due to loss of productivity and recovery efforts
Loss of productivity – think SPIT here, the loss of productivity from dealing with hundreds or thousands of spam messages Cost of recovery	Management confidence, shareholder confidence Regulatory losses such as HIPAA fines, PCI fines, and SOX regulatory reparation Insurance costs escalate, errors and omissions, etc.

2. What would the plan involve? Clearly there is a structure that can be followed such as the outline for a plan to mitigate the breaches in VoIP. These might include a template as follows (this comes right out of the RFC):

   a. Overview – the goals and objectives in handling the incident:
   - Assure integrity of critical VoIP systems (IP PBX, voice mail, gateways, proxies, registrars, etc.).
   - Maintain and restore service (mitigate DoS, mitigate ransom threats).
   - Figure out how it happened (what systems were exposed, what failed in the IPS, IDS systems).
   - Avoid escalation and further incidents (stop it from occurring and then handle future risks).
   - Prioritize efforts based on some managerial criteria.
   - Avoid negative publicity (the media will have a field day if they find out).
   - Find out who caused the incident (external, internal, accidental, or deliberate).
   - Punish the attackers (pursue and prosecute).

b. Evaluation – Determine the seriousness of the incident. This may well involve setting up a criterion as to the degree of complexity of the incident:
- Does it affect a whole system or perhaps just a certain link?
- Is the attack a multisite attack?
- Is it a media problem (access links, cable cuts, etc.)?
- How many components are involved (routers, gateways, proxies, DNS, DHCP)?
- Is confidential or proprietary information involved?
- Is all voice mail down or just a few mail boxes?
- How many people are internally affected?
- What is the cost of the internal lost productivity?
- What resources are needed to solve the problem (vendor, internal, other)?
- What is the severity of an outage (department, whole company)?
- What about the frequency (recurring problem vs. a one-time incident)?

c. Notification – Who should be notified about the incident and specifically have they been preselected as team members?
- Explicit notification means that whatever the event, the notification must be very specific indicating exactly what has occurred, in a concise manner not overly verbose but enough to react, and the notification must be fully qualified so that there are no false alarms.
- Complete and factual; it does no good to try to sugarcoat a notification. The information has to be complete regardless of how embarrassing, or complicated. If the information is not complete, then the solution will be hindered or the problem may become worse.
- Nonexaggerated; the way the notification is provided should be to the level of the recipient. In a technical world such as VoIP, one must be careful when notifying nontechnical people and using terms that they do not understand. Moreover, highly emotional reporting does nothing to convey the information properly.
- Who should be notified? The team should already be established as stated above. There should be a primary point of contact (PoC), technical and financial teams, IT audit, and possibly the vendor who is providing the product under attack. There may also be members of the media relations and legal departments notified to provide damage control with the general public. Others as appropriate can be inserted.

d. Response – What should the response to the incident be to minimize damage, mitigate losses, and expedite recovery and control?
- Containing the damages is the first issue. Once the attack is noted, the first set of actions is to stop it as fast as possible. So if a denial-of-service attack is noticed on a specific gateway or proxy (e.g.), then the first thing might be to shut that server down so the attack cannot permeate through the entire network. The act of containing the attack should follow preplanned activities. A list of activities and strategies should be part of the process.

- Eliminating the cause will follow the containment. If the action can be stopped from continuing, then it must be eliminated. If the problem is ransomware, one should have a complete image backed up of the servers, gateways, etc. That way if the malware does make it into the system, then if it cannot be cleaned, a replacement image is necessary. Another issue is if a proxy, for example, has been compromised and a redirection or forking of the routing has been introduced, that software must be reinstalled (possibly after reformatting a disk or reinstalling the OS).
- If backup images are installed, then a copy of the backup may have to be checked for the malware to prevent proliferation of the attack.
- Recovering from the attack/incident is the next step. Recovery means that the systems are brought back online and operations return to normal. At that point it is also important to work with the vendor(s) whose product is involved to be sure that all patches are installed to prevent reoccurrence of the attack.
- Following up after the attack has been mitigated is a critical step and a document containing lessons learned should be prepared. After any attack an analysis of what happened, how it happened, and how quickly it was addressed should be one of the first orders of business. In particular after the attack/incident steps must be documented to rectify any shortcomings in the response plan and normal operations. Moreover, if the response teams had any difficulty in performing the necessary steps, this is a time to determine if retraining or revised procedures are needed. Earlier it was mentioned that documentation is a requirement. This serves many issues not the least of which is a chronology of how things progressed during the response, but also for legal reasons it may be necessary to have a step-by-step documentation of what actions were taken. An estimate of the damages that occurred and any incidental costs of recovery may also be needed for insurance purposes.

Putting all things in perspective, if one were to look at the risks associated with the maintenance of a VoIP system, then relationships are intertwined by a number of hooks from the various interactions as shown in Figure 7.1. Note that risk is at the center of the graphic and everything else feeds into that risk. Included in the risk are hackers (as one would expect) but also the technology, compliance, and users (including executives, IT staff, and end users).

Another issue that must be pointed out comes from a US Department of Energy, circa 1982 statement regarding the security of a network that reads as follows:

The biggest mistake companies make relative to network security is underestimating the knowledge and persistence of those people attempting to break into them.

That said, it should be understood that hackers and miscreants spend inordinate amounts of time trying to penetrate networks and cause either disruption or loss or chaos and/or they attempt to steal services. The VoIP managers, on the other hand, are trying to maintain status quo on operations, install new services and systems, and

FIGURE 7.1

The risk factor is affected by many components.

satisfy the needs of the end user population. Therefore, the internal personnel do not have the time to address every security issue, whereas the hackers have as much time as they need.

Internal issues

It has always been said that most organizations are shocked to discover that 80% of the attempted breaks in a network occur from internal users. This could be disgruntled employees, or regular employees just trying to access systems and services for personal gain (such as free long distance or proprietary information). Consider that an internal employee has knowledge of how the systems work. They know passwords and may even swap passwords with other internal users. Remember that in Chapter 1 the issue of employees using the company network for their own gain occurred when employees went on vacation to Mexico. Before leaving for vacation to a resort hotel, the employees configured their telephones (VoIP) to "call forward all calls." Then, after forwarding their lines to the resort hotel in Mexico, they called their friends and told them they could be reached by calling their business phone number, which forwarded to the hotel operator in Mexico. Then the caller just asked for the employee by name and the operator transferred the call to the employee's hotel room. If this was an isolated incident, then one could say "it couldn't happen to me." However, there are many recorded situations like that. Consequently organizations have to take a serious look at internal systems and services. As an aside to this discussion, there are those in the industry who feel the internal threats are not as prevalent as external threats and break-ins. These same naysayers also state that the reason is that most organizations do not know they are being hacked from outsiders or if they discover that an outsider has hacked into the system, it gets hidden. The reason for hiding such an incident is clearly for public image:

- The IT/telecommunications folks in the company do not want management to know they did not have the proper protection in place, else it might cost their jobs.
- Marketing managers don't want the word to get out to the industry for fear that they will lose customer confidence.
- Financial managers don't wish to let the banking community know they have been breached for fear of loss of future funding for projects.
- Operational management doesn't want to look foolish to their peers and they do not want to lose shareholder confidence.
- Senior managers may fear reprisals from regulatory and compliance agencies.

With the list above, it is conceivable that the number and frequency of external breaches are higher than what the industry as a whole perceives. Let's not forget the issues also pointed out in Chapter 1 such as the Target security breach (although not VoIP related, it still gives a wake-up call that breaches of all sorts are possible). Also there were the T.J. Maxx, Adobe Software, MasterCard International, and Visa breaches and penetrations. One cannot ignore the facts and statistics that these forms of occurrences happen on a regular basis. Moreover, many of the breaches occurred with the aid of an internal user who knew how the systems worked, what some of the procedures are, and passwords and nuances of each system. So it cannot be ignored that even if an external event occurs, there is a reasonable probability that it was a combined internal/external attack.

Another issue with the internal user is the fact that employees (contractors or third parties) who have access to internal systems create a new wave of risk. It is no secret that organizations are also losing valuable intellectual property regularly. The many security initiatives already discussed above focus their energy and prevention on threats from cyber criminals and hackers, the less obvious risk in the theft of corporate assets. As already stated that equates to the internal employees. In most cases these are highly trusted employees. As stated above, because they know the internal operations of the systems, they move, share, and potentially expose valuable corporate data just to get their work done. In other cases, they might purposefully take confidential information with them if they leave the company. Some employees actually may not realize that taking confidential or proprietary information to their new job is illegal and morally wrong. They might also involve a third party outside in a conversation (VoIP) and divulge information that is proprietary (knowingly or unknowingly). The three parties – the employee, the current organization, and the new employer – are all at risk. There can be no winner in any of these situations. Remember the threats to IP telephony (which can include IM) include:

1. Loss of privacy
2. Loss of integrity (voice or data)
3. Impersonation (man in the middle)
4. Theft of information (eavesdropping, illegal passing it on, etc.)

5. Denial of service (takes down the whole telephone network)
6. Interception of calls (redirection, impersonation, forking)
7. Malware embedded in the signaling and media session

Security needs to be stressed and employees educated regarding the risks associated with passing information along to others, or taking it from the company. Many employees have a sense of ownership that they worked on the development of a product, project, software, etc., and therefore they own it. Or at least they feel they have a share in ownership. Thus, they do not have any qualms about taking it.

TOLL FRAUD – A BIG THREAT

Toll fraud and phone hacking is a multibillion dollar industry with monetary damages more than double those of credit card fraud. Toll fraud can be simply explained as any instance where a subscriber attempts to defraud the telephone company, the telephone company attempts to defraud a subscriber, or a third party attempts to defraud either of them. As already seen above, the numbers can be staggering. Although tool fraud has been around for years before VoIP, it becomes a much bigger problem when the Internet is used as the vehicle for carrying voice. In the past there were always certain countries that were the "hot buttons" for fraud. For example, the telephone carriers were known to produce a monthly list of countries where toll fraud was prevalent. These are countries where there is little regulation and the end user can literally charge whatever they choose for terminating a call. An example is the list shown in Figure 7.2. In this figure these are commonly exploited area codes,

- Many Commonly Exploited Area Codes.
- The Following List is Just a Start and May Not Apply to Your Organization ...
  - Research the Problem for Your Particular Area

Country	Area Code	Blocked CM Pattern
Bahamas	242	9.1242xxxxxxx
Anguilla	264	9.1264xxxxxxx
Antigua/ Barbuda	268	9.1268xxxxxxx
Barbados	246	9.1246xxxxxxx
Bermuda	441	9.1441xxxxxxx
British Virgin Islands	284	9.1284xxxxxxx
Cayman Islands	345	9.1345xxxxxxx
Dominica	767	9.1767xxxxxxx
Dominican Republic	809	9.1809xxxxxxx
Grenada	473	9.1473xxxxxxx

Country	Area Code	Blocked CM Pattern
Jamaica	876	9.1876xxxxxxx
Montserrat	664	9.1664xxxxxxx
Puerto Rico	787	9.1787xxxxxxx
St. Kitts and Nevis	869	9.1869xxxxxxx
St. Lucia	758	9.1758xxxxxxx
St. Vincent and the Grenadines	784	9.1784xxxxxxx
Toll Charge	900 / 976	9.1900xxxxxxx / 9.1976xxxxxxx
Trinidad and Tobago	868	9.1868xxxxxxx
Turks and Caicos Islands	649	9.1649xxxxxxx
US Virgin Islands	340	9.1242xxxxxxx

FIGURE 7.2

List of toll fraud countries.

albeit not totally inclusive. The chart shows the countries and the area codes that are prevalent, and then blocking pattern that should be input to the system (call manager). So, for example, a call is attempted to dial 9 (for an outside access), 1 (for long distance), and 242 (e.g., the area code for the Bahamas). So 9 + 1 + 242 + 123-2456 (or any other seven-digit telephone number in this area code) would be blocked by the VoIP system. This helps but is not a panacea.

There are too many examples of toll fraud from employees and outsiders. One such example is a company in Australia whose VoIP PBX was hacked and had over 11,000 internationally placed calls costing more than US$120,000. Africa has always been a hot country for toll fraud and an incident over a single weekend in South Africa resulted in a bill of more than $12,000. In Chapter 1 the incident of reselling VoIP calls was cited that amounted to over US$1 million.

There is an organization that tracks a lot of the fraud and losses experienced by the carriers and users alike. This organization, the Communications Fraud Control Association (CFCA),[4] conducts annual surveys of the losses experienced. By tracking the losses, the organization's members can apply common practices to limit the losses.

According to the CFCA survey in 2011 top five fraud loss categories reported by operators were[5]:

- US$4.96 billion – Compromised PBX/voice mail systems
- US$4.32 billion – Subscription/identity theft
- US$3.84 billion – International revenue share fraud
- US$2.88 billion – Bypass fraud
- US$2.40 billion – Credit card fraud

In 2013 the survey showed the top five fraud loss categories reported by operators as[6]:

- US$5.22 billion – Subscription fraud
- US$4.42 billion – PBX hacking
- US$3.62 billion – Account takeover/identity theft
- US$3.62 billion – VoIP hacking
- US$3.35 billion – Dealer fraud

There were some reclassifications of the methods and types in 2013 that account for the label differences. However, the global revenues and the losses are on an upward trend. For example, in Figure 7.3 is a table that compares the revenues and losses between 2011 and 2013. The total global revenues were US$2.1 trillion and US$2.2 trillion, respectively. The losses were US$40.1 billion and US$46.3 billion, respectively. And although the percentage of losses was low (1.88% and 2.09%, respectively), this is a significant number. What this means is that fraud in dollars

[4]CFCA.org.
[5]Source: CFCA 2011 Loss Survey; the global losses in 2011 were reportedly US$40.1 billion.
[6]Source: CFCA 2013 Loss Survey; the global losses in 2013 were reportedly US$46.3 billion.

2001 versus 2013 Losses

Loss Summary

	2011	2013
Global Revenue (in Billion Dollars)	21,00,000.00	22,00,000.00
Total Losses (in Billion Dollars)	40,100.00	46,300.00
Percentage of Losses	1.91	2.10

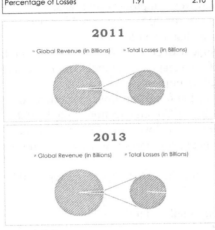

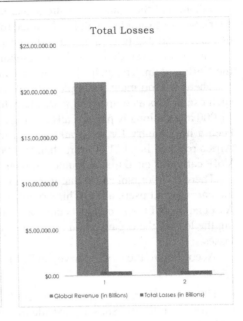

FIGURE 7.3

Comparison of losses.

increased over the two comparative years and about 0.21% of the total in that same time frame. This is a marked trend upward; however, with all the emphasis on fraud it should be noted that the following is the downward trend since 2005, for example:

	2005	2008	2011	2013
Revenues (in trillion dollars)	1.2	1.7	2.1	2.2
Global fraud loss (in billion dollars)	61.3	60.1	40.1	46.3
Percentage of losses	5.11	3.54	1.88	2.09

The CFCA also attempts to list the top 10 countries where toll fraud originates as follows (in their respective order):

1. The United States, 7%
2. India, 4%
3. The United Kingdom, 4%
4. Brazil, 3%
5. Philippines, 3%
6. Latvia, 3%

7. Pakistan, 3%
8. Somalia, 3%
9. Spain, 3%
10. Bulgaria, 2%

Moreover, the survey by the CFCA in 2013 lists the top 10 countries where toll fraud terminates (in their respective order) as follows:

1. Latvia, 10%
2. Gambia, 8%
3. Somalia, 7%
4. Sierra Leone, 6%
5. Guinea, 6%
6. Cuba, 4%
7. East Timor, 4%
8. Lithuania, 4%
9. Taiwan, 4%
10. The United Kingdom, 4%

One final table that should be noted from the CFCA survey is the fraud losses by method in 2013 (in no specific order):

Method	In billion USD
PBX hacking	4.4
Account takeover/identity takeover	3.6
VoIP hacking	3.6
Subscription fraud	5.2
Proxy fraud	0.8
Signaling manipulation	0.9
Unauthorized abuse of access	1.2
Network/IT abuse (internal fraud/employee theft)	1.3
Phishing/pharming (Internet fraud)	1.7
Voice mail hacking	2.0
Social engineering	2.0
Abuse of network, device, or configuration weaknesses	2.7
SMS faking or spoofing	1.6

There are other methods, but it should be obvious that the threats are real and the losses are significant. These are the most prevalent methods that one must address. In each of the methods listed above, the threats were discussed in earlier chapters outlining many of these along with some of the recommended solutions.

From a business perspective, there can be no doubt that the risks far outweigh the costs associated with the implementation of a solid security plan. The threats are both internal and external as can be seen from the table above. The numbers are staggering; although a mere 2% of the global revenue being captured by the carriers and providers, a US$46.3 billion loss is a number that should sound a wake-up call to anyone. Another factor to consider is as follows.

VoIP is now the most prevalent form of voice communications and as the acronym suggests, it is Voice over IP, meaning the calls terminate over the network. Keeping this in the forefront, network security professionals must add another service to their list of networked services to protect: requiring them to implement policies and procedures that mitigate breaches and theft of service.

SUMMARY

Although this was a lengthy discussion regarding the exposure and the losses experienced by carriers and users alike, there are untold cases of organizations that have not been published. As mentioned there are many reasons an organization will not report security breaches (theft, toll fraud, eavesdropping, loss of proprietary information). As pointed out some organizations may not even know they are being attacked or that a breach has occurred. Others fear reprisals from their management, or shareholders. Still there can be the loss of information that leads to loss of business image.

Although the list of risks and breaches addressed many organizational types of industry, there is one area that has not been totally addressed – military applications. Today one only needs to view the local newspapers to recognize that cyber security is under attack by host countries around the world. Military advantage and technical advancements are some of the common goals that countries spy/steal information from each other. This book does not address many of the military secure networks that follow FIPS 140-2 guidelines because that is a whole discussion in itself.

Suffice it to say that no network is safe. When looking at the network build the protection in layers so that a compromise of any one system or component/feature does not compromise the whole system. Recognize that a sound VoIP security strategy is dependent on a sound data security strategy. Understand that the only pure security system is a rock. Everything else is a balance between risk avoidance and cost. Finally filter all of the systems and packet flows as much as possible.

Approaches to VoIP security

8

BEFORE WE START

In the last chapter the analysis was on the RFC in that it describes what is really necessary to secure the VoIP systems and the actual VoIP conversations. Well, that is what the whole book is about so this should not be a surprise. Several suggestions have been made about how to secure the VoIP network such as using encryption on the media and the control channels. Additionally use firewalls that are VoIP enabled (aware), and use all the techniques possible to authenticate the users (such as certificates to authenticate the phone, and username/password combination to authenticate the person). Throughout the discussions, there were also suggestions for using DoS prevention using an application layer gateway (ALG). There are myriad capabilities if one takes the time to research and use them. Thus, this chapter will attempt to fold in all the topics to build upon and secure the network and the actual voice. It is not the intention of this chapter to recommend any one product, nor to recommend any specific vendor solution. In Chapter 1 it was mentioned that there is no Holy Grail out there (no one-stop shopping). Thus, the intent is to highlight best practices and recommendations to make security a reality.

BUILD IT IN LAYERS

If one could begin at the top of a ladder, then step down one rung at a time; it would become obvious that from the top-down approach there must be some steps that extend all the way to the ground. So too, if we look at a network using the reliable old OSI model, the need for security at different layers comes into play. For example, up at the higher level of the model resides the application layer; thus, if an ALG is used, it would protect the data at the highest levels of the model. But another application layer device, for example, might include the IP PBX.

1. Should the IP PBX be considered, then the following might be areas that come into play:
   a. If the IP PBX is Windows Server based (such as Win2k, Win2008, Win7, etc.), then minimize the Windows services where possible. This is a particular point that many hackers are adept at attacking certain parts of a Windows Server. Thus, if the services are minimized to only the ones needed to drive the application (PBX), then other aspects are not accessible (e.g., Cisco CallManager, ADTRAN NetVanta BCS).
   b. If the system is Unix/Linux based, then minimize the services there too. Many IP PBXs are Linux based (e.g., asterisk PBX, which is a high target for hackers, Ericsson MX-One, Avaya IP Office).
   c. Whatever the operating system, if it is Windows based, then make sure that the NTFS file system is used (as opposed to FAT16 or FAT32).
   d. Make sure that the RADIUS server (IAS) and IIS are secured.
   e. Lock down access to SQL.
   f. Use IDS/virus protection.
2. Assuming that the IP PBX is secure, next look at the firewalls and access control lists (ACLs). In this case the issue is to control the addressable devices on the network (LAN) such as to allow/deny access based on firewall ACLs, including:
   a. Allow only call control information (such as SIP or whatever signaling protocol is used).
   b. Allow lookup to an LDAP server.
   c. Allow management protocols in both signaling and media access.
   d. Control the source addresses (remember that SIP uses ports 5060 and 5061, H.323 uses TCP port 1720) to set up a call connection, and the source addresses for a user should fall within the scopes of the LAN.
3. One must not ignore the end points (phones, fax machines, servers, and PCs using a softphone). Much discussion has already been devoted to the actual end points, including the use of authentication (with certificates and username/password combinations) and encryption (using SRTP and ZRTP or any other encryption tool available). In addition to authentication at the endpoint level there should be a mechanism to control the ports at the local layer 2 or layer 3 switches. Some of the steps might include:
   a. Make the phone authenticate to the network and the IP PBX/VoIP server.
   b. Enforce the phone to also use 802.1X port authentication at the local port/switch level.
   c. Ensure the RADIUS server authenticates and authorizes the end user (mutual certificate swap or server certificate and username with password).
   d. Use separate VLANs for voice and data network devices. If a PC is using a softphone, then block the data port from crossing the VLANs to the voice ports.

e. Disable the voice VLAN on the PC.

f. Do not allow GARP on the voice VLAN; use GARP protection.

A word about GARP is probably needed here as this is the first time it is being mentioned. GARP stands for Gratuitous Address Resolution/Registration Protocol. It is a tool that was meant to be used as a helpful tool on a LAN, like so many other tools and protocols. However, the use of GARP for malicious purposes has become a risk. For example, most IP-based phones have the capability to use or disable GARP. By disabling GARP, protection is added to prevent the IP phone from replying to GARP requests. Normally when a phone wants to resolve an address for another device on the LAN (i.e., resolve the IP to a MAC address) the phone (or any other device for that matter) will send out an Address Resolution Protocol (ARP) request.

The IP stack provides a protocol for resolving addresses. The ARP is used to take care of the translation of IP addresses to physical addresses and hide these physical addresses from the upper layers. Generally, ARP works with mapping tables (referred to as the ARP cache). The table provides the mapping between an IP address and a physical address. In a LAN (like Ethernet or an IEEE 802 network), ARP takes the target IP address and searches for a corresponding physical address in a mapping table. If it finds the address, it returns the 48-bit address back to the requester, such as a device driver or server on a LAN. However, if the needed address is not found in the ARP cache, the ARP module sends a broadcast onto the network, as shown in Figure 8.1.

A device that owns the IP address replies with an ARP reply back to the requesting device. The reply contains the MAC address of the device sending

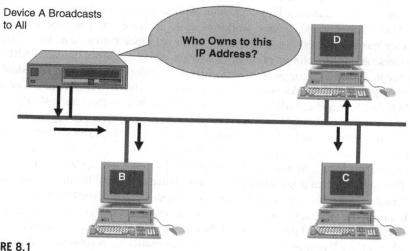

FIGURE 8.1

ARP request.

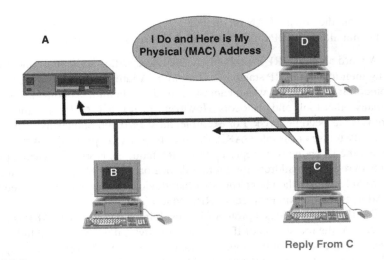

FIGURE 8.2

ARP reply.

the reply, so that the ARP table can now be updated with the mapping of the IP to MAC addresses. See Figure 8.2.

Another protocol, called proxy ARP or promiscuous ARP, allows an organization to use only one IP address (network portion of address) for multiple networks. In essence, proxy ARP maps a single IP network address into multiple physical addresses.

The ARP protocol is a useful technique for determining physical addresses from network addresses. However, some workstations do not know their own IP address. For example, diskless workstations do not have any IP address knowledge when they are booted to a system. They know only their hardware address. The *reverse* address resolution protocol (RARP) works in a manner similar to ARP except, as the name suggests, it works in reverse order: it provides an IP address when given a MAC address. So an end device sends out a RARP request with its MAC address and the ARP server returns an IP address to the device. RARP is often used on LANs for booting the machines to the network. See Figure 8.3.

Now suppose an IP device (phone) receives a gratuitous (unrequested) ARP response providing a MAC address to IP address mapping that differs from the one it already had. So the end device (phone, PC, etc.) will update its ARP table. This is good when using some IP protocols [such as Virtual Routing Redundancy Protocol (VRRP)] and the tables need to be updated; when the router wants to update all the end devices on gateway addresses, the router will send out a GARP request to all devices so that they can update their tables. Conversely, when a GARP request (unsolicited) is sent for malicious purposes it is designed around a man-in-the-middle attack or a hijack attack; then the acceptance of the GARP request is not good. Thus, disabling GARP makes the phone ignore the

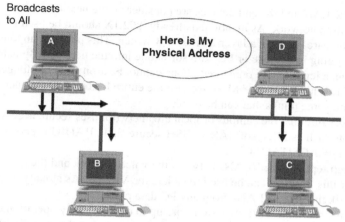

FIGURE 8.3

RARP request.

GARP requests and adds some level of security. Remember too, the statistics still point to the fact that 80% of the reported intrusions were from internal users who have access to the LAN and could easily generate GARP requests. So as seen in Figure 8.4 the phone device will not listen to the GARP messages from a malicious device announcing itself and therefore prevents the malicious device from assuming the identity of a different device (default router possibly) to become a man in the middle. This effectively blocks a tool called Ettercap.[1]

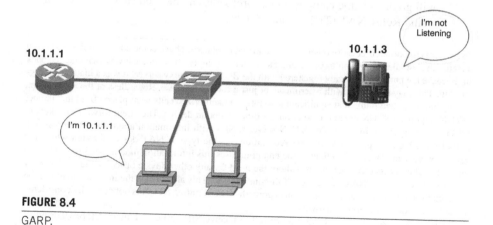

FIGURE 8.4

GARP.

---

[1]Ettercap works by putting the network interface into promiscuous mode and by ARP poisoning the target machines. Thereby it can act as a "man in the middle" and unleash various attacks on the victims. Ettercap has plug-in support so that the features can be extended by adding new plug-ins.

4. Once the LAN and the end devices are considered, the next area is the distribution network. As mentioned already, 802.1X should be used to secure unused (spare) ports in a layer 2 or layer 3 switch. This prevents anyone from just plugging in a phone or PC with softphone into the network. By using this function, a legitimately registered phone cannot be arbitrarily unplugged and moved to a hidden place.[2] Moreover, on the entire LAN or campus network there are some things that can be done:

    a. Make sure that the campus or local area network uses secure access using tools such as Microsoft IAS, or SSH secure shell, RADIUS servers, AAA, or TACACS/TACACS+.
    b. Keep separate the VLANs between the voice network and the data network. For this IP filters can be used to isolate the VLANs. As already mentioned block the voice VLANs from any PC data ports.
    c. Make sure that IPS/IDS systems are up to date and fully operational.
    d. Limit the number of protocols/ports being opened in the firewall. The more pinholes opened in a firewall, the greater the risk of penetration. A pinhole is a path through a firewall, through which a flow passes.
    e. Can be used to masquerade as someone else.
    f. Attack performed by reconfiguring a phone to have the same SIP user ID as another phone.
    g. Could be massively applied to redirect all calls for entire enterprise to a different entity.

5. The next area to tighten down is the access to the outside world.

    a. Eliminate the use of NAT across the Internet. When dealing with VoIP aware firewalls and VoIP aware NAT devices it is important to limit what will go outside the campus. Other protocols can be used such as Traversal Using Relay NAT (TURN) and STUN.[3]

---

[2]Why this is important is because others have found that third parties have come into a building and taken a legitimate but idle phone, unplugged it, and moved it to an empty office where it was then plugged back in. Because the phone had already registered with the IP PBX (or proxy server) it was a matter of reregistering. This may have been with a certificate or just a cached database. Regardless of the mechanism, the organization then found that significant amounts of unauthorized calls were placed from that phone.
[3]STUN requires a STUN client on the phone or other endpoint device. The client forwards packets to a STUN server on the Internet. The STUN server replies with information about the IP address and ports from which the packets were received and detects the type of NAT device through which the packets were sent. The STUN client at the end point uses this information in constructing headers so that external contacts can reach them without the need for any other device or technique. STUN only works with less secure NATs, so-called "full-cone NATs." This also means the internal client will be exposed to an attack from anyone who can capture the STUN traffic. STUN is not generally considered a viable solution for enterprise networks.

TURN allows an end point behind a firewall to receive SIP traffic on either TCP or UDP ports. This solves the problems of clients behind symmetrical NATs that cannot rely on STUN to solve NAT traversal. TURN connects clients behind a NAT to a single peer to provide the same protection as that created by symmetrical NATs and firewalls. The TURN server acts as a relay; any data received is forwarded. The client on the inside can then be on the receiving end, rather than the sending end, of a connection that is requested by the client on the inside.

b. At the external access, install intrusion detection tools that can effectively mitigate the damages and the DoS attacks, such as an ALG. Many tools are now available from the vendors. An intrusion detection system monitors a host or a network for suspicious activity patterns such as those that match some preprogrammed or possibly learned rules about what constitutes normal or abnormal behavior.

c. Also at the entry point, make sure that sensors are installed to sense when a DoS or DDoS attack is being launched. Sensor networks destined for harsh environments should already be designed to continue functioning in the event of a failure. This robustness and disaster recovery program against physical challenges may prevent various types of DoS attacks. Sensors are particularly important in wireless LAN environments where a number of similar and yet different attacks can occur.

SOME BEST PRACTICES FOR INFRASTRUCTURE SECURITY

Given some of the infrastructure issues listed above, a summary of some best practices can address the points made by stating:

1. Manage switches and routers with SSH, HTTPS, and out-of-band (OOB) and permit lists.
2. Separate the voice and data VLANS.
   a. Use private addresses, which helps to isolate the addresses from the public Internet; avoid NAT wherever possible.
   b. Use dedicated VLAN IDs for trunks in the network.
   c. Never use VLAN 1. That is the single most common mistake that people make. When they do not change the default VLAN 1, it is the target of the attackers where they can find and penetrate the networks. Preferably disable VLAN 1.
   d. Disable unused ports as already stated. Put all the unused ports in an unused VLAN to keep them off the voice and data networks.
   e. Use 802.1X authentication for all ports on the switches.
3. Actively use ACLs.
   a. Group assets along a bitwise boundary.
   b. Restrict and/or control ARP, GARP, ICMP redirect, and TCP Intercept.
   c. Only allow sources from known scopes in the address pools. Limit the scopes to those in use.
   d. Protect the QoS of all the packets and any VLAN tagging.
4. With firewalls and NAT use a voice ALG.
   a. They perform stateful inspection of voice signaling protocols.
   b. They support all of the VoIP protocols now (including SIP, SCCP, H.323, and MGCP).
   c. They can be implemented and are available in both firewalls and NAT devices.

    d. Firewall ALG inspects signaling packets to discover the UDP port that the RTP stream uses; then it dynamically opens a pinhole for the UDP port and watches for an end-of-call signaling to close the pinhole.

    e. NAT ALGs modify the private originating source IP address and port number (the socket) in the signaling packet to a publicly addressable NAT'ed IP address and port.

5. Layer 2/layer 3 caveats:

    a. Port security and private VLANs are not supported on trunk ports, including auxiliary VLAN ports for phones. Both can be used on servers.

    b. Firewall and NAT ALGs presume that both the signaling path and the media path pass through the firewall and/or the NAT. If this does not happen, then it unnecessarily opens up a pinhole in the firewall and it turns the NAT device into a media termination point (MTP).

    c. It should be understood that ALGs are not as efficient in complex firewall implementations.

6. Physical security is important too!

    a. Remember the physical plant in all network designs; all too often this is overlooked.

    b. Access to equipment and equipment rooms must be controlled. This means that when there is a special room that houses the IP PBX and/or the added equipment such as media gateways, proxy servers, DNS and DHCP servers, etc., this room must be secured from public access. A caveat here is that most organizations try to squeeze out just enough room for the equipment at hand. Sometimes this room is shared with other types of equipment such as switching systems or maybe even a janitorial closet.[4] Regardless of the conditions, it is imperative that the equipment room be locked and access controlled. The servers could be exposed to anyone who may walk by if the room is not locked and secured. This allows anyone to access and possibly reconfigure the system, which is highly undesirable.

    c. Pay particular attention also to the rest of the room; for example, are there any containers, or water pipes, etc.? It is all too easy to overlook the fact that these facilities are not conducive to a secure and safe operating procedure. The security plan should include such and audit to make sure that things like this won't happen. One quick point here is that security includes the following items: confidentiality, integrity, and availability.[5] If the room presents the wrong access methods, or the wrong environmental conditions, the equipment is likely to fail. Thus, availability cannot be assured. It should also be noted that the availability of the telephone systems in the past has always been considered a 99.999% requirement because of the lifeline responsibility.

---

[4]This is a true statement where the author actually conducted a tour of a facility and found that the IP PBX shared a janitorial closet.

[5]This is jokingly referred to as the CIA.

d. In all equipment rooms pay particular attention to maintain the environment within the limits specified by the manufacturer. In many instances equipment rooms were designed for air conditioning (cooling) and power (battery backup and commercial) based on the switching racks. Now that VoIP is being used, these rooms are also used to provide backup power and Power over Ethernet (PoE) to every telephone end point. This creates a huge demand for cooling and added power in the rooms. However, many of these rooms are not sized suitably to handle the added demand. Keep this in mind when laying out the network.

e. Although there is some benefit for security purposes to centralize resources in a secure room, many of the critical resources may require that they are dispersed for a redundancy and recovery plan. Do not lose sight of what must and can be consolidated and what equipment should be dispersed.

f. Make sure that the access panels for the power and air conditioning are secured. It should be understood that killing power can be a very effective DoS attack, especially in line with item number 3 above.

g. Dealing with a mixed-use situation, such as using the PC switch ports on an IP phone,[6] may create more difficult security practices. Think if the use of the extra port is necessary. If it is not necessary and not in use, disable it.

7. Use dynamic ARP inspection.

    a. Dynamically binds IP address to MAC address to prevent fraudulent addresses.

    b. Automatically creates a VLAN ACL (VACL) to provide access control on all traffic. The VACL is used as a packet filter and packet redirect to enhance security.

    c. In the event of a loss of link, it will automatically reset.

    d. All hosts using dynamic ARP inspection must support DHCP.

    e. It is possible to configure and provide a manual IP to MAC address binding, but it is too tedious.

8. At the VoIP gateways do the following:

    a. All VoIP gateways only allow VoIP call control from the IP PBX Manager (or Call Control Manager Cluster).

    b. All VoIP gateways should deny any H.323, MGCP, Skinny, or SIP connection attempts originating from the data network.

      – There is no way to enforce a centralized plan if any PC can arbitrarily use the VoIP gateway for initiating calls.

      – Not doing this creates a DoS vulnerability on the VoIP network.

      – Also opens the door for a session hijacking situation.

---

[6]Remember that an IP phone is a three-port (or more) switch that provides a switch port for the phone, a PC, and then the Ethernet connection. Some phones may have as many as four or five ports.

9. Consider phone hardening – many of the phone systems out there today have a phone load that introduces the phone hardening. This helps raise the bar against security vulnerabilities.
   a. Use 802.1q packets tagged with the voice VLAN tag blocked on the PC port.
   b. This helps to block malicious sniffing of voice streams from the PC port on the phone.
   c. Blocks intentional sniffing in troubleshooting and monitoring situations.
   d. Stops the use of VOMIT.[7]
   e. Allows the phone to be configured to ignore the GARP messages.
   f. Both features are typically configurable options on the phone administration page.
10. Application hardening in the IP PBX:
   a. Disable the autoregistration feature in the IP PBX. Although this is useful for a bulk deployment, such as the initial deployment of hundreds of phones, it should only be a temporary use.
   b. Harden the operating system, such as Win2k (2000, 2003, 2008, and now 2012). Typically the OS is shipped in a default Win state, but there are fixes that are downloadable from the vendors and from Microsoft.
   c. Make sure that virus protection is installed on the OS.
   d. Use dedicated servers for the functions that an IP PBX may be used for such as TFTP/FTP, Syslog, XML transport of data, music on hold, and voice processing/mail. On dedicated servers these features can be offloaded and protected separately.
   e. Where possible disable services in the OS that are not needed, for example, DHCP, IIS, IAS, and TFTP for subscribers.
   f. Use various levels of administration for the system. For example, help desk functions may be able to display only, whereas superuser can configure security and features.
   g. Limit extension mobility so that persons cannot pick up a phone and move it to a hidden place where it can be abused for tolls, fraud, interception, etc.
   h. Wherever possible, limit the area codes as already described to prevent toll fraud.
   i. Limit the Call Forward All calls that will prevent an authenticated user from using the system for toll fraud.
      – Forward a phone call from a work phone to a home phone, have relatives call toll-free office number, and then transfer that call from office to employee home.
      – A second example is forwarding a work phone number to a hotel or resort in a foreign country while on vacation, and then having friends from home call the resort for free.

---

[7]VOMIT is voice over misconfigured IP telephones as discussed in Chapter 1.

- When an employee needs to make international calls from home (personal), they can use the web to forward their work phone to a desired international number; then employee calls the work number (from home) that has been forwarded.
- Turning off the forward all feature can stop this, but sometimes it may be legitimate. Therefore, it must be done on a case-by-case basis.

11. Block call forwarding from voice mail ports.

   a. Also be careful that no access to the voice mail ports (admin) is available through remote access (modem or web-based access). This way the VM system cannot be used to forward calls similar to the discussion in item number 10 above.

   b. Only allow access to maintenance personnel from remote when scheduled and absolutely needed. If a technician needs access, turn it on only for the duration of work and turn it off after completed.

12. Social engineering – Be careful that the operators are trained on social exploits such as when a caller connects and asks to be transferred to extension "9011," which is usually the code for gaining outside access "9" and the code for international dialing "011." This exploit comes from a hacker calling and saying something like "Hello this is the Telephone Company testing your circuits. Please transfer me to extension 9011." Of course, once the transfer is done (if done), the caller has access to call any international number in the world and run up a monstrous telephone bill.

INTEGRATING NETWORK SECURITY

Having stated all of the best practices above, there should be some form of hierarchy to network security. This means that somewhere, as described earlier, a decision should be made to link the security policies and procedures for VoIP with the security policies and procedures in place for the network. For example, looking at Figure 8.5, one could apply rules that state:

1. If a user is demonstrating any form of malicious behavior, such as attempting to gain access to network resources that are not authorized, then the system policy should be that the user will not gain access to the network. If the device cannot authenticate to the port level switching system, then, again, no access shall be given.

2. Above the malicious behavior on the chart, if the user or device is creating any policy violations such as using an unauthorized device, a wrong procedure, or even an application that has not been approved for the network, then it is likely that an alarm indication will be sent and the user may or may not gain access. This really boils down to a "flip of the coin" as some violations may be minor (e.g., trying to use a different soft phone than approved, or using a video application that is not authorized). Conversely if the user appears to be attempting to break into a system of service, then the violation is considered

FIGURE 8.5

Net security.

major and no access will be allowed. Additionally if a signature of a virus or a sniffing tool is detected (e.g., Ettercap), then service will be denied to that user.

3. At the top of the chart is a strict enforcement policy that states the user will use user-based authentication to the RADIUS server, and if the user fails authentication, then he/she will be denied access no matter what. Additionally, the encryption policies such as IPSec or SRTP protocols will be used, but if the user does not enable these required protocols, then, again, no access will be allowed. At this level on the pyramid, there will be no exceptions. The user either adheres to the security policies or gains no access to the VoIP network.

So the IP telephony service dictates that new security initiatives be added to the existing IT security plan and enforcement must be equal to or greater than the existing IT policies. For example, the new initiatives may include the following as a minimum:

1. New infrastructure capabilities – These include the fact that PoE to every phone should be a requirement. The reason for this decision is that voice has always been considered a lifeline service. The "always available" dial tone is a requirement for this service. If a person takes ill or becomes threatened, that person needs the assurance that when they pick up the phone to dial "911" or any other assigned number, the dial tone will always be there. When the phones are plugged into a local outlet (using the provided power brick) and power goes down, the phones will typically not work. That is unless PoE is provided to every phone. Now in order to provide PoE to every phone, more backup power (UPS) is needed in every closet in order to power all the phones. As mentioned, the closets are normally small and will be tight, so trying to add power in these

rooms may be a challenge. Also, with the added heat that will be generated in the closets, more air conditioning will be needed, stressing the already tight spaces. In some cases, there may be a need for more closets to house all this equipment. Thus, the infrastructure for the phones is a must. In addition to the requirements for the phones, there will be the IP PBX, SBC, media gateways, and myriad other devices that will also have to be backup powered in order for the phone system to work.

However, data access has rarely been considered a lifeline service. If power is down, then the access to the computer screen and data must wait until the power is restored and the systems reinitialized. One cannot power all the PCs and printing services in a building at a reasonable cost. Therefore, the infrastructure for the data side is unchanged. Think however if the use of a softphone is employed. This may require the PCs to be backed up if no hard phones are in place and all the phones are powered by softphones. This is a consideration that must be taken into account. One possibility now with the proliferation of tablets and laptops is to eliminate the desktop devices and run on batteries in the laptops/tablets to power the softphones. Each of these considerations must be considered.

2. Another security initiative is to include the hardening of the IP PBX server as already described. Regardless of the operating system (Windows Server based or some form of Unix/Linux based) look at minimizing the services on the servers so that access is limited and services are moved to dedicated servers (such as DHCP, DNS, IAS, RADIUS, etc.).

   While looking at the server hardening, consider the hardening of the phones as discussed above such as turning off the autoregistration, locking down the admin screen for configurations, turning off replies to GARP, and using certificates to register.

   Look also at hardening the MTPs with virus protection, firewalls that are VoIP aware, and the limited access methods.

   Also add to the security of the media gateways. Make sure there are no back doors to access these devices. If there are, close them. Use ALGs that will assist in intrusion detection systems/intrusion prevention systems and allow only certain access methods through the ALG. Add to the gateways an ALG that will prevent DoS attacks,

3. Next be very specific to have the vendors install systems that require device authentication. Already discussed in previous chapters is the use of a certificate of some sort to authenticate and authorize the devices (phones, GWs, MTPs, etc.); preferably a mutual certificate swap is recommended, but if not a mutual certificate, then at least a single certificate (and possibly a dongle or single access key such as a Secure ID) should be used. Also use the 802.1X standard for port authentication for the devices. Only authenticated devices will connect to a port on the local Ethernet switch and others that cannot authenticate will be denied access to the network.

4. Beyond having all devices authenticated and authorized, ensure that human authentication and authorization is enforced. This means that beyond the device gaining access to the network, no privileges or phone access is available unless the user authenticates. Once again this can be with the certificates, a username/password combination, or a token (like a CAC card in military systems or a Secure ID dongle). By ensuring both device and person authentication, the risks are minimized considerably.

5. Ensure that when installing the VoIP system the integrity and privacy of call signaling and media channels can be preserved. Of course, this means using the encryption methods discussed (i.e., SRTP, ZRTP) and where possible using VPN or IPSec to secure the channels. Probably the single largest effort that will surface is the integrity of these channels. Once the system is connected to the Internet especially, there is little that can be done to control the cross-web connections. Thus, using strong encryption, make sure that the AES 256 encryption standard is applied in the network works. But, what of the call that is going to a random off-net user? That is where the risks build. You cannot encrypt the media channel, for example, unless the opposite end can decrypt. So perhaps you are using a VoIP ISP (called ITSP) to provide the transport of encrypted traffic and signaling channels to an end point (tail-end hop off) where the call is carried on a secure channel until the end of the ITSP's network, and then decrypted and sent to the far end on a very short PSTN link. Consider asking what the ITSP can provide and to what areas this can be provided.

6. While discussing the integrity and security of the traffic, consider also the integrity and security of control channels, provisioning access methods and any other signaling necessary. Whenever a call is being initiated in either H.323 or SIP, we know that there are session description parameters exchanged. So when an "invite" from SIP is sent out from Bob to Alice, we know that Bob will send the SDP message first along with the invite. See Figure 8.6 where Bob sends a SIP Invite to Alice. Note the first line includes the parameters.

The parameters are described in RFC 2327 in which session descriptions are explained as follows:

An SDP session description consists of a number of lines of text of the form <type> = <value>. <type> is always exactly one character and is case-significant. <value> is a structured text string whose format depends on <type>. It also will be case-significant unless a specific field defines otherwise. Whitespace is not permitted either side of the '=' sign. In general <value> is either a number of fields delimited by a single space character or a free format string.

A session description consists of a session-level description (details that apply to the whole session and all media streams) and optionally several media-level descriptions (details that apply onto to a single media stream).

An example SDP description is shown in Figure 8.7.

Note that the SDP example conveys information that has the IP address and port numbers of the sender and the receiver. It also has e-mail contact

Bob

Alice

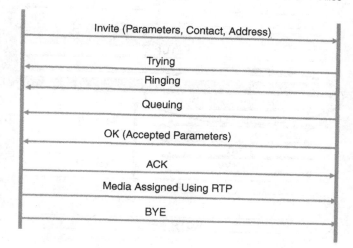

FIGURE 8.6

SIP Invite.

v=0

o=mhandley 2890844526 2890842807 IN IP4 126.16.64.4

s=SDP Seminar

i=A Seminar on the session description protocol

u=http://www.cs.ucl.ac.uk/staff/M.Handley/sdp.03.ps

e=mjh@isi.edu (Mark Handley)

c=IN IP4 224.2.17.12/127

t=2873397496 2873404696

a=recvonly

m=audio 49170 RTP/AVP0

m=video 51372 RTP/AVP31

m=application 32416 udp wb

a=orient:portrait

FIGURE 8.7

SDP example.

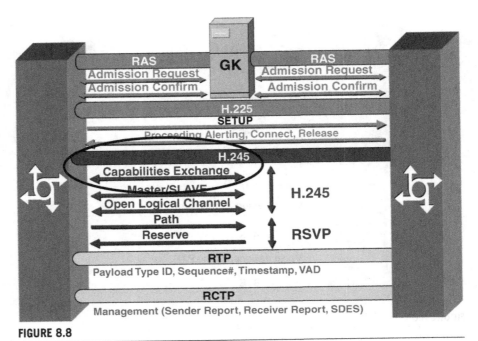

FIGURE 8.8

SDP in H.323.

information and it describes the media channels (both audio and video with an application also being described). This is a lot of information in the signaling channel that will aid a hacker in interception, man in the middle, hijacking, and/ or bandwidth stealing. By changing any of these parameters the hacker could either disrupt or hijack the session.

In Figure 8.8 H.323 parameter description is shown. What this means is the SDP information is exchanged in the negotiation stages of the call setup (in the H.245 protocol) regardless of the VoIP protocols being used.

7. The next area to consider in the security initiatives is to be sure that configuration tools are locked down so that a hacker cannot gain access to the system components and reconfigure them; for example, a redirection or a forwarding element should not be available to anyone for the taking. Along with this thought, an area that should also be protected is the management of the system. Particularly, the reports and alarms should not be available to others; these tools should be locked down and secured. Preferably the management tools should be offloaded from the VoIP server and maintained on a dedicated server that is well secured. A Syslog server may serve as a home for the management and reports.

When looking at the above initiatives, the building in layers concept comes back as a means of implementation. Shown in Figure 8.9 is a pyramid to look at working from the bottom up.

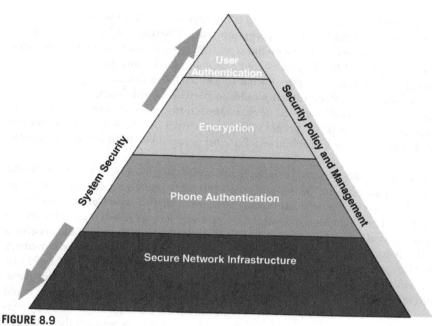

FIGURE 8.9

Integrated security.

At the bottom of the pyramid is the title Secure Network Infrastructure. This is where layer 2 and layer 3 security can be implemented. In this portion is where the 802.1X architecture controls the access to the port-based security. As already addressed, it is at this layer 2 position that no access will be granted unless the device can authenticate. Moreover, at this bottom rung of the pyramid, intrusion detection and intrusion prevention will come into play. Firewalling with VoIP aware firewalls and VoIP aware NAT devices can be implemented. Monitoring all activities for any form of malicious behavior will shut down the ports that display this form of malfeasance. Note this is the secure network access.

Looking at the second rung on this pyramid is the phone authentication. Once again with a mutual certificate-based system or a certificate and a dongle architecture, the phone will not authenticate and be authorized to the network or to the IP PBX unless this portion of the security management is met. At the network level (layer 2 or 3) the phone will be granted access to the LAN on successful authentication to the network devices (layer 2 or layer 3 switches using the 802.1X protocol and a MAC level authentication). At the IP PBX the phone will also have to authenticate to the server. This is that second step of authentication in which the mutual certificate swap or a server certificate and dongle authentication takes place. This is what is used for most system-based access methods in a data network, and should be used similarly in a VoIP environment.

At the next level up on the pyramid is the security stage for securing the media and the control channels. Here encryption and VPN/IPSec will come into play. The encryption should be between the signaling devices, such as media gateways, ALGs, firewalls and NAT devices, and SBCs along with any MTP devices. VPN end-to-end is a prime example of what to use for these devices (e.g., gateway to gateway); using an IPSec tunnel would be perfect for this connection. The gist of this layer is to handle trusted device connections; it would not be appropriate to attempt a VPN or IPSec tunnel with an unknown device that is not under our control. That could be a problem as a false tunnel could be built to a nonsupported device.

At the top of the pyramid is the user and specifically user authentication. As the human interface between the two end points (phone to phone) a user should authenticate to the server using what has already been discussed such as username and password, or a token device or a mutual certificate swap. Regardless of the methodology, the goal is to allow only authorized and authenticated users to make and receive a call. If this part is neglected, then the possible resultant toll fraud could be extremely high. Moreover, if an unauthenticated user can get on the network, the risks of sniffing, eavesdropping, and hijacking all exist. One cannot be too careful in this event. Additionally if the data port on a phone is not locked down, a potential hacker could use the data port as an access means to try to usurp the basic phone security by running a sniffer (VOMIT, Wireshark, Ettercap) and try to breach between the voice and data VLANs (basically jumping the wall between the VLANs). The least amount of access given reduces the amount of attempted cracking and hacking tools that can be used with any effect.

Notice on the sides of the pyramid are two distinct labels. On the left side is an integrated approach. This is what is meant by integrated security, taken as a system-wide approach. Any of these pieces on the pyramid can be implemented individually but total system security is not achieved. In fact, a false sense of security would be present if only pieces were attempted rather than a holistic approach. On the right side of the pyramid is what must be brought together. Security policies must be integrated with both the data and the VoIP side of the network, as well as a single set of management tools that can monitor the entire system. Admittedly, there may be some unique tools that pertain only to the voice (because of the media and signaling channels) but they would still be integrated into a homogenous system to monitor, prevent, and react whenever something happens. The goals of this holistic approach would be to increase end user productivity such that once authenticated and authorized, they should not have to worry about security breaches that will affect them. Another clear and present goal is the asset management and protection. As VoIP managers, it is incumbent on our security awareness and propagation. Any breach is an embarrassment; repeated breaches will cost our organizations money, confidence, risk of lawsuits, and loss of job security. If all plays out appropriately, the final result will be a secure network, secure voice, and reduced overall operating expenses.

ADDITIONAL THOUGHTS AND ITEMS

In this section are given some additional thoughts that should be addressed when protecting and integrating the VoIP system into the data network. It is extremely important to use a multilayered approach on the VoIP network.

- No matter what, the goal is to preserve the QoS of the VoIP while at the same time providing the necessary security of the control, signaling, and media channels.
- If the configuration menu on the phone relies on FTP, make sure to use nondefault username/password for the FTP account.
- If the configuration menu on the phone relies on TFTP, you must implement an auditing process of the configuration files. Additionally, make sure that the default username and password are changed to a unique one.
- When looking at social engineering issues understand that for a hacker, spoofing Caller ID and called party information with VoIP is very easy. End users must be made aware of this possibility and trained not to trust the Caller ID being displayed. One such spoofed call displayed that a call was coming from a very high-ranking executive in an organization whereby the help desk personnel gave out the username and password to the caller allowing the caller access to the senior executive's account.
- Audits on the VoIP systems should be done often to ensure a malicious attacker has not compromised the system. If a malicious user does compromise the system, they can redirect outbound calls.
- When integrating the VoIP system, be careful not to allow access to customer information or employee information from the PSTN. This holds true with the data network.
- Wherever possible all access to the in/out PSTN should be protected with a PIN or an access code/password combination that is unique.
- Whatever happens, do use a VPN for the traffic and control information that traverses the Internet or the PSTN.
- When implementing VoIP on the corporate LAN be sure to use SRTP if it is available. If SRTP cannot be used, then segregate VoIP traffic data traffic with the separate VLANs. If that cannot be done, consider installing a completely separate physical network.
- Be careful with SRTP on the Internet, as the headers could be exposed, compromising the encryption techniques and keys.
- If possible, use separate DHCP servers for the voice and data networks. Also make sure that the DNS servers are secure.
- Whenever possible do not allow remote management, but if it must be used, then use SSH or IPSec to secure the management.
- Do not assume that the vendor(s) will automatically secure all the components and protocols used in the VoIP network.

Registration spoofing

Already discussed is the trick that hackers attempt to spoof the registrar server into thinking that they are someone else. This spoofing technique manipulates the register message to the server. Any spoofing is bad, but when a hacker can use a spoofed registration, it leads to some of the following issues:

- It can either be a precursor to a DoS attack or be effectively used as a DoS attack itself.
- Spoofing allows the hacker to masquerade as someone else and preferably a high-ranking member of the organization with sufficient permissions to gain access to any part of the system.
- It is performed by reconfiguring a phone to have the same SIP user ID as another phone. Capturing a register message on the LAN and then manually replicating that register information is relatively simple with many of the tools (e.g., SiVus).
- Once spoofed the spoofed device could redirect all calls for entire enterprise to a different entity. Although this would be recognizable fairly soon and then shut down, if a portion of the enterprise traffic is redirected, the results could be worse.

SUMMARY

Integrating VoIP onto a network can pose significant risks to the already existing data network. It can also open many opportunities for hackers to launch attacks against the voice side of the network because they do function differently. As a result the above lists (although not all inclusive) should provide enough thought-provoking areas that will make the system administrator dig even further to prevent any opening of holes in an existing network. The integrated VoIP system also opens the entire network to a new public access mechanism called the PSTN. This means that two different exposure points exist: the Internet and the PSTN. Whenever creating an integration plan strong encryption is a must (prefer AES-256). Passwords for the system must be strong and unique. However, do not store the password files on the VoIP server; instead use a separate server for that role.

For an IP PBX a best practices guide should be used that provides:

- Internal control and audit:
  - Develop policy and perform assessments.
  - Eliminate unnecessary modems.
  - Centralize architecture.
- When vendors use modems for support:
  - Turn them off when not needed.
  - Use centralized remote access.
  - Audit usage.

- Authentication:
  - Make passwords strong and unique.
  - Use two-factor authentication, where possible: tokens (e.g., SecurPBX Agent or RSA SecurID[8]).
- Filter traffic between PSTN/gateways and PBX/IP network:
  - Telephony firewall
- Build separate DHCP servers:
  - One for voice (IP phones)
  - One for data (PCs)
- Disable automated phone registration:
  - Prevents rogue IP phones from grabbing a directory number from the IP PBX
- Monitor MAC addresses within voice segment.
- Filtering in all segments should limit devices in unknown segments from connecting to IP PBX.

The bottom line is:

- VoIP security is the users' responsibility.
- Vulnerabilities of voice and data systems carry over to the VoIP services.
- Risks as already shown are far too big to ignore.
- There are no single turnkey solutions.
- Your best approach is to implement security best practices with unique VoIP security measures.

---

[8]SecurPBX token authentication is provided by www.voiceinnovate.com; RSA SecurID Token is provided by www.emc.com.

Final thoughts

BEFORE WE START

This chapter is a summary of the thoughts discussed herein as well as a different way of looking at things. There can be no simple "one-size-fits-all" solution to securing a VoIP network or a VoIP service. Internet telephony service providers, VoIP component manufacturers, and end users alike all look for a single solution, but to no avail. So perhaps the best way to close this book out is to try and summarize the thoughts and suggestions contained in the preceding chapters. It should not be a surprise that there will be some redundancies in this summary. To paraphrase a saying that was used in different training sessions: "I am going to tell you what I am going to tell you and then I am going to tell you what I told you!" So please understand that these final thoughts are more of a reiteration and a statement of the importance of the facts that have been laid out here. The intent of any book like this is to spur the thought process and hopefully encourage you, the reader, to take a hard look at the service and network to find any holes that still might exist. Things change too fast to document any guidelines that will stay current for any length of time. So this section will try to give you an opportunity to rethink your network.

WHAT WE HAVE ALREADY COVERED

A few of the things already covered include the following:

1. Encryption of the network control and signaling information as well as the media stream (RTP) is a must. AES encryption, either 192 or 256, is the best choice today. Move beyond DES and triple DES.
2. VPNs should be used to carry the VoIP in a secure tunnel whenever possible. SSL VPNs work well with the VoIP systems as well as software-based VPN clients.

3. IPSec delivers the strongest security today when it can be deployed. Refer to the RFC for this great tool.
4. Autoregistration of telephones on an IPPBX should be turned off to prevent a rogue device from registering on the network. If used, autoregistration can be used for bulk deployments but then turned off.
5. Wherever possible use dedicated servers for TFTP, music on hold (MOH), and XML to isolate these in a walled garden away from the normal servers. Moreover, offload these functions from the PBX servers.
6. Use multiple layers of administration so that a nonessential account cannot get access to security, and additions and changes to the operating systems.
7. Be aware of extension mobility, such that before a phone can be moved to a different place on the network, it must use port authentication on the switch (L2/L3) as well as user authentication.
8. One of the single largest problems with VoIP is toll fraud. Use a good prevention program to eliminate or at least minimize the risk. This includes the exploits of call forwarding all calls, restricted access to voice mail ports, and prevention of transferring calls to extension "9011."
9. Use separate DHCP servers when possible, one for voice and one for data.
10. Protect the signaling gateways, media gateways, and session border controllers from remote access. Use a strong password and use a VoIP aware firewall. Consider any device that sits out on the network and build in the necessary protection.
11. Application layer gateways will aid in preventing unauthorized access and DoS attacks as listed.

Vendor issues

As stated earlier, trying to get multiple vendor solutions to play well together can be a daunting challenge. This in no way is reflecting poorly on the vendor; it means that the end user must be proactive when dealing with vendors.

1. Become an active part of the team; don't leave all the work and decisions to the vendor(s) alone.
2. Ask tough questions regarding the way that the system works and what the potential risks are. Most of the vendors know what the issues are with their systems and with interoperability. This should not be the very first installation they are doing; they should have a series of past experiences and lessons learned.
3. Ask how long it normally takes them to rectify a problem (either known or a new issue that surfaces). What has their track record been in solving and securing their systems?
4. Ask the vendors what standards they support and what RFCs they follow. For example, RFC 3261 defines how SIP works and how to assure interoperability with most vendors. RFC 3261 is the updated version of RFC 2543 and there are approximately 150 differences between the two RFCs. Does the vendor support the 3261 over the original 2543? Has the vendor complied with the changes to allow interoperability between vendors?

5. How does their system deal with SIP support? Does it use a GUI to ease its use?
6. Does their system offer high availability and possibly load balancing throughout the system? This is a measure of not just uptime but also performance. Does the system use a form of clustering? (Preferably yes.)
7. How does the system handle IP defragmentation on all standard and nonstandard ports? The goal here is to find out how the vendor handles the networking of the system and the mitigation of a DoS attack. The ping of death may be an example to consider here in how the vendor system handles this component.
8. Does the vendor system allow the setting and defining of separate rules and actions to follow for different media types, or is a one-size-fits-all approach used?
9. Can the end user track individual calls through the system to mitigate DoS and hijacking? Can the vendor offer support against "zero-day" attacks and advanced persistent threats?
10. Can redirection of the signaling protocols be disabled to prevent misuse of this feature?
11. Can the reinvite messages, hold, and conference calling features be limited? This can prevent abuse of number of connections attacks.
12. Does the system allow static NAT for incoming and outgoing calls as an option? Can NAT be hidden from the calling/called parties?
13. Does the system offer extensive reports and logging capabilities (registration attempts/failures; call detail recording logs, etc.)? Is a Syslog server used for offloading the reports for later analysis?
14. Does the system support fill QoS features and prioritization? Will the system integrate with the parameters of the network resources in providing QoS as an integrated service?
15. How adaptable is the system to implement a toll bypass scheme? Can legacy systems (key systems, TDM PBXs, etc.) be integrated into a toll bypass arrangement, and then migrated to an IPPBX solution over time?
16. How does the system facilitate telecommuters in the network? Are there any special considerations or constraints? How many users will the system support?

The above list is not all inclusive, but these are some of the areas that would have to be discussed with each vendor providing a component or a "total solution." It may be wise to have a joint meeting with all vendors providing any component in a VoIP network. From a personal perspective, by allowing all vendors to come together and discuss your networking plans and goals, they get to hear about how each other's products work and how they may have to integrate together. Then, there is no excuse if they promise a solution and do not fulfill it; moreover, this helps to minimize the finger-pointing when something does not play well with another vendor's products. The time to learn what will and will not work together is before the system is bought and installed. At that point, the vendors still have a vested interest in full disclosure. This predeployment approach should be first on the agenda.

Controlling the risks

Without saying, one of the first things to control risks in voice mail and PBX systems includes reading the documentation. This may sound somewhat general knowledge but it is often a skipped step by end users and providers alike. Voice system manuals will (should) provide a lot of step-by-step procedures and instructions on how to properly configure the system and secure it. There is also a publication by NIST 800-24[1] that addresses finding the holes in your PBX that makes for good reading. Although the NIST publication does not address the VoIP world, it addresses many of the same issues.

Another area that needs to be considered is the way to integrate the VoIP system into the IT security plans. VoIP has very similar network issues as the data network, but it also includes many protocol-specific and device-specific issues on its own that go beyond the data network. As for internal audits and control there should be a mechanism to:

1. Centralize all of the telephony and telecommunications service requests so that stringent control can be maintained.
2. The VoIP telephony or IT management should develop policies and procedures for the systems and where possible integrate them into the IT security policy so that the wheel is not reinvented here.
3. Assessments need to be performed. Check the vendor instructions and documentation on what to test and how often.
4. Periodically test and recheck everything as new exploits are discovered regularly.

When evaluating the effectiveness of the security there may be a few added benefits offered by the vendor (either at a cost or free) such as reporting instructions on how to surface a potential issue. The same hold true in a multivendor environment (or third-party arrangement).

1. Look for and report unusual patterns that show up in real time or in the logs.
2. Consider consolidating the logs (here is where the Syslog server can come into play) so that a single point of logging can be readily reviewed.

Consider an option from either the long-distance supplier or third-party insurer if toll fraud insurance is available. Remember this is the single largest exploit on VoIP at the time and the numbers can be staggering.

Incorporate and/or add a PBX disaster recovery and continuity plan to the security measures. Remember confidentiality, integrity, and availability are the three keys to maintaining security on VoIP. Availability falls under the category of a recoverable system in the event of some disaster such as virus, malware (including ransomware), and a malicious physical attack on the hardware or software of the system. There can be no substitute to a good plan in place to recover in the event of a major breach. This process therefore includes maintaining control over physical access to the system and components. The data processing center is locked and controlled via secure card access. Think of the closets spread around the building where

---

[1]This is a bit dated but it has some good information in it. It was produced in 2001.

the data switches and patch panels are located. Are they also secure? Now think of the closets used for telephone connections. Are they as secure as the closets housing the data processing equipment?[2] Now that the systems are converging, they need to be controlled as much as the data components.

PBX best practices

From the perspective and at a minimum here are a few things that should be done at little or no cost, but that will provide a great return for the effort:

1. Eliminate unnecessary modems or access ports.
2. Use a centralized architecture (or centralized cluster) if possible.
3. When a distributed architecture is used lock it down.
4. When vendors use remote access for diagnostics and patches, turn the access off when not needed.
5. Centralize and protect any remote access systems.
6. Audit the use of any remote system access (this includes access to remote IPPBXs, voice mail systems, conference bridges, call centers, gateways/gatekeepers, SBC, firewalls/NAT, ALGs, proxies).
7. Whenever anyone needs to access these systems or components make sure they must authenticate before getting on. Use strong passwords and make them unique.[3] Always reset the default passwords and authentication practices.
8. When possible consider using a two-factor authentication or better (i.e., SecurPBX tokens and/or biometric capabilities).
9. Use a telephony firewall that can filter traffic between the PSTN/gateways and the PBX/IP network.
10. Already mentioned but included in the IPPBX strategy is to use separate DHCP servers: one for the voice network and one for the data network. Consider also using access control procedures that only allow certain ports to be used for DHCP requests and a different DHCP port for the DHCP response. Use a DHCP snooping feature to handle these requests and responses. This will aid in preventing a DHCP spoofing attack.
11. Along with item number 10 above, consider using a MAC filter to monitor and manage MAC addresses within the voice segment of the network. This filtering should limit devices in unknown segments from connecting to the IPPBX.

Some steps that may assist in developing a security plan like any other plan include:

1. Use a business strategy, because the plan has to protect the business from unknown adversaries.
2. Plan the network with security in mind, segment where possible, and isolate where it makes sense.

---

[2]Remember the discussion of a janitor closet where the telephone panels are located. The telephone systems were never controlled the same as the data closets.
[3]It is remarkable how many organizations still leave the default passwords in place and the default authentication.

3. Appoint a project manager as a liaison between the groups.
4. Conduct a network assessment of existing network infrastructure.
5. Add to the network plan a VoIP architecture design as an integrated system, not just an overlay.
6. Implement the VoIP and test it every step of the way.
7. Optimize the VoIP network and document the operation.

Some additional recommendations include:

1. Don't use any form of a shared media device (such as a hub or low-end switch).
2. Conduct regular inspections and look for any snooping devices.
3. Ensure VoIP sent out across a public network is encrypted. End-to-end encryption is not the only option; consider link-level encryption too.
4. Lock down any VoIP server that contains confidential information (i.e., usernames, employee IDs, department IDs, etc.) and treat the servers like any other confidential database server.
5. Possibly place the IPPBX or the telephony server on a separate segment of the network protected by a VoIP aware firewall.
6. Build redundancy into the VoIP network. This does not mean that two networks are required but critical components should be backed up with suitable redundancy.
7. QoS, scalability, manageability, and security of IP telephony should be logically deployed on logically different IP segments. Ideally, two separate networks would be used, but this conflicts with the goal of convergence.
8. Voice and data segmentation and switched architectures enhance security and aid in the eavesdropping attacks known today.
9. While separate VLANs help, filtering and routing between them is better.
10. Configure access control lists in the layer 3 switches to limit ports and addresses that can access the voice VLAN. A possibility of a VLAN Management Policy Server (VMPS) allows the switch to dynamically assign VLANs to users based on the MAC address. This is an added benefit.

SUMMARY

Suffice it to say that no network is safe. When looking at the network build the protection in layers so that a compromise of any one system or component/feature does not compromise the whole system. Recognize that a sound VoIP security strategy is dependent on a sound data security strategy. Understand that the only pure security system is a rock. Everything else is a balance between risk avoidance and cost. Finally filter all of the systems and packet flows as much as possible.

The bottom line is that:

1. VoIP security is a user's responsibility.
2. Vulnerabilities of voice and data networks and systems carry over to a VoIP network and system, only more so.

3. The risks are far too large to ignore; no action is not a solution.
4. No Holy Grail exists; there is no one solution that fits all systems and networks and for the most part there is no single solution that addresses all components of a network.
5. It is up to the organization to implement security best practices with unique VoIP security measures.

Therefore, a wrap-up of thoughts to consider might include the following:

1. Make sure that the network and security infrastructure (including all the components) are voice optimized/aware and capable of including all the unique needs of a VoIP system. Normal policies and procedures used for a TDM architecture will not work for a VoIP system. Various protocols that must open ports dynamically to establish a call require opening and closing these ports on demand. When using a NAT device, inspection of the traffic protocols is required at the network layer as well as the application layer. Thus, a VoIP aware NAT device is essential.
2. Bandwidth, latency, and QoS are crucial for network security. Theft of bandwidth is a high risk in the network today, causing severe latency that may cause dropped calls, or worse yet frustrate the end users because of poor QoS causing them to seek alternative services that are expensive and dilute the security of the organization.
3. No matter what has already been done, new exploits are discovered everyday leaving system exposed and vulnerable. Because the IPPBX system is at the heart of the VoIP network, make sure that updates and patches are conducted regularly. Where possible a test bed may be needed to install the patches and updates and be assured that these will not conflict with other ongoing systems. The last thing that should happen is a flash update causing a new vulnerability being exposed because of the patch. Isolate the system (server) from the rest of the network and test the changes.
4. Conduct regular security audits. Think like the "bad guy" who is trying to penetrate the network.
5. When any flaw or vulnerability is uncovered remediation, immediately if possible, is a must.
6. Always secure the remote access from employees; use a VPN wherever practical.
7. Eliminate any backdoors in the systems that are used by vendors for diagnostics and testing. Secure the access and turn it off when not needed.
8. Disable any unsecure features such as FTP and Telnet; disable local administration and management accounts when not needed.
9. Use encryption whenever the VoIP is crossing the internet. Wherever encryption, authentication, and authorization are optional, use them.
10. Set up the network to take advantage of separate VLANs for voice and data. Although this does not totally eliminate risk from a savvy internal user, it does aid in minimizing the overall risks.

Test it, test it, and test it again. Good luck.

Index

Printed in the United States
By Bookmasters

Printed in the United States
By Bookmasters